Praise for *Sams Teach Yourself Android™ Application Development in 24 Hours*, Fourth Edition

"This latest edition of *Sams Teach Yourself Android Application Development in 24 Hour*s is just what you've been waiting for if you've been waiting to get into Android development. Freshly updated with what you need to know for developing applications using Android Studio for Android Lollipop (Android 5) with Material Design, this book covers what you need to know to get started building applications for Android."

—**Ray Rischpater**, Author and Engineering Manager at Microsoft

"The new edition of *Sams Teach Yourself Android Application Development in 24 Hours* covers a lot of new features. The book takes you from the beginning through to uploading your own app into the store. All the screen shots in this edition use the new and official Android IDE (the amazing Android Studio IDE)."

—**Fady A. M. Ibrahim**, Android Instructor, Benha Faculty of Computer and Information

"Any developer who wants to get up to speed quickly on Android will appreciate this introduction. Beyond the SDK fundamentals, there's plenty of good information on the things real-world Android apps are made of, such as maps, images, and navigation. This is a great way to dive head-first into Android development, or just to become Android-literate in record time."

—**Jonathan Taylor**, VP, Mobile Technology, Priceline.com

The authors knock it out of the park for new Android developers and experienced ones who want to extend their prowess. This book is perfectly set-up for a sports technology oriented person like me to teach me the basic principles, give me design knowledge, and then cap that off with how to add and manipulate data. Data-driven applications are the life's blood of every fantasy sports player and the authors' ability to break down the path to success with real-life exercises to put these principles into action is a Grand Slam!"

—**Rick Wolf**, President, Fantasy Alarm, and Co-Founder, Fantasy Sports Trade Association

Carmen Delessio
Lauren Darcey
Shane Conder

Sams **Teach Yourself**

Android™
Application
Development

Fourth Edition

in **24**
Hours

800 East 96th Street, Indianapolis, Indiana, 46240 USA

Sams Teach Yourself Android™ Application Development in 24 Hours, Fourth Edition

Copyright © 2016 by Carmen Delessio, Lauren Darcey, and Shane Conder

Several images in this book use scenes from the online movie Big Buck Bunny to illustrate the use of online video and using a VideoView control. This movie and related material is distributed under a Creative Commons license. For more information on the movie, go to http://www.bigbuckbunny.org/.

Blender Foundation | http://www.blender.org

Copyright © 2008, Blender Foundation / http://www.bigbuckbunny.org

Some images in this book are reproduced or are modifications based on work created and shared by Google and used according to terms described in the Creative Commons 3.0 Attribution License.

See https://developers.google.com/site-policies.

Screenshots of Google products follow these guidelines: http://www.google.com/permissions/using-product-graphics.html

The following are registered trademarks of Google:

Android, Google Play, Android TV, Android Wear, Google, and the Google logo are registered trademarks of Google Inc., and are used here with permission.

Flickr and Flickr API are registered trademarks of Yahoo!.

No Flickr end-user images appear in this book.

ISBN-13: 978-0-672-33739-0

ISBN-10: 0-672-33739-8

Library of Congress Control Number: 2015906279

Printed in the United States of America

First Printing July 2015

Trademarks

Warning and Disclaimer

Special Sales

For information about buying this title in bulk quantities, or for special sales opportunities (which may include electronic versions; custom cover designs; and content particular to your business, training goals, marketing focus, or branding interests), please contact our corporate sales department at corpsales@pearsoned.com or (800) 382-3419.

For government sales inquiries, please contact governmentsales@pearsoned.com.

For questions about sales outside the U.S., please contact international@pearsoned.com.

Acquisitions Editor
Laura Lewin

Development Editor
Sheri Cain

Managing Editor
Kristy Hart

Project Editor
Andy Beaster

Copy Editor
Keith Cline

Indexer
Larry Sweazy

Proofreader
Sarah Kearns

Technical Editors
Ray Rischpater
Valerie Shipbaugh

Publishing Coordinator
Olivia Basegio

Interior Designer
Gary Adair

Cover Designer
Mark Shirar

Composition
Nonie Ratcliff

Contents at a Glance

Part IV   Next Steps

Table of Contents

Preface

What I wish I knew when I started Android development....

Android has become a leading platform for smartphones, tablets, and other devices. The goal of this book is to introduce the Android platform and start you on the path to creating professional-grade apps.

In 24 hours of topic-based material, you learn the concepts of Android development and move on to specific topics like working with data in the cloud, handling bitmaps and videos in an app, and using new features (such as `CardView` in the Lollipop versions of Android). The coverage of material design and Lollipop features will take you far. The Lollipop version of Android will give way to Android M in the future. Android M will focus on performance improvements.

In the early days of Android, author Carmen Delessio worked on a significant Android project for a large media company. The app launched and was a success. But, it could have been built in a more "Android way." With the authors having built many Android apps since then, the material in this book is largely guided by the idea of including "what I wish I knew then."

This book is not intended to be an encyclopedia of all things Android. Plenty of Android resources are available, and the documentation on the Android developer site has never been better. This book starts you on the path to developing professional Android apps and can be used as a guide to the additional material.

New in the Fourth Edition

There are two major changes from the third edition to the fourth edition of this book.

New features in Android are covered. The updates include significant coverage of material design, including `RecyclerView` and `CardView`. New notification features are covered. An introduction to Android Wear and Android TV is included. Significantly, this edition uses Android Studio throughout rather than Eclipse. All development screenshots and examples use Android Studio.

The second change is this book starts by covering four important components of Android. In the first hour, you learn about activities, intents, intent services, and broadcast receivers. Subsequent hours drill more deeply into these broad concepts. This change highlights what is happening when an app runs and puts even more emphasis on doing things the "Android way."

Who This Book Is For

The examples in this book are created so that someone with programming knowledge can understand them, but Android apps are developed in Java. You will find the book much more valuable and useful if you are familiar with Java concepts and syntax. If you are knowledgeable in C or C# and understand object-oriented concepts, you should be able to understand the level of Java code in this book. You should know what classes and methods are.

If you are a Java programmer with an interest in Android development, this book introduces you to Android and gets you on track for professional Android development.

If you have started Android development, but have not proceeded past the basic examples, this book is for you. It covers topics such as downloading data, using a database, and creating content providers. This book can take you from the basics to real development in a series of understandable steps.

How This Book Is Organized

The book is organized into four broad sections:

Part I, "Android Fundamentals." This first part introduces Android concepts and uses examples to show how to start activities, pass data, and handle core functionality. It covers activities, intents, resources, and background processing.

Part II, "Creating the User Interface." When you create the user interface, you learn about components and layouts. You cover bitmaps and video views. You also learn about navigation within an app, and you cover material design—the new design from Google that is used in Android.

Part III, "Working with Data." Working with data means both retrieving data over a network and storing it. You learn about using a SQLite database and using content providers.

Part IV, "Next Steps." This last part covers other features to investigate further, open source projects of interest, and how to publish your app.

You can find online updates, contact the author, and ask questions about this book on http://talkingandroid.com/. Links to source code are posted there.

Source Code for the Book

Nearly every chapter in this book includes an example that has source code available online. The code is on GitHub and organized by chapter. You will find the code here: https://github.com/CarmenDelessio. Code for an individual chapter should be easy to find. For example, the complete project code for Hour 10 is here: https://github.com/CarmenDelessio/Hour10application.

About the Authors

Carmen Delessio is an experienced application developer who has worked as a developer, technical architect, and CTO in large and small organizations. Carmen began his online development career at Prodigy, where he worked on early Internet applications, shopping apps, and fantasy baseball. He is a graduate of Manhattanville College and lives in Pound Ridge, New York, with his wife, Amy, and daughter, Natalie.

Lauren Darcey is responsible for the technical leadership and direction of a small software company specializing in mobile technologies, including Android and iOS consulting services. With more than two decades of experience in professional software production, Lauren is a recognized authority in application architecture and the development of commercial-grade mobile applications. Lauren received a BS in computer science from the University of California, Santa Cruz.

Shane Conder has extensive application development experience and has focused his attention on mobile and embedded development for well over a decade. He has designed and developed many commercial applications for Android, iOS, BREW, BlackBerry, J2ME, Palm, and Windows Mobile—some of which have been installed on millions of phones worldwide. Shane has written extensively about the tech industry and is known for his keen insights regarding mobile development platform trends. Shane received a BS in computer science from the University of California, Santa Cruz.

Dedication

For ASL and NMLD.

"To the Valiant of heart, nothing is impossible." – Jeanne d'Albret
—Carmen Delessio

Acknowledgments

This book would not exist without the help and guidance of the team at Pearson (Sams Publishing). Thanks to Laura Lewin for constant encouragement and Olivia Basegio for her incredible work on the project. Sheri Cain helped take this book to another level with her feedback. Her diligence and hard work kept this project constantly moving forward.

Technical editors are an important part of every book. Ray Rischpater was an incredible help. Valerie Shipbaugh did her technical review by placing herself in the role of a reader who was new to Android. The feedback and guidance from Ray and Valerie make this a better book.

We Want to Hear from You

As the reader of this book, you are our most important critic and commentator. We value your opinion and want to know what we're doing right, what we could do better, what areas you'd like to see us publish in, and any other words of wisdom you're willing to pass our way.

We welcome your comments. You can email or write directly to let us know what you did or didn't like about this book—as well as what we can do to make our books better.

Please note that we cannot help you with technical problems related to the topic of this book.

When you write, please be sure to include this book's title and author as well as your name and email address. We will carefully review your comments and share them with the author and editors who worked on the book.

Email: feedback@samspublishing.com

Mail: Reader Feedback
           Sams Publishing
           800 East 96th Street
           Indianapolis, IN 46240 USA

Reader Services

Visit our website and register this book at http://www.informit.com/register for convenient access to any updates, downloads, or errata that might be available for this book.

PART I

Android Fundamentals

HOUR 1
Introducing Android

What You'll Learn in This Hour:

▶ Defining Android

▶ Understanding Android development

▶ Beginning Android Studio

In this book, you learn about using Android development tools, creating user interfaces, and getting information over a network to create fun and interesting apps. Learning Android development certainly means the ability to create an app that runs on an Android device such as a phone or a tablet. It also means understanding how different parts of the Android platform work together. In this chapter, you learn about core features of the Android platform and how they interact.

Defining Android

This hour lays the foundation for what you learn throughout the rest of this book. You can begin by thinking about what Android is.

Operating System

On one level, Android is an operating system (OS) that runs on phones, tablets, and other devices (such as TVs). A device manufacturer has the job of installing the Android OS on their devices.

The Android OS includes the set of features that the user sees and interacts with. When Android adds new features for the camera, a new visual design, or a new way for the user to unlock the phone, those features are in the OS.

NOTE

What Is Lollipop?

The current version of Android is called Lollipop. It is also known as Android 5.0. Each version of Android includes an application programming interface (API) level that refers to the developer features that were introduced in that release. Lollipop has API level 21. Earlier versions of Android were also named for desserts, including Cupcake, Donut, Eclair, Froyo, Gingerbread, Ice Cream, and KitKat. You can learn more about Lollipop at http://developer.android.com/about/versions/"lollipop. html. Android M has been announced as the next version of Android. Android M will focus on performance

---

Development Environment

Android includes a powerful development environment that enables developers, like you, to create apps that run on Android devices. You have access to Android-specific classes in the Android framework.

In the past, the primary tool for Android development was the Eclipse, but the latest tool for Android development is known as Android Studio. This book uses Android Studio for examples. The Android concepts are the same regardless of the integrated development environment (IDE) you choose. You learn more about Android Studio later in this chapter. Figure 1.1 shows the project-creation process in Android Studio. You can choose an Android version as your target version.

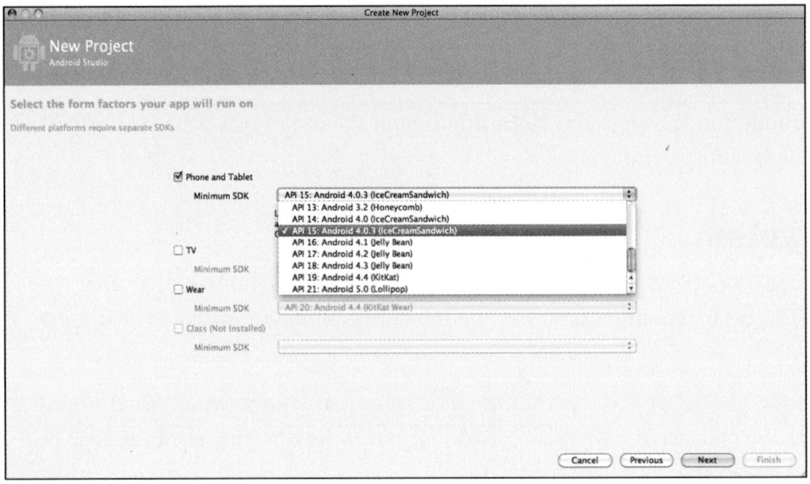

FIGURE 1.1
Setting up a project in Android Studio.

Mobile Platform

Android is a mobile platform. Being an OS with a development environment that gives access to OS features makes Android a platform. A marketplace to sell apps completes the picture.

Android is a big deal!

- ▶ Available in 190 countries
- ▶ Supported by 300 manufacturers
- ▶ 1 million Android devices activated daily
- ▶ 1.5 billion apps per month downloaded

As a developer, you learn about using Android development tools and how to create apps.

Understanding Android Development

This section's goal is for you to understand some basic things about what is happening when an Android app runs.

Four things in the Android framework can help you understand how Android works and what is going on in an Android app. This is not an exhaustive list of everything important in Android, but it is enough for you to consider what is happening when an Android app runs.

Getting the Big Picture

The following four things can help you understand the "big picture" for Android:

- ▶ Activities
- ▶ Intents
- ▶ IntentServices
- ▶ BroadcastReceivers

Introducing Activities

An `Activity(android.app.Activity)` is a core component of the Android platform. An activity is typically associated with a screen in the application. That means that most activities start and then show a user interface.

When an Android app launches, some activity must be launched. This launch activity is specified as the entry point to the app.

The launch activity is specified in the Android manifest file.

NOTE

The Android Manifest File

The Android manifest file, AndroidManifest.xml, is the central configuration file for an Android application. It includes things such as the name of the application, the icon for the application, and a set of permissions that the application requires. Each activity in the app must be defined in the manifest file.

You can create an app that uses one `Activity` or many. For apps that have more than one activity, each must be defined in the manifest. The launch activity is often used to start other activities.

The most common way to start one activity from another is to use the `startActivity()` method. The `startActivity()` method is passed an `Intent` as a parameter.

Introducing Intents

An `Intent(android.content.Intent)` is used to make a request to the Android operating system. An `Intent` contains all the information needed by the Android OS to start a task. When you want to start an `Activity`, you must create an `Intent` that specifies that `Activity`.

When the `startActivity()` method is called with the intent parameter, the Android system matches the intent action with the appropriate activity on the Android system. That activity is then launched.

One job of the Android OS is to associate intents with actions. An `Intent` can be specific, such as a request for a specific activity to be launched, or an `Intent` can be less specific and request that any activity that matches certain criteria be launched. A specific `Intent` is known as an explicit `Intent` and a less-specific `Intent` is known as an implicit `Intent`. With an implicit `Intent`, the OS presents a list of applications that can handle the task.

Intents can pass data between activities. You can use an `Intent` in this way by including additional data, called extras, within the `Intent`.

To package extra pieces of data along with an intent, you use the `putExtra()` method with the appropriate type of object you want to include.

Introducing IntentServices

A service in Android is a task that runs independently of an activity. A `Service(android.app.Service)` can be launched from an activity and work in the background. That means while the user is interacting with the user interface of an `Activity`, a `Service` can be running in the background and doing work. When an `Activity` updates, the user interface that work is occurring on is the *UI thread*. For efficient and responsive apps, use background processing and move work off of the UI thread.

An `IntentService(android.app.IntentService)` provides a convenient and simple way to implement a service. Like an `Activity`, an `IntentService` must be defined in the manifest file. An `Intent` is launched with a call to `startService()` with a parameter that is the `Intent` associated with the `IntentService`.

Introducing BroadcastReceivers

A service runs independently of an `Activity`, but often an `Activity` should be notified when a service completes. An `IntentService` can send a broadcast when it completes. By now, you might not be surprised to learn that when the `IntentService` sends a broadcast, it uses an `Intent` as the parameter. The `IntentService` calls the `sendBroadcast()` method with an intent as a parameter.

A `BroadcastReceiver(android.content.BroadcastReceiver)` receives an intent from the `sendBroadcast()` method. The broadcast receiver acts on the intent.

Together intent services and broadcast receivers can be considered a "publish and subscribe" system. The intent service publishes that some event has occurred, and the broadcast receiver is subscribed to the event. One job of the broadcast receiver is to determine whether it should handle the event. It does that by checking the contents of the intent. The broadcast receiver determines whether it should act on the action supplied by the intent.

Putting It All Together

Both activities and services are tasks that run within an Android app. Android developers often write code that makes things happen in an activity or service. You've also learned that intents are used to make things happen on Android. Intents are used to launch both an `Activity` and an `IntentService`.

`BroadcastReceivers` listen for intents and act on them. A broadcast receiver is often associated with a specific intent service.

One way to bring these ideas together is to consider what is going on in Android when you look at a web page in the Chrome app and decide to share it.

You know that apps launch an activity when they start, so the Chrome app starts by launching an activity. As you browse web pages, you have the option to share a page, as shown in Figure 1.2.

When you decide to share a web page, a list of apps that are capable of sharing a web page appears, as shown in Figure 1.3. How do you think that might happen?

FIGURE 1.2
Share a web page from the Chrome app.

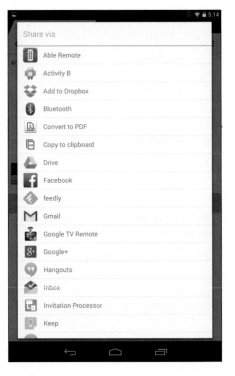

FIGURE 1.3
List of apps that can share a web page.

The Chrome app is sending an intent to share web page URL. Any app that has a broadcast receiver that handles a web page URL is shown to the user by the Android system. (In Hour 2, "Understanding Intents," you make an app that adds itself to that list.)

Classes and Methods

In Android, activities, intents, intent services, and broadcast receivers are all specific classes defined in the Android framework. From this point on, when a new class is introduced in this book, the full class name is provided. Classes are included in packages.

Activity Class

For example, the `Activity` class (`android.app.Activity`) is in the android.app package.

TIP

Using Android Online Documentation

Each class that is available for you to use as an Android developer is documented online on the http://developer.android.com site. For example, the `Activity` class is documented at http://developer.android.com/reference/android/app/Activity.html/. The documentation is organized by package name.

Classes include fields that are properties of the class, and methods that are operations that the class can perform. You commonly override the methods of a class to specify what you want your implementation of the class to do.

An `Activity` includes the method `onCreate()`. It is in the `onCreate()` method that you specify what should be done when your activity is created.

Intent Class

An `Intent(android.content.Intent)` defines an action to be taken and the data needed for that action to occur. The constructor that defines an `Intent` often contains both the action and the data. Let's look at some examples for defining intents in code.

The following code defines an intent that launches an activity name `HelpActivity`. The `putExtra()` method in this code adds an additional piece of data to the `Intent`. Note that by convention the package name for the application is used as part of the name for the extra data:

```
Intent intent = new Intent(getApplicationContext(), HelpActivity.class);
intent.putExtra("com.example.LEVEL", 23);
startActivity(intent);
```

When the `HelpActivity` class launches, the `getIntent()` method can be used to retrieve the intent. Then the extra information can be extracted and used. That code looks like this:

```
Intent receiveIntent = getIntent();
int helpLevel=receiveIntent.getIntExtra("com.example.LEVEL", 1);
```

The parameters to the `getIntExtra()` method are the name of the parameter and a default value.

In addition, after an `Intent` is defined, extra data can be added with the `putExtra()` method.

IntentService Class

An `IntentService(android.app.IntentService)` includes the `onHandleIntent()` method that is called to process the request. It is passed an `Intent` as a parameter to decide what to do. It is where the work associated with the `Intent` is done.

BroadcastReceiver Class

A `BroadcastReceiver(android.content.BroadcastReceiver)` has an `onReceive()` method that is called when the `BroadcastReceiver` receives an intent broadcast. When a task associated with the `Intent` needs to be performed, it is done in the `onReceive()` method.

Tying Up Loose Ends

Much of the functionality in an Android app takes place in activities and services. An `IntentService` is a specific type of `Service(android.app.Service)`. A service is a long-running operation that does not require user interaction. Intents are used to start both services and activities. A broadcast receiver is started when either an activity or service sends an intent via the `sendBroadcast()` method.

When you begin creating apps, you can focus on adding functionality to activities. As your app gets more sophisticated and does things like retrieve data from the network, you will find more of a need to use services.

An `Application(android.app.Application)` is an object that can be used for maintaining global application state. When we define activities and services within the manifest file, they are defined as part of the application.

Both the `Application` class and `Activity` class are extended from the `Context(android.content.Context)` class. The `Context` class contains global information about an application environment. In later chapters, you learn about application properties; those are accessed via a `Context`. Contexts are used to start activities and services. Because an activity is a `Context`, it can launch other activities.

You can retrieve the application context for the current process by using the `getApplicationContext()` method, like this:

```
Context context = getApplicationContext();
```

Because the `Activity` class derives from the `Context` class, you can use the `Activity` object instead of retrieving the application context explicitly when you're writing code inside your `Activity` class.

After you have retrieved a valid application context, you can use it to access application-wide features and services.

Beginning Android Studio

Android Studio is an IDE for Android development. It includes an environment for developing code and a visual environment for creating user interfaces for your apps.

Installation

You can find the online documentation for installing Android Studio at http://developer.android.com/sdk/installing/studio.html. Download the complete Android Studio package and follow the installation instructions. You will have a development environment that includes the following:

▶ Android software development kit (SDK) tools to design, test, and debug your app

▶ An Android platform to compile your app

▶ An Android system image to run your app in the emulator

TRY IT YOURSELF ▼

Downloading and Installing Android Studio

All examples in this book use Android Studio. Follow these steps to install Android Studio as your development environment:

1. Go to http://developer.android.com.

2. Follow the steps to download Android Studio.

3. Unzip and install Android Studio.

4. Check for software updates and explore the environment.

Creating a Project

When you start Android Studio, several options are presented. Choose to create a new project. You are asked to name your application and to enter a company domain. If you have a domain name that you plan on using for your development, you can enter it. If you intend to sell apps on the Google Play market or other Android app stores, the package name is very important. It is a way to uniquely identify your apps.

Choose the SDK that supports Phone and Tablet apps. The other options are Wear and TV apps. You can set the minimum SDK to API 14: Android 4.0 (IceCreamSandwich).

Choose to add a blank activity, as shown in Figure 1.4.

You are asked to name your activity. You can leave the default of `MainActivity`.

Android Studio now creates your project.

Your goal is to install Android Studio and to understand some of the basics of the user interface. There is no need to add new code or to change the user interface at this point. This is a good opportunity to understand where the code is in the project and to take a close look at the manifest file.

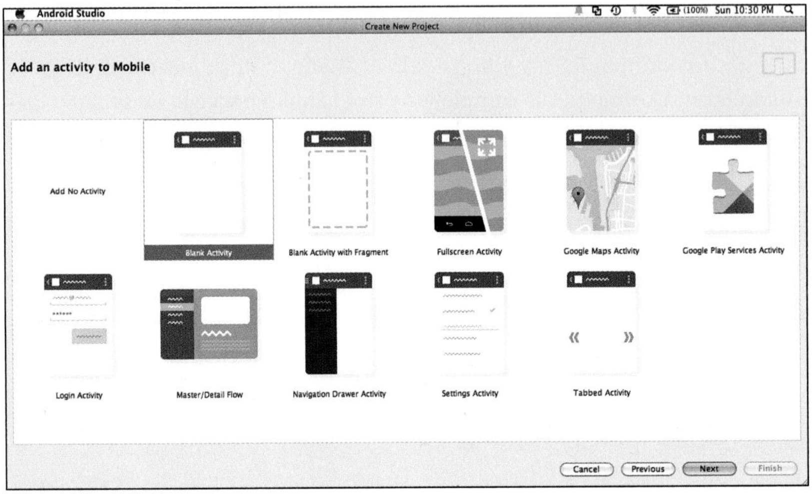

FIGURE 1.4
Add a blank activity.

▼ TRY IT YOURSELF

Exploring the Project

You have already installed Android Studio and created a new project. Follow these steps to open the code for the Activity in the editor and then open the code for the manifest file in the editor:

1. Choose the Java folder.

2. Select the name for the package that you created.

3. Open the Java code for the activity. The result should look like Figure 1.5.

4. Choose the Manifests folder.

5. Open the AndroidManifest.xml file (see Listing 1.1).

The activity you created via Android Studio includes an `onCreate()` method and several methods for adding menu options.

You learned that each activity must be defined in the manifest file and that a launch activity must be defined. Listing 1.1 shows the complete manifest file. In line 10, the full name of `MainActivity` is specified. It is associated with an intent filter that includes the category `android.intent.category.LAUNCHER` in line 14. That defines this as the launch activity.

Also note the package and application-level definitions.

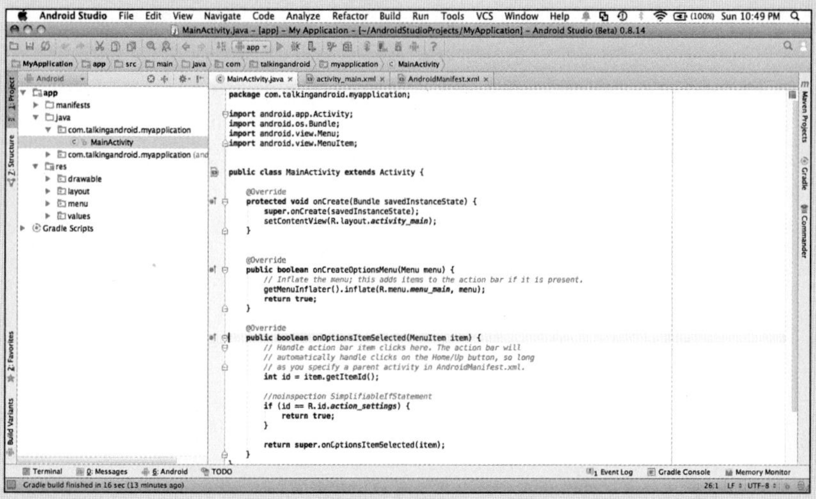

FIGURE 1.5
Viewing code for an `Activity` in Android Studio.

LISTING 1.1   AndroidManifest.xml

```
 1:  <?xml version="1.0" encoding="utf-8"?>
 2:  <manifest xmlns:android="http://schemas.android.com/apk/res/android"
 3:      package="com.talkingandroid.myapplication" >
 4:      <application
 5:          android:allowBackup="true"
 6:          android:icon="@drawable/ic_launcher"
 7:          android:label="@string/app_name"
 8:          android:theme="@style/AppTheme" >
 9:        <activity
10:            android:name="com.talkingandroid.myapplication.MainActivity"
11:            android:label="@string/app_name" >
12:            <intent-filter>
13:                <action android:name="android.intent.action.MAIN" />
14:                <category android:name="android.intent.category.LAUNCHER" />
15:            </intent-filter>
16:        </activity>
17:      </application>
18:  </manifest>
```

Summary

Android is a popular OS and platform. This chapter introduced you to Android and explained what occurs when an Android application is running. You learned that activities and services perform operations in Android and that intents are used to pass data and initiate tasks. Intent services and broadcast receivers can be considered to be a simple "publish and subscribe" system within Android. Intents are always being passed around in Android. Though your initial focus will be on activities and the user interface associated with application development, these concepts should help your overall understanding of Android; you revisit them in detail in subsequent chapters.

This chapter also introduced Android Studio, and you learned how to create an activity with a new project.

Q&A

Q. Must I use Android Studio for Android development?

A. No, Android Studio is the focus of the Android Tools Team, and new development is occurring on that platform. Eclipse has been used for Android development in the past. The direction is to move from Eclipse to Android Studio.

Q. Should I develop for Lollipop?

A. As you saw when you created a new project in Android Studio, you can specify a minimum SDK to support. For certain development, such as Android Wear and Android TV development, you must use Lollipop. For phones and tablets, it might make sense to use the latest SDK but support a lower SDK version. The particulars of your app drive this decision.

Workshop

Quiz

1. How does an `Activity` differ from a `Service`?
2. How does an application know which activity to launch when it starts?

Answers

1. A `Service` will never have a user interface, and it runs in the background. An `Activity` usually has a user interface, and it runs on the UI thread.
2. A launch activity is defined in the manifest file. When an application starts, it launches the activity defined in the manifest.

Exercise

For this chapter, make sure that you installed Android Studio and created a simple project. Explore the Java code for the activity that you created.

HOUR 2
Understanding Intents

What You'll Learn in This Hour:

▸ Starting an activity by using intents

▸ Using implicit intents

▸ Handling an implicit intent

Hour 1, "Introducing Android," provided an introduction to `Intents`. You learned that an `Intent` initiates an action, and can include additional data for that action. In this hour, you use an `Intent` to start a new `Activity` and you learn about some of the `Intents` that are built into Android that you can use in your apps. Finally, you develop an app that will be launched from another app via an `Intent`. When a user shares a web page URL from the web browser, your app will be included in the list of available apps that can handle that `Intent`.

Using Intents to Start an Activity

To launch one `Activity` from another, you will use an `Intent`. To start one `Activity` from another, you need to create two activities. You should create one `Activity` called `MainActivity` and a second called `SecondaryActivity`. `MainActivity` is defined in the manifest file as the launch `Activity` and launches when the app is started.

To start the `SecondaryActivity`, you create a button in the user interface for `MainActivity`. That button includes code to create to start `SecondaryActivity`.

You do all of this using Android Studio.

The steps in this process are as follows:

1. Create a new project called Hour2Application.

2. Add a new blank `Activity` called `MainActivity`.

3. Put a `Button` on the user interface for `MainActivity`.

4. Create a second `Activity` called `SecondaryActivity`.

5. Add code to `MainActivity` that starts `SecondaryActivity` when the button is clicked.

Creating the User Interface in Android Studio

In Hour 1, you installed Android Studio and went through the steps of creating a project with a blank `Activity`. To begin this chapter, do the same thing by creating an application called Hour2Application that includes a blank `Activity` called `MainActivity`.

Expand the folders in the project so that you can find MainActivity.java in the Java folder and activity_main.xml in the res/layout folder. When you select activity_main.xml in the res/layout folder, Android Studio displays the user interface, as shown in Figure 2.1.

FIGURE 2.1
Viewing activity_main.xml in Android Studio.

In the view of Android Studio in Figure 2.1, the project structure is in the left section, the visual editor for the user interface is in the center, and the details for the selected property are shown in the component tree on the right.

Because your goal is to add a button to the user interface, you can drag and drop a button from the palette to the user interface. The result will look like Figure 2.2.

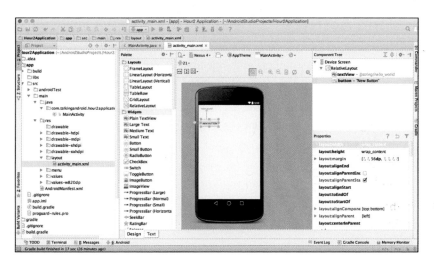

FIGURE 2.2
Adding a `Button` to `MainActivity`.

You can change the text on the button by changing the text property. Select the button component in the user interface and you will see both the component tree and set of properties. The
component tree lists all the components in the user interface. When the button component is
selected, you can change the text property. In this case, change it to Start Second Activity, as
shown in Figure 2.3.

FIGURE 2.3
Update the user interface in Android Studio.

Creating a Second Activity

At this point, using Android Studio, you have created a single `Activity` called `MainActivity` and added a button to the user interface. You now add code to `MainActivity` so that when the button is clicked, it opens your second `Activity`. Now you need to create the second `Activity`.

When you created a new project, you were prompted to create an `Activity`. You chose to create a blank `Activity`, and `MainActivity` was created.

To create `SecondaryActivity` using Android Studio, select the Java folder and right-click to open the menu. Choose New, Activity, Blank Activity, as shown in Figure 2.4.

FIGURE 2.4
Create a new activity.

Continue to create `SecondaryActivity`. When you complete the wizard, the `Activity` should look like Figure 2.5. You can choose whatever company URL you want to be your package name. If you intend to create apps to put on the Google Play marketplace, you must use a unique package name. Typically, you use a reverse domain name convention. If your web domain is mydomain.com, for instance, your package name begins with com.mydomain.

`SecondaryActivity` includes a `TextView(android.widget.TextView)` in the user interface that says "Hello World." As you might have noticed, this `TextView` is included in each `Activity` that is created via Android Studio. You should change the text in this `TextView` to indicate that this is the `SecondaryActivity`.

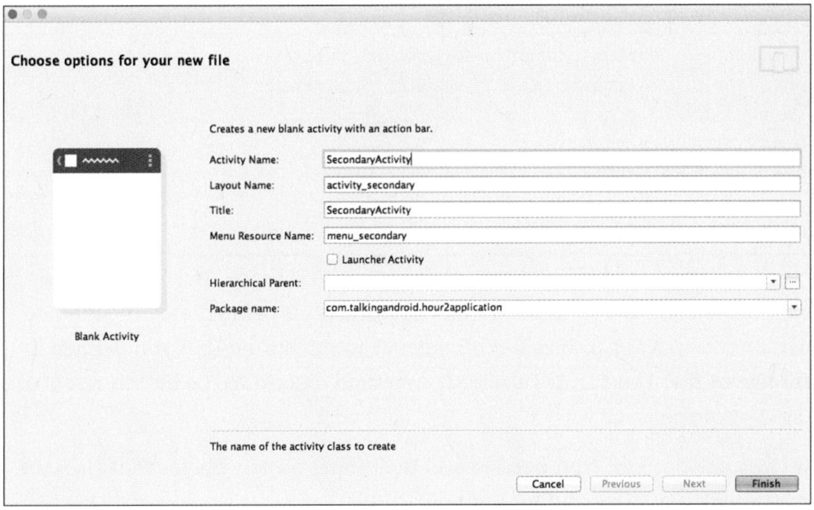

FIGURE 2.5
Create SecondaryActivity.

Adding Code to Start an Activity

You have learned about Intents and Activities. You have used Android Studio to create the foundation for a simple application in which MainActivity will start SecondaryActivity. The next step is to add code to MainActivity to detect when the button is clicked and to start SecondaryActivity.

MainActivity.java was generated with your project. The generated code includes a method called onCreate(). The onCreate() method runs when MainActivity is created in the app. The onCreate() method is used to define a Button and to specify an action to occur when the Button is clicked. You can think of the Android framework as having events that occur. and a listener that listens for those events. To detect that the button is clicked, you add an onClickListener(). The code in Listing 2.1 defines a Button (android.widget.Button) and adds a listener.

A button named activityButton is defined in line 1. The setOnClickListener() method for activityButton is called on line 2. A View.OnClickListener(android.view.View.OnClickListener) object is passed as a parameter. The View.OnClickListener is defined inline in the code. To implement an OnClickListener, the onClick() method must be defined and overridden. The onClick() method is on line 4.

That seems complicated for this snippet of code in Listing 2.1! There is a lot going on. It is easy to look at code as setting an OnClickListener for the activityButton.

LISTING 2.1   MainActivity.java Clicking a Button

```
1: Button activityButton =  (Button) findViewById(R.id.button) ;
2:   activityButton.setOnClickListener(new View.OnClickListener() {
3:      @Override
4:      public void onClick(View view) {
5:        // add code here for button click
6:      }
7:   });
```

Here are a few more things to consider: In line 1, `activityButton` is defined with the method `findViewById(R.id.button)`. `R.id.button` is a reference to the button that you defined in the activity_main.xml layout file. The `findViewById()` method associates the button resource to the `Button activityButton`.

When you use a new class like `Button`, you need to add the proper import file for that class. In this case, add two new imports for `View` and for `Button`:

```
import android.view.View;
import android.widget.Button;
```

TIP

Adding Imports On the Fly

There is a preference setting in Android Studio that proves very helpful when it comes to imports. The preference is for the Editor. Choose Preferences, Editor, Auto-Import, and add a check mark to Add Unambiguous Imports On the Fly. Then, when you use a class like `Button`, the `import` statement is added automatically. See Figure 2.6 for the settings.

Listing 2.2 adds code to create an `Intent` called `startIntent` on line 5. The `startIntent` is used as a parameter to `startActivity()` on line 6.

The `Intent` in line 5 is passed two parameters. A `Context` (`android.content.Context`) is passed as the first parameter. The application context is retrieved by calling the `getApplicationContext()` method. The second parameter refers directly to the `SecondaryActivity` class.

LISTING 2.2   MainActivity.java Starting an Activity

```
1: Button activityButton =  (Button) findViewById(R.id.button) ;
2:   activityButton.setOnClickListener(new View.OnClickListener() {
3:      @Override
4:      public void onClick(View view) {
5:        Intent startIntent = new Intent(getApplicationContext(),SecondaryActivity.
class);
```

```
6:        startActivity(startIntent);
7:      }
8:   });
```

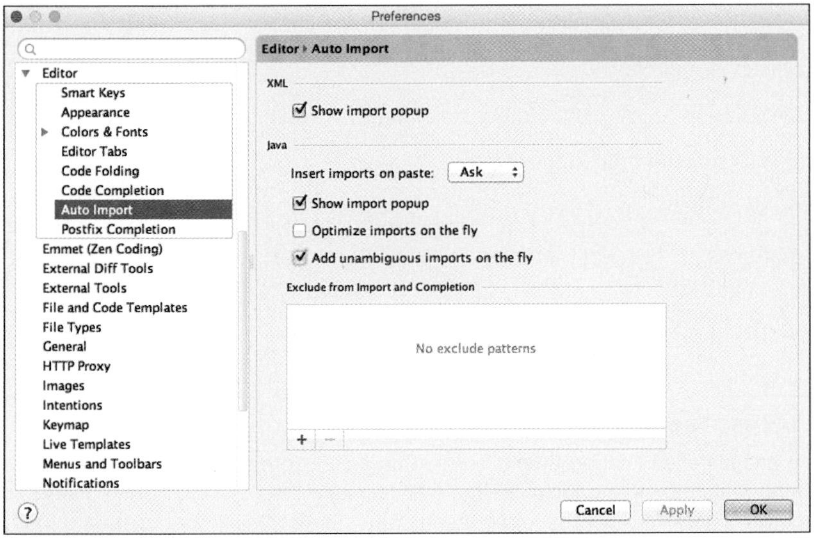

FIGURE 2.6
Setting imports on the fly preference.

Running the App

You've created a simple app to open one `Activity` from another. `MainActivity` shows a button called `activityButton` that starts `SecondaryActivity`.

In Android Studio, you can run this code in the emulator. Android tools include the Android Virtual Device Manager. An Android Virtual Device is referred to as an AVD. An installation of Android Studio includes an AVD.

To see the list of available virtual devices, choose Tools, Android, AVD Manager. A list of available devices will be displayed. You can add new virtual devices using AVD Manager.

You can start the app from the Android Studio Run menu. You are asked if you want to choose a running device or to start a virtual device on the emulator. You can start a virtual device. If you have an Android phone or other device connected by USB, it should be detected, and you can use it to run the app.

▼ TRY IT YOURSELF

Running an App in the Emulator

Creating an AVD and running an app in the emulator enables you to try different devices and configurations virtually:

1. Create a new project in Android Studio.

2. Create a new AVD. Choose Tools, Android, AVD Manager.

3. Run the app for your project in the emulator.

4. Use the AVD you created.

5. You do not need to change the app that Android Studio generates.

WARNING

Updating to the Latest Tools

When you downloaded and installed Android Studio, you set up a complete development environment. It includes Android Studio itself and tools like the AVD Manager. You can check for updates to Android Studio by choosing Check for Updates in the menu. You can also check for updates to the software development kit (SDK) by choosing Tools, Android, SDK Manager. In the SDK Manager, you will see the currently installed version of Android SDK Tools and whether updates are available.

Passing Data Between Activities

It is possible to pass data from one `Activity` to another using `Intents`. To do that, you must enhance the code for `MainActivity` to include extra data in the `startIntent` and add code in `SecondaryActivity` to receive this data and use it.

In `MainActivity`, one line of code is added to the `Intent` definition. The `putExtra()` method passes a key and a value. In this case, the key is `com.talkingandroid.MESSAGE`, and the value is `"Hello SecondaryActivity"`:

```
Intent startIntent = new Intent(getApplicationContext(), SecondaryActivity.class);
startIntent.putExtra("com.talkingandroid.MESSAGE","Hello SecondaryActivity" );
startActivity(startIntent);
```

You also need to make changes to `SecondaryActivity` to receive this data. The goal is to change `SecondaryActivity` to receive the data and show the passed message in a `TextView`.

You are going to add a `TextView` called `message` to the secondary_activity.xml layout file. Open the activity_secondary.xml file under the res/layout folder. You can edit the layout in either design mode or text mode. Find the `TextView` that was generated and verify that it has a property called `id`. In the design view, you can find the `id` property and enter `message` as the new `id`. In the text view, you will see `android:id="@+id/message"`.

In the `onCreate()` method of `SecondaryActivity`, you get the passed `Intent` by calling the `getIntent()` method. After you have the `Intent`, you can get the `String` that was passed by using the `getStringExtra()` method with the same key that was used in `MainActivity`.

Listing 2.3 shows the `getIntent()` method on line 1 and the `getStringExtra()` method on line 2. The passed message is displayed by called `setText()` on line 4.

LISTING 2.3   SecondaryActivity.java Received Passed Intent

```
1:    Intent= getIntent();
2:    String message = Intent.getStringExtra("com.talkingandroid.MESSAGE");
3:    TextView messageTextView = (TextView) findViewById(R.id.message);
4:    messageTextView.setText(message);
```

Figure 2.7 shows both activities for this app.

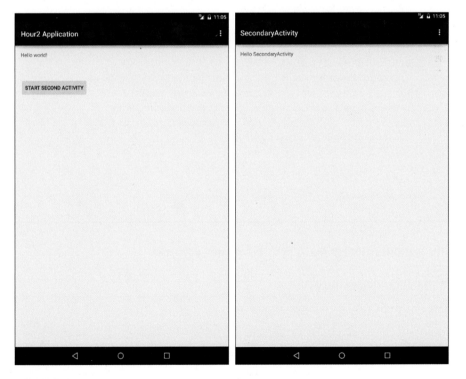

FIGURE 2.7
`MainActivity` and `SecondaryActivity`.

Listings 2.4 and 2.5 show the code for MainActivity.java and SecondaryActivity.java. When Android Studio generates `Activity` code, the methods `onCreateOptionsMenu()` and `onOptionsItemSelected()` are included. This code handles menus. The sample code does not use a menu, and that code is excluded from Listings 2.4 and 2.5.

LISTING 2.4 MainActivity.java

```
 1: package com.talkingandroid.hour2application;
 2: import android.content.Intent;
 3: import android.support.v7.app.ActionBarActivity;
 4: import android.os.Bundle;
 5: import android.view.Menu;
 6: import android.view.MenuItem;
 7: import android.view.View;
 8: import android.widget.Button;
 9:
10: public class MainActivity extends ActionBarActivity {
11:     @Override
12:     protected void onCreate(Bundle savedInstanceState) {
13:         super.onCreate(savedInstanceState);
14:         setContentView(R.layout.Activity_main);
15:         Button activityButton =  (Button) findViewById(R.id.button) ;
16:         activityButton.setOnClickListener(new View.OnClickListener() {
17:             @Override
18:             public void onClick(View view) {
19:                 Intent startIntent = new Intent(getApplicationContext(),
20:                                     SecondaryActivity.class);
21:                 startIntent.putExtra("com.talkingandroid.MESSAGE",
22:                                    "Hello SecondaryActivity" );
23:                 startActivity(startIntent);
24:             }
25:         });
26:     }
27:     // menu code excluded
28: }
```

In Listing 2.5, the message passed in the `Intent` is read and displayed.

LISTING 2.5 SecondaryActivity.java

```
 1: package com.talkingandroid.hour2application;
 2: import android.content.Intent;
 3: import android.support.v7.app.ActionBarActivity;
 4: import android.os.Bundle;
 5: import android.view.Menu;
```

```
 6: import android.view.MenuItem;
 7: import android.view.TextView;
 8:
 9: public class SecondaryActivity extends ActionBarActivity {
10:     @Override
11:     protected void onCreate(Bundle savedInstanceState) {
12:         super.onCreate(savedInstanceState);
14:         setContentView(R.layout.Activity_secondary);
15:         Intent= getIntent();
16:         String message = Intent.getStringExtra("com.talkingandroid.MESSAGE");
17:         TextView messageTextView = (TextView) findViewById(R.id.message);
18:         messageTextView.setText(message);
19:     }
20:     // menu code excluded
21: }
```

Explicit and Implicit Intents

Intents include an action and may include additional data. In the case of the startIntent defined in MainActivity.java, the action is to start SecondaryActivity. The data passed was a message. Because the specific Activity to start was specified, this is an explicit intent.

An implicit Intent is defined by an action and data, but the specific action to take is resolved by the Android operating system. The action might be to display a map or to open a web page. The data contains the details of the map or the page. With an implicit Intent, if multiple apps can handle the action, those apps are presented to the user. As mentioned in Hour 1, an example of this is sharing a web page. Many applications can handle that Intent.

Using Implicit Intents

Many actions can be performed using an implicit Intent. They include showing a web page, showing a map, making a phone call, and picking an image from the device to use in your app.

Actions that show content are easy to use and can add a lot of value to the apps that you create. The Intent class defines a constant called ACTION_VIEW for actions that display content to the user.

To test some common view Intents, you can add update the user interface and code for MainActivity. You will add buttons to activity_main.xml and additional code to MainActivity. java. First you will do this for showing a location on a map and then for opening a web page.

CAUTION

What Happens If the Intent Is Not Handled?

Intents make Android powerful, and there are many built-in `Intents`. However, it is possible that an `Intent` that you are using is not available on a particular device. Your code should check to see whether the `Intent` is handled. That can be done by calling the method `Intent.resolve Activity()`. If the `Intent` is resolved, an `Activity` exists to handle it. Typically, `Intents` are available on devices for common actions. At times, the emulator may not handle certain Intents.

Opening a Map to a Specific Location

Apps that show maps handle the `ACTION_VIEW` `Intent`, including data that includes specific geographic coordinates. The data passed is a URI (Universal Resource Identifier) in a specific format. You can launch the Maps application to a specific set of coordinates using the following URI format string:

```
geo:latitude,longitude
```

Creating an Intent Using Latitude and Longitude

Taken together, latitude and longitude provide coordinate system for specifying any point on earth. Latitude is used for the north-south position. Latitude is represented in degrees, with the equator being 0 degrees and the poles being 90 degrees denoted by north and south. Longitude is used for the east-west position. Greenwich, England is designated as the prime meridian, with a longitude of 0 degrees. The latitude for other locations is defined by the degree of difference from the prime meridian from 180 degrees to –180 degrees indicating east and west. North is 90 degrees, and south is –90 degrees.

To show an example of how using an `Intent` for maps works, you can use a preset latitude and longitude. The coordinates of Google headquarters, known as the GooglePlex, are 37.4220° N, 122.0840° W.

That translates to 37.422, –122.084 for your `Intent`. To begin defining the `Intent`, you define a `String` as follows:

```
String geoURI = "geo: 37.422, -122.084";
```

This geo URI also include a zoom level, which is a number between 1 and 23, where zoom level 1 shows the whole earth, level 2 shows a quarter of the earth, and each larger number shows a closer view. The following URI format string is used for zoom:

```
geo:latitude,longitude?z=level
```

Here's how to format a URI string with the zoom level set to 8:

```
String geoURI = " geo: 37.422, -122.084"?z=8";
```

You use a string in this format and pass it to the `parse()` method of the `Uri` class to create the `Uri` that is used as the data for the `Intent`. You can then use that `Uri` with the `ACTION_VIEW` `Intent`, as follows, to open a map:

```
Uri geo = Uri.parse(geoURI);
Intent geoMap = new Intent(Intent.ACTION_VIEW, geo);
startActivity(geoMap);
```

Showing the Map

You add a button in `MainActivity` that will open a map when clicked. To do that, you pass `startActivity()` and the `Intent` that uses `ACTION_VIEW` and a URI that specifies latitude and longitude. Your code checks to see whether there is an `Activity` that can handle the `Intent`. If you are using a device to test, you might have several apps available.

NOTE

Using Maps in the Android Emulator

You can find online instructions for setting up Google Maps on the Android emulator. It is not a straightforward process. If you do not have access to a device, try using the map code as shown in Listing 2.6 and considering adding a message that displays to indicate that no map app is available. The emulator will have a browser, and you can work with the `ACTION_VIEW` for a web page in the emulator.

Add a button to the user interface in activity_main.xml. By default, Android Studio assigns the name `button2`. As you develop more complex apps, you want to use more meaningful names, but for now it is okay to use `button2`. Change the text on `button2` to say, "Show Map".

Figure 2.8 is a screenshot of Android Studio with the changes made to android_main.xml.

You will add code to MainActivity.java to show a map when the Show Map button has been clicked. The code is similar to what you did to start the second `Activity`. You will create the button and add an `onClickListener()`. The difference is the `Intent` definition.

Listing 2.6 shows the additional code that is added to MainActivity.java. The `String geoURI` is defined in line 5 using the format for location and a zoom level of 23. An `Intent` called `mapIntent` is created on line 8 and used in the `startActivity()` method on line 9. Line 8 uses the `resolveActivity()` method to determine whether an `Activity` exists that will handle the specified `Intent`.

FIGURE 2.8
Adding a Show Map button in Android Studio.

LISTING 2.6   MainActivity.java: Intent to Handle Location

```
 1: Button mapButton =   (Button) findViewById(R.id.button2) ;
 2: mapButton.setOnClickListener(new View.OnClickListener() {
 3:     @Override
 4:      public void onClick(View view) {
 5:          String geoURI = "geo:37.422,-122.084?z=23";
 6:          Uri geo = Uri.parse(geoURI);
 7:          Intent mapIntent = new Intent(Intent.ACTION_VIEW, geo);
 8:          if (mapIntent.resolveActivity(getPackageManager()) != null) {
 9:              startActivity(mapIntent);
10:          }
11:      }
12: });
```

On some devices, the mapIntent may be handled by the Google Map app or the Google Earth app; the user is given a choice of which app to use. Figure 2.9 shows the app chooser screen and result of showing the GooglePlex at zoom level 23.

Displaying a Web Page

Creating an Intent to view a web page is similar to showing a location on a map. For viewing a web page, the Intent.ACTION_VIEW is used. The URI to use is created from the string for the web page to view. To view the Google search page, use http://www.google.com.

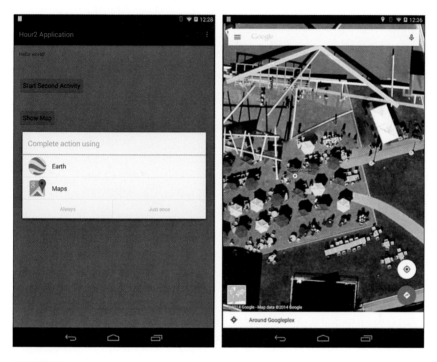

FIGURE 2.9
Showing GooglePlex using geo `Intent`.

Putting it all together, the code to create an `Intent` and start an `Activity` to show a web page is shown in Listing 2.7.

LISTING 2.7   Creating an Intent to Show a Web Page

```
1: String webURI = "http://www.google.com";
2: Uri web = Uri.parse(webURI);
3: Intent webIntent = new Intent(Intent.ACTION_VIEW, web);
4: if (webIntent.resolveActivity(getPackageManager()) != null) {
5:     startActivity(webIntent)
6: }
```

Using an Intent to Display a Web Page

It is common to display web pages in apps when needed. Opening a web page is an easy way to provide help or additional information to the user. You can update a web page independently of pushing out a new version of an app:

1. Add a new `Button` for opening a web page to activity_main.xml.

2. Use `findViewById` to access the new `Button` in MainActivity.java.

3. Add an `onClickListener()` to the `Button`.

4. When the `Button` is clicked, create an `Intent` to open a web page. (Refer to Listing 2.7.)

5. Start an `Activity` using the event.

More Actions

Many actions are available in addition to the `ACTION_VIEW` actions that you tried in this chapter. You can use `ACTION_DIAL` to dial a phone number and `ACTION_SEND` to send an email or text message. Actions such as `ACTION_PICK` can be used to select an image.

You have defined `Intents` using an action and additional data in the form of a URI. For more complex actions, you may create the `Intent` and then add multiple extras. For example, you could create an `Intent` with `ACTION_SEND` and add parameters for the recipient and subject. Any `Activity` that handles this `Intent` will be presented to the user, including email apps:

```
String[] recipient = {"carmendelessio@gmail.com"};
Intent emailIntent = new Intent(Intent.ACTION_SEND);
emailIntent.putExtra(Intent.EXTRA_EMAIL, recipient);
emailIntent.putExtra(Intent.EXTRA_SUBJECT, "About Android in 24");
emailIntent.putExtra(Intent.EXTRA_TEXT, "Hi Carmen, ");
```

Handling an Implicit Intent

You have created an app to handle several kinds of `Intents`. When you are creating an Android app, it is a good practice to determine whether there are one or more existing built-in `Intents` that might help in your development effort. Need to take a picture, pick a photo, or send a text message? There's an `Intent` for that.

You can also handle `Intents` that come from other apps. Currently, `SecondaryActivity` checks the `Intent` for data that was passed from `MainActivity`. You can modify `SecondaryActivity` to handle text being passed from other apps. That will require changes to the manifest file and changes to the code. The manifest file will be changed to show that

SecondaryActivity accepts ACTION_SEND actions for plain-text messages. The code is changed to do three things. First, it checks to verify that the Intent is not null. Then it checks to see if the Intent has data passed from MainActivity. If there is no data from MainActivity, there will be a check to see whether data has been passed from another app. If any plain-text data has been passed, that data is displayed.

The changes to AndroidManifest.xml indicate that SecondaryActivity will handle ACTION_SEND. In Listing 2.8, the Intent filter is added. SecondaryActivity responds to the SEND action for plain-text data. That is indicated on lines 5 and 7.

LISTING 2.8   AndroidManifest.xml for SecondaryActivity.java

```
1: <Activity
2:   android:name=".SecondaryActivity"
3:   android:label="@string/title_Activity_secondary" >
4:   <Intent-filter>
5:       <action android:name="android.Intent.action.SEND" />
6:       <category android:name="android.Intent.category.DEFAULT" />
7:       <data android:mimeType="text/plain" />
8:   </Intent-filter>
9: </Activity>
```

Changes are required in the code in SecondaryActivity.java to check for an Intent and to see which type of Intent is being passed. You want SecondaryActivity to display a message from MainActivity.java and to display any text passed via an Intent that uses the ACTION_SEND action.

All changes for SecondaryActivity.java occur in the onCreate() method. Listing 2.9 shows the changes to the onCreate() method.

In line 6 of Listing 2.9, the method getIntent() is called to populate a variable named intent. Line 7 checks to see whether the intent is null. If it is not null, two more checks are made. To check the type of extra data, the method hasExtra() is used. In line 8, the hasExtra() method is passed com.talkingandroid.MESSAGE as a parameter. That is the check to see whether this code has launched from MainActivity.java. If it has, the extra data is retrieved. Similarly, on line 10, a check is made to see whether the Intent has an extra called Intent.EXTRA_TEXT. That is one of the predefined extras that is used with the SEND action. If the Intent.EXTRA_TEXT is available, it is used and displayed.

LISTING 2.9   SecondaryActivity.java Handling Implicit Intent

```
1: @Override
2:   protected void onCreate(Bundle savedInstanceState) {
3:           super.onCreate(savedInstanceState);
4:           setContentView(R.layout.Activity_secondary);
```

```
5:          String message = "no data from Intent";
6:          Intent= getIntent();
7:          if (Intent != null) {
8:              if (Intent.hasExtra("com.talkingandroid.MESSAGE")) {
9:                  message = Intent.getStringExtra("com.talkingandroid.MESSAGE");
10:             } else if (Intent.hasExtra(Intent.EXTRA_TEXT)) {
11:                 message = Intent.getStringExtra(Intent.EXTRA_TEXT);
12:             }
13:         }
14:         TextView messageTextView = (TextView) findViewById(R.id.message);
15:         messageTextView.setText(message);
16:     }
```

So, what happens when an app sends an `Intent` that can be handled by
`SecondaryActivity`? You can check by using the browser app and sharing a page. The URL
of the page is displayed in `SecondaryActivity`. Figure 2.10 shows how a web page is shared
from the browser app in the emulator, the app chooser window, and the shared page URL being
displayed in `SecondaryActivity`.

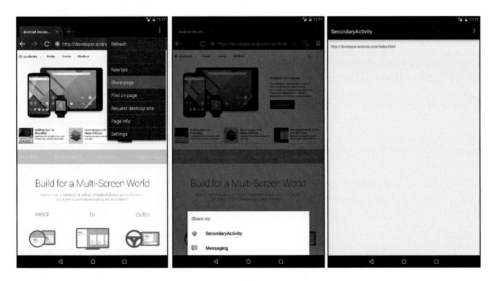

FIGURE 2.10
Starting `SecondaryActivity` via implicit `Intent`.

Summary

In this hour, you used `Intents` to start an `Activity` that you created and to start activities
that are built in to Android such as showing a location on a map or launching a web browser to

a specific page. In each case, the `Intent` consisted of an action to take and the data required to fulfill that action. You also saw how to create an `Activity` that responded to an `Intent` fired from another app. `Intents` are used throughout Android. You can create an app with your own set of activities, but each time you call the `startActivity()` method, you are using an `Intent`.

Q&A

Q. **What other `Intents` can I use?**

A. The documentation for Android at http://developer.android.com has information on additional `Intents`. Looking at the documentation for the `Intent` (`android.content.Intent`) class can also be helpful. You might also sometimes find that a third-party app has published an `Intent` that you can use. The issue you may encounter in that case is determining whether the user has the third-party app installed so that you can use the published `Intent`! Typically, in cases like that, there is information on how to handle that case.

Q. **Can I specify the exact app to use for an implicit `Intent`?**

A. This concept comes up when you want to share data from your app and want to specify which apps can handle the shared data. The best advice is to let the intent resolution system do its job and show the list of apps that can handle the `Intent`. The user might have a preferred email or messaging app that will show up in that list.

Workshop

Quiz

1. What must be updated so that an `Activity` in your app can handle an implicit `Intent`?

2. How does the code in `SecondaryActivity` determine what data it has available to display?

Answers

1. To handle an implicit `Intent`, the `Activity` definition on the AndroidManifest.xml file must be modified to include an `Intent` filter that specifies the `Intent`. The code in the `Activity` should handle the `Intent`.

2. If an `Intent` is successfully retrieved, a call to the `Intent.hasExtra()` method is used to determine whether the extra data that is expected is available. Specifically, a check is made to determine if the extra `com.talkingandroid.MESSAGE` or `Intent.EXTRA_TEXT` is available.

Exercise

The `Intent` to dial a telephone number is well-documented online at http://developer.android. com. Read about this `Intent` and implement a button in MainActivity.java that dials a specific phone number when clicked. Check the documentation on the `Intent` for making a phone call. How is it different?

HOUR 3
Understanding Resources

What You'll Learn in This Hour:

▶ Resources in your project

▶ Understanding common resources

▶ Providing alternative resources

▶ Internationalization: Using alternative-language resources

▶ Asset and raw data

In both Hour 1, "Introducing Android," and Hour 2, "Understanding Intents," you created projects using Android Studio and updated specific resources like the layout files. In this hour, you take a detailed look at Android resources and how to use them. Resources include simple values such as strings and values that you will use in your app and more complex resources like layout files. You can specify alternative resources based on different conditions. For example, resources can be specified for device attributes like screen size and for locales. This chapter covers different types of resources, and you learn about using alternative resources.

Resources in Your Project

Android applications are made up of functions (Java code, classes) and data (including resources such as graphics, strings, and so on). Android application resources are stored under the /res subdirectory of the project.

Create a new project in Android Studio called Hour3Application. The generated project includes a number of resources that are helpful to understand.

The generated project includes a single activity and an associated layout file. That layout file is a resource. The layout file includes a TextView that is populated with the words "Hello World." The text "Hello World" is stored in a resource file. The generated project also includes image resources and dimension resources.

There are several options for viewing the project structure in Android Studio. Figure 3.1 shows the project set to the Android view. Note the drop-down option is set to Android.

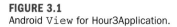

FIGURE 3.1
Android View for Hour3Application.

In the Android view, you can see the resource folder (res), and subfolders for drawable, layout, menu, and values. There are four icons in the drawable folder, activity_main.xml is in the layout folder, menu_main.xml is in the menu folder, and four XML files are in the values folder.

Figure 3.2 shows the same information in the *project view* in Android Studio. The specific folder names are displayed. The four icons of different densities exist in four separate folders.

You can review the contents of the res folder. The following files and directories have been created:

▶ **/res folder:** Required folder where all application resources are managed. Application resources include animations, drawable graphics, layout files, values like strings and numbers, and raw files.

▶ **/res/drawable:** Application icon graphic resources are included in several sizes for different device screen resolutions.

▶ **/res/layout/activity_main.xml:** Layout resource file used by Hour3Application to organize controls on the MainActivity screen.

▶ **/res/menu/activity_main.xml:** A menu for the Activity can be defined here. You use menus in the chapters on the ActionBar and navigation.

▶ **/res/values/:** Default folder to find values to be used in this app.

 /res/values/strings.xml: File where string resources are defined.

 /res/values/styles.xml: File where style resources are defined.

 /res/values/dimens.xml: File where dimension resources are defined.

▶ **/res/values-820dp/:** Folder to find values for devices that are at least 820 device independent pixels wide.

 /res/values-820dp /dimens.xml: File where dimension resources are defined for these devices.

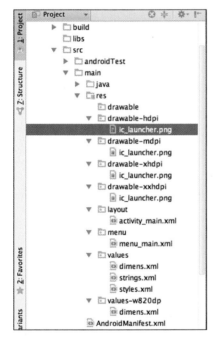

FIGURE 3.2
Project View for Hour3Application.

The folder structure created by Android Studio when you use the wizard to create an activity includes the most common resources and illustrates the basic concept of providing an alternate resource depending on the device where the app is running. Images in the drawable folders are appropriate for devices with different screen densities. In the project, alternative dimensions are provided for devices with a minimum width of 820 devices independent pixels. You learn more about additional resource folders and providing alternative resources in the section "Providing Alternative Resources."

▼ TRY IT YOURSELF

Viewing Your App Resources

Android development requires coding in Java. It also requires you to understand what resource files are and how to work with them. As a first step, you examine the resources created in a new project:

1. Create a new project.

2. Find the res folder in the project.

3. In the values folder, open the strings.xml file.

4. Modify the contents of the strings.xml file for the `hello_world` element.

5. Check the layout file for the activity in design mode to see that the changes you made are displayed.

Understanding Common Resources

Common resources for a project include layout files, image drawables, string definitions, and more.

Using Resources

As you have seen, resource files are stored within /res subdirectories. Filenames follow these rules:

▶ Resource filenames must be lowercase.

▶ Resource filenames may contain letters, numbers, underscores, and periods only.

▶ Resource filenames (and XML name attributes) must be unique.

Referencing Application Resources

All application resources are stored within the /res project directory structure and are compiled into the project at build time. Resources can be used in programs. One application resource can also be referenced in another resources.

To reference a resource from within your `Activity` class, you will be using the `getResources()` method to access the resources. Then, you make the appropriate method call based on the type of resource you want to retrieve.

For example, to retrieve a string named `hello_world` defined in the strings.xml resource file, use the following method call:

```
String greeting = getResources().getString(R.string.hello_world);
```

When you use the string resource `hello_world` as a value for another resource, the format to use is as follows:

```
@[resource type]/[resource name]
```

For example, the same `String` used earlier would be referenced as follows:

```
@string/hello_world
```

A `TextView` is created in activity_main.xml file that references the `hello_world` string resource using this format. Open activity_main.xml and view the file in text mode rather than in design mode. You will see a reference to the `hello_world` string resource in the first line:

```
<TextView android:text="@string/hello_world"
    android:layout_width="wrap_content"
    android:layout_height="wrap_content" />
```

Working with Simple Resources

Simple resources such as string, color, and dimension values are defined in XML files under the /res/values project directory in XML files. These resource files use XML tags that represent name/value pairs.

Working with Strings

You can use string resources anywhere your application needs to display text. You define string resources with the `<string>` tag, identify them with the `name` property, and store them in the resource file /res/values/strings.xml.

Here is an example of the string resource file that was created when you created the Hour3Application:

```
<?xml version="1.0" encoding="utf-8"?>
<resources>
    <string name="app_name">Hour3Application</string>
    <string name="hello_world">Hello world!</string>
    <string name="action_settings">Settings</string>
</resources>
```

String resources have a number of formatting options. Strings that contain apostrophes or single straight quotes must be escaped or wrapped within double straight quotes. Table 3.1 shows some simple examples of well-formatted string values.

TABLE 3.1   **String Resource Formatting Examples**

String Resource Value	Will Be Displayed As
Hello, World	Hello, World
"Hello, World"	"Hello, World"
Mother\'s Maiden Name:	Mother's Maiden Name:
He said, \ "No.\"	He said, "No."

You can access a string resource programmatically in several ways. The simplest way is to use the `getString()` method within your `Activity` class:

```
String greeting = getResources().getString(R.string.hello);
```

Working with Colors

You can apply color resources to screen controls. You define color resources with the `<color>` tag, identify them with the `name` attribute, and store them in the file /res/values/colors.xml. This XML resource file is not created by default and must be created manually.

Android Studio makes it easy to do this. When you choose the values folder and right-click to open the menu, you will see the option to create a new resource file. Figure 3.3 shows this. Create a new file called color.xml. When prompted for a filename, enter *color*.

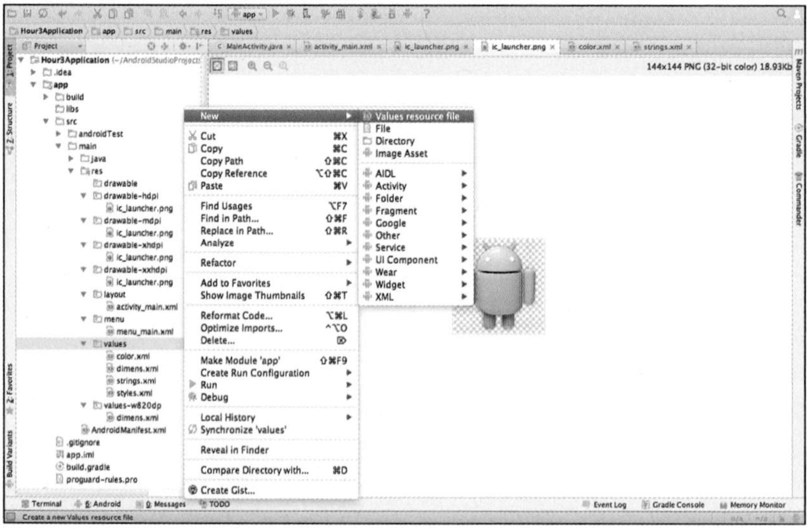

FIGURE 3.3
Creating a resource file.

Here is an example of a color resource file:

```xml
<?xml version="1.0" encoding="utf-8"?>
<resources>
    <color name="background_color">#006400</color>
    <color name="app_text_color">#FFE4C4</color>
</resources>
```

This resource file defines `background_color` and `app_text_color`. These resources can now be used in the app either programmatically or in other resource files. For example, these can be used in components in layout files. In the "Try It Yourself" section, you define a new color and use it for the background in your activity.

The Android system supports 12-bit and 24-bit colors in RGB format. Table 3.2 lists the color formats that the Android platform supports.

TABLE 3.2 Color Formats Supported in Android

Format	Description	Example
#RGB	12-bit color	#00F (blue)
#ARGB	12-bit color with alpha	#800F (blue, alpha 50%)
#RRGGBB	24-bit color	#FF00FF (magenta)
#AARRGGBB	24-bit color with alpha	#80FF00FF (magenta, alpha 50%)

TRY IT YOURSELF ▼

Creating a Color and Using It in Your Activity Layout

Here, you create a color resource file, define a new color, and then use that color in the layout file for your activity:

1. Create a color.xml using Android Studio.

2. Add color resources like `background_color`, as previously shown.

3. Open activity_main.xml in design mode.

4. Select the `relative_layout` component and find the `background` property.

5. Set the `background` property to the `background_color` resource (you can click the property in Android Studio and select `background_color`) from the project list (see Figure 3.4).

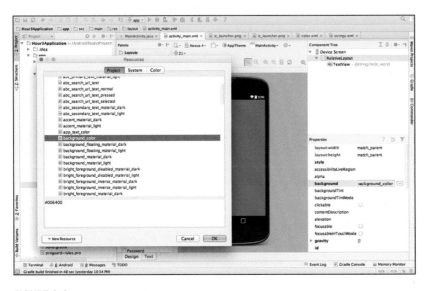

FIGURE 3.4
Using a color resource.

Working with Dimensions

Dimension resources are helpful for font sizes, image sizes, and other physical or pixel-relative measurements. You define dimension resources with the `<dimen>` tag, identify them with the name property, and store them in the resource file /res/values/dimens.xml.

In Android Studio, two dimension resource files are defined. A default file is used by most devices, and a separate file is used for devices that have 820dp of available width. Device-independent pixels are referred to as dp. Seven-inch and 10-inch devices will have a width of at least 820dp.

The dimens.xml resource file defines margins that are used in the activity_main.xml file to specify padding.

This is the dimens.xml file in the values folder. Each margin is defined as 16dp:

```
<resources>
    <!-- Default screen margins, per the Android Design guidelines. -->
    <dimen name="activity_horizontal_margin">16dp</dimen>
    <dimen name="activity_vertical_margin">16dp</dimen>
</resources>
```

This is the dimens.xml file in the values-w820dp folder. In this case, a larger horizontal margin is specified. You can check the activity_main.xml file to see how these dimension values are used:

```
<resources>
    <!-- Example customization of dimensions originally defined in res/values/
         dimens.xml (such as screen margins) for screens with more than 820dp
         of available width. This would include 7" and 10" devices in landscape
         (~960dp and ~1280dp respectively). -->
    <dimen name="activity_horizontal_margin">64dp</dimen>
</resources>
```

Each dimension resource value must end with a unit of measurement. You should use density-independent pixels as logical pixels for a device. The unit of measure is a dp. For fonts, use scale-independent pixels, referred to as sp.

The use of device-independent pixels and scale-independent pixels is highly recommended. In Android, there are not fixed screen sizes, so using device-independent values helps to ensure that your layout displays well on different devices.

NOTE

Density-Independent Pixels

Screens have a density expressed in dots per inch (dpi). A density-independent pixel (dp) has the size of 1 physical pixel on a device with a 160dpi screen. So, a density-independent pixel is equivalent to 1 physical pixel on a medium device. For higher-density screens, the number of physical pixels increases with the dpi:

  1 device-independent pixel = 1 physical pixel on a 160dpi screen

  1 device-independent pixel = 1.5 physical pixels on a 240dpi screen

Physical pixels can be determined from the dpi as follows: px = dp * (dpi / 160), where px is physical pixels, dp is the number of device-independent pixels, and dpi is the dpi of the device. Ten device-independent pixels is equivalent to 15 physical pixels on a 240dpi screen.

Working with Drawable Resources

Drawable resources, such as image files, must be saved under the /res/drawable project directory hierarchy. Android devices have different sizes and different pixel-density screens. Android provides a mechanism to show an appropriate image for each type of screen. When applications provide multiple versions of the same image for different pixel-density screens, the appropriate image is shown for the screen.

The Android project generates four drawable directories: drawable-mdpi (medium density), drawable-hdpi (high density), drawable-xhdpi (extra-high density), and drawable-xxhdpi (extra extra-high density). The system picks the correct version of the resource based on the device the application is running on. All versions of a specific resource must have the same name in each of the drawable directories.

You can drag and drop image files into the /res/drawable directory using Android Studio.

The most common drawable resources used in applications are bitmap-style image files, such as PNG files. These files are often used as application icons and button graphics, but may also be used for a number of user interface components.

In addition to graphics files, you can also create specially formatted XML files to describe other drawables.

For example, you can create a shape in the drawable folder. The shape defined by the following XML is a rectangle with a thick red border. If you right-click the drawable folder, you are given the option of creating a new drawable resource file. The following was saved in a new file called background_shape:

```xml
<?xml version="1.0" encoding="utf-8"?>
<shape xmlns:android="http://schemas.android.com/apk/res/android"
android:shape="rectangle">
        <stroke android:width="20dp" android:color="#ff0000" />
        <padding android:left="20dp" android:top="20dp"
        android:right="20dp" android:bottom="20dp" />
</shape>
```

When this shape is used as the background in the `relative_layout` in activity_main.xml, a red border is displayed, as shown in Figure 3.5.

FIGURE 3.5
Defining a shape drawable.

Using Style

The styles.xml generated with Android Studio defines a default app theme. Different theme options are available in different versions of Android.

Android styles can be used to set a multiple attributes for a view. Rather than setting font size to 20sp in 10 `TextViews`, you can define a custom style for these views.

Consider a more complex example. If you want to define a `TextView` with blue text color, italics, and a font size of 20sp, you could define each of those individual values, or you could define a style that uses all of those characteristics and assign that style to the `TextView`.

These two snippets of XML code show the same result when it comes to displaying a `TextView`. In the first snippet, the values are set directly in the `TextView` attributes:

```
android:text="TextView"
android:textColor="#0000ff"
android:textSize="20sp"
android:textStyle="italic"
```

In the second case, we define a style called `CustomText` in the styles.xml file in the res/values folder:

```
<style name="CustomTextStyle"  >
    <item name="android:textColor">#0000ff</item>
    <item name="android:textSize">20sp</item>
    <item name="android:textStyle">italic</item>
</style>
```

Then, we use the style we defined in a `TextView` with the following line:

```
style="@style/CustomTextStyle"
```

The result is that the `TextView` controls are displayed in an identical manner. Figure 3.6 shows the `TextView` in activity_main.xml set to `CustomTextStyle`.

By defining and using styles, you can give your app a distinct look and feel. Your results will be consistent, and you can change the look of the app easily by changing the contents of the style files.

FIGURE 3.6
Simple style applied to `TextView`.

Providing Alternative Resources

There are different versions of images in different resource folders. That is an example of using the alternative resources based on the device running the app. By having a drawable-mdpi folder, you are specifying to the system where medium-density images can be found. That concept can be extended to create folders for different types of alternative resources.

In addition to the drawable density qualifiers like `mdpi`, you can use size qualifiers of `small`, `normal`, `large`, and `xlarge`.

To create an alternate layout for an extra-large screen, you append `xlarge` to the layout folder:

```
/res/layout-xlarge/activity_main.xml
```

Screen orientation can also be addressed by using alternative resources. To support portrait and landscape orientation, the qualifiers `port` and `land` are available.

Table 3.3 shows a list of import resource directory qualifiers. Note that the Android software development kit (SDK) version can be directly targeted using resources.

Resources qualifiers can be used in combination. This is a valid resource directory for landscape orientation on an extra-large device:

```
res/layout-xlarge-land/my_layout.xml
```

TABLE 3.3 Important Resource Directory Qualifiers

Directory Qualifier Type	Values	Comments
Language	`en, fr, es, zh, ja, ko, de, and so on`	ISO 639-1 two-letter language codes
Region/locale	`rUS, rGB, rFR, rJP, rDE, and so on`	ISO 3166-1-alpha-2 region code in ALL UPPERCASE, preceded by a lowercase `r`
Screen dimensions	`small, normal, large, xlarge`	Screen size and density ratio
Screen aspect ratio devices	`long, notlong`	Screen aspect ratio to handle "wide screen" devices
Screen orientation	`port, land`	Portrait mode, landscape mode
Dock mode	`car, desk`	Device is in a specific dock state
Night mode	`night, notnight`	Device is in night or day mode
Screen pixel density	`ldpi, mdpi, hdpi, xhdpi, nodpi`	Screen density that the resource is for
Touch screen type	`notouch, stylus, finger`	No Touch screen, Stylus-only, Finger Touch screen
Is keyboard available	`keysexposed, keyshidden, keyssoft`	Keyboard available, Keyboard not available to user, resources used only with software keyboard
Primary non-touch screen navigation method	`nonav, dpad, trackball, wheel`	Four-key directional pad, track-ball, scroll wheel
SDK version	`v1, v2, v3, v4, v5, v6, v7, v8, v9, v10, v11, v12, and so on`	The SDK version's API level (for example, v4 is Android SDK 1.6, while v11 represents 3.0)

Internationalization: Using Alternative Languages Resources

It may be beneficial to provide your app in different languages. You can create alternative resource files that specify the languages that you want to support. If you use resources throughout your app, your strings.xml file will contain every instance of text in the app. Providing the app in a new language will require creating an alternative language-specific strings.xml file.

At a high level, a locale is specified by language code and country code. For example, the constants en_US, en_GB, and en_AU represent the English language as spoken in the United States, Great Britain, and Australia, respectively.

The only locale that is guaranteed to be available is en_US locale. Not all devices will have all locales. A device sold in the United States will likely support en_US and es_US (English and Spanish for the United States), but will not necessarily support en_GB (English Great Britain).

Handling Locales with Android

Much like other operating systems, the Android platform has a system setting for locale. This setting has a default setting that can be modified by the mobile operator. For example, a German mobile operator might make the default locale Deutsch (Deutschland) for its shipping devices. An American mobile operator would likely set the default locale to English (American) and include an option for the locale Español (Estados Unidos)—thus supporting American English and Spanish of the Americas.

A user can change the system-wide setting for locale in the Settings application. The locale setting affects the behavior of all applications installed on the device. Some apps may support the selected language, and others may not. If the app does not support the selected language, the default language for that app will be used.

When an Android application uses a project resource, the Android operating system attempts to match the best possible resource for the job at runtime. In many cases, that means checking for a resource in the specific language or regional locale. If no resource matches the required locale, the system falls back on the default resource.

Developers can include language and locale resources by providing resources in specially named resource directories of the project. You can localize any application resource, whether it is a string resource file, drawable, animation sequence, or some other type. It is important to consider setting locales for layout resources. Layouts that are carefully reviewed in English may need to change for other languages. A short word in one language may be a long word in another language. If your buttons just fit in a layout, they may need to change for other locales.

Specifying Default Resources

A default resource is a resource that has no resource qualifiers.

Default resources are the most important resources because they are the fallback for any situation when a specific, tailored resource does not exist (which happens more often than not).

Specifying Language-Specific Resources

To specify strings for a specific language, you must supply the resource under a specially named directory that includes the two-letter language code. For example, English is en, French is fr, and German is de. Let's look at an example of how this works.

Say that you want an application to support English, German, and French strings. To do so, follow these steps:

1. Create a strings.xml resource file for each language. Each string that is to be localized must appear in each resource file with the same name, so it can be programmatically loaded correctly. Any strings you don't want to localize can be left in the default (English) / res/values/strings.xml file.

2. Save the French strings.xml resource file to the /res/values-fr/ directory.

3. Save the German strings.xml resource file to the /res/values-de/ directory.

Android can now grab the appropriate string, based on the system locale. However, if no match exists, the system falls back on whatever is defined in the /res/values/ directory. This means that if English (or Arabic, or Chinese, or Japanese, or an unexpected locale) is chosen, the default (fallback) English strings are used.

Similarly, you could provide German-specific drawable resources to override the default graphics in the /res/drawable/ directory by supplying versions (each with the same name) in the /res/drawable-de/ directory.

Android Studio makes this particularly easy to create folders with proper qualifiers because these are provided as options when you create a new resource file!

Summary

This hour examined the structure of an Android project and took a look at how to create and use common resources.

Once defined, resources can be accessed programmatically and can be used by other resources. String, color, and dimension values are stored in specially formatted XML files, and graphic images are stored as individual files. Application user interfaces are defined using XML layout files. It is possible to provide alternative resources based on device specifications such as screen density and size. Alternative resources can also be provided based on the locale supported by the device.

Q&A

Q. Must string, color, and dimension resources be stored in separate XML files?

A. Technically, no. However, it is a good practice to follow. Keeping the resource types separate keeps them organized.

Q. What are some of the technical and practical benefits of using resources?

A. Using resources keeps your code cleaner and more readable. In practice, using resources for colors, text, and styles allows you to consistently and quickly change the look and feel of your app just by changing the resource files.

Workshop

Quiz

1. True or false: Resource filenames can be uppercase.

2. Specify a resource folder for layouts that are in portrait mode and support a large screen?

3. True or false: You can provide alternative resources for a specific version of the Android SDK, such as KitKat.

Answers

1. False. Resource filenames may contain letters, numbers, and underscores and must be lowercase.

2. The resource folder is res/layout-large-port.

3. True. Refer to Table 3.3 for the list of resource directory qualifiers.

Exercises

1. Add a new color resource with a value of `#00ff00` to your project. Within the `activity_main.xml` layout file, change the `textColor` attribute of the `TextView` control to the color resource you just created.

2. Add a new drawable graphics file resource to your Hour3App project (for example, a small PNG or JPG file). In Android Studio, add an `ImageView` control to the layout. Then set the `ImageView` control's `src` attribute to the drawable resource you just created. View the layout in the Android Studio.

HOUR 4
Activities and Fragments

What You'll Learn in This Hour:

▶ Working with `Activities`
▶ Understanding the `Activity` lifecycle
▶ Introducing fragments

You have created several activities so far. You used intents to start activities and modified layout files to change the user interface for an `Activity`. In this hour, you retrieve a result from an activity and understand what it means to handle configuration changes. You learn about all the methods within an `Activity` and how they relate to the `Activity` lifecycle. Fragments and their relationship to activities are introduced.

Working with Activities

You will do a quick review of how you have worked with `Activities` so far. Then, new concepts like starting an activity to get a result are introduced.

A Quick Review

In Hour 2, "Understanding Intents," you learned that `Intents` are used to start tasks in Android. You used an `Intent` to start one activity from another. In addition, you were able to pass data from one activity to another. To start an `Activity`, pass data to define an `Intent` and add data using the `putExtra()` method, like this:

```
Intent startIntent = new Intent(getApplicationContext(), SecondaryActivity.class);
startIntent.putExtra("com.talkingandroid.MESSAGE","Hello SecondaryActivity" );
startActivity(startIntent);
```

For all the examples in which you used an `Activity`, all the code was added to the `onCreate()` method. You learn more about that method and others later in the section "Understanding the Activity Lifecycle."

Activities must be defined in the AndroidManifest.xml file. When you create an `Activity` using Android Studio, the manifest file is updated directly. If an activity is not defined in the manifest file, a fatal error occurs when the code runs. The fatal error includes a helpful message that asks: "`Have you declared this activity in your AndroidManifest.xml?`"

Using Layouts

In every `Activity` that you created, you also created an XML layout file for the user interface. The `Activity` displays the view from the layout by calling `setContentView()` with the layout resource name. For example:

```
setContentView(R.layout.activity_main);
```

For each widget in the layout that you want to use in the `Activity`, you call the `findViewById()` method. The resource id is passed to the `findViewById()` method. If you define a `Button` with the resource ID set to `button` in the layout file, you access the `Button` in your `Activity` by using the following:

```
Button okButton = (Button) findViewById(R.id.button);
```

The `okButton` is now a variable that can be used in your code.

Returning a Result: Using StartActivityForResult

You have created activities, started activities, and passed data from one activity to another using intents. Another way that activities interact is the case where one activity starts a second activity with a request to return a result. Whatever data is collected in the second activity is passed to the first activity as the result.

Consider an example app with a `MainActivity` that launches a second `Activity` called `MessageActivity`. The purpose of `MessageActivity` is to accept one line of input from the user. The resulting message is passed back to `MainActivity` and displayed. Figure 4.1 shows what this will look like.

▼ **Using StartActivityForResult, Part I: Creating MainActivity**

To start one `Activity` from another, you must create two activities. Here, you set up `MainActivity`:

1. Create a new project.
2. The project should have a blank activity called `MainActivity`.
3. Delete the `TextView` HelloWorld in the activity_message.xml.
4. Modify activity_main.xml to include a `TextView` and a button (see Figure 4.1).
5. Add an `onClickListener()` for the button.

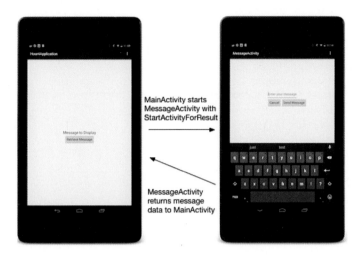

MainActivity starts
MessageActivity with
StartActivityForResult

MessageActivity
returns message
data to MainActivity

FIGURE 4.1
MainActivity requests information from MessageActivity.

At this point, MainActivity can start MessageActivity and handle a result being returned from MessageActivity.

MainActivity has a layout with a TextView and a Button. When MainActivity receives a result from MessageActivity, the text entered in MessageActivity will be displayed.

So, MainActivity has two jobs: start MessageActivity and handle the result returned from MessageActivity.

You can create a new Android Studio project called Hour4Application and follow along to create MainActivity.

You start with MainActivity and then build MessageActivity. Your layout file activity_main.xml will have a TextView with the resource ID textView and a Button with the resource ID button. You can use Android Studio to create this layout file.

For reference, Listing 4.1 shows the layout file with the two widgets defined. This is similar to what you should see whether you open the activity_main.xml file to view in text mode. Assuming that you create your layout file visually, there may be differences. In Listing 4.1, the TextView widget definition begins on line 9. The ID is specified on line 14. Similarly, the Button widget definition begins on line 18, and the ID is specified on line 22.

LISTING 4.1 Layout File

```
 1:  <RelativeLayout xmlns:android="http://schemas.android.com/apk/res/android"
 2:      xmlns:tools="http://schemas.android.com/tools"
android:layout_width="match_parent"
 3:      android:layout_height="match_parent"
 4:      android:paddingLeft="@dimen/activity_horizontal_margin"
 5:      android:paddingRight="@dimen/activity_horizontal_margin"
 6:      android:paddingTop="@dimen/activity_vertical_margin"
 7:      android:paddingBottom="@dimen/activity_vertical_margin"
 8:      tools:context=".MainActivity">
 9:      <TextView
10:          android:layout_width="wrap_content"
11:          android:layout_height="wrap_content"
12:          android:textAppearance="?android:attr/textAppearanceLarge"
13:          android:text="Message to Display"
14:          android:id="@+id/textView"
15:          android:layout_centerVertical="true"
16:          android:layout_centerHorizontal="true" />
17:
18:      <Button
19:          android:layout_width="wrap_content"
20:          android:layout_height="wrap_content"
21:          android:text="Retrieve Message"
22:          android:id="@+id/button"
23:          android:layout_centerHorizontal="true"
24:          android:layout_below="@+id/textView" />
25:  </RelativeLayout>
```

`MainActivity` will start `MessageActivity` and handle any result that `MessageActivity` sends back. To start `MessageActivity`, you set up the `onClickListener()` event for button. That is similar to what you have done in earlier chapters. Handling the result from `MessageActivity` is something new (see Listing 4.2).

On lines 13 and 14, variables are defined for the `TextView` and `Button`. The `Button` is called `getMessageButton`, and the `TextView` is called `messageTextView`. These are defined for the entire `MainActivity` class. In Java, variables defined this way are called *fields*. Line 12 defines a constant called `MESSAGE_REQUEST_CODE` that is an int with a value of 0.

Lines 20 and 21 in the `onCreate()` method use the familiar `findViewById()` method for the called `getMessageButton` and `messageTextView`. To handle the button click event, `getMessageButton` calls the `setOnClickListener()` method. On line 25, a new `Intent` named `getResult` is created. On line 27, the call to `startActivityForResult()` is made. As you take a closer look, you see that the intent defined on lines 25 and 26 was created using `MessageActivity.class`. The `getResult` intent is used to start `MessageActivity`.

The `startActivityForResult()` method takes two parameters. The first is the intent to start. In this case, that is the `getResult` intent associated with `MessageActivity`. The second is an integer value that is used to track the request. In this case, `MESSAGE_REQUEST_CODE` is passed.

Listing 4.2, through the `onClickListener` defined on lines 24–30, is used to display the user interface and to start `MessageActivity` when the button is clicked.

The other job of `MainActivity` is to handle any result returned from `MessageActivity`. That is done in the `onActivityResult()` method on line 32. You want to check several things in the `onActivityResult()` method. You need to check the `requestCode` to see whether it matches a previous request. You check for two possible states in the result. It is often possible for the user to cancel a request. The two possible result codes that can be returned are `OK` and `Cancelled`. Those are constants that are defined in the `Activity` class, so you can use `Activity.RESULT_OK` and `Activity.RESULT_CANCELED` to check.

In Listing 4.2, the `requestCode` is checked on line 34 to verify that it matches `MESSAGE_REQUEST_CODE`. On line 35, the `resultCode` is checked to see whether it matches `Activity.RESULT_OK`. If it does, the data returned from `MessageActivity` displays in the `TextView` `messageTextView`.

How is the data passed back to `MainActivity`? The data is passed in an `Intent`, of course. In the `onActivityResult()` method, one of the parameters is an `Intent`. On line 26 of Listing 4.2, the message data is retrieved from that intent by checking for an extra data field using the key `"MESSAGE_DATA"`. The `String` data retrieved is then displayed in the `TextView`.

You have seen how `MainActivity` starts `MessageActivity` with the goal of getting a result and how `MainActivity` handles the `MessageActivity`. Now you can consider how `MessageActivity` collects a message and passes it to `MainActivity`.

LISTING 4.2   MainActivity.java

```
 1:  import android.app.Activity;
 2:  import android.content.Intent;
 3:  import android.support.v7.app.ActionBarActivity;
 4:  import android.os.Bundle;
 5:  import android.view.Menu;
 6:  import android.view.MenuItem;
 7:  import android.view.View;
 8:  import android.widget.Button;
 9:  import android.widget.TextView;
10:
11:  public class MainActivity extends ActionBarActivity {
12:      public final static int MESSAGE_REQUEST_CODE = 0;
13:      TextView messageTextView;
14:      Button getMessageButton;
15:
```

```
16:       @Override
17:       protected void onCreate(Bundle savedInstanceState) {
18:           super.onCreate(savedInstanceState);
19:           setContentView(R.layout.activity_main);
20:           messageTextView = (TextView)findViewById(R.id.textView);
21:           getMessageButton = (Button) findViewById(R.id.button);
22:           getMessageButton.setOnClickListener(new View.OnClickListener() {
23:               @Override
24:               public void onClick(View v) {
25:                   Intent getResult = new Intent(getApplicationContext(),
26:                                       MessageActivity.class);
27:                   startActivityForResult(getResult, MESSAGE_REQUEST_CODE);
28:               }
29:           });
30:       }
31:
32:       @Override
33:      protected void onActivityResult(int requestCode, int resultCode, Intent
data){
34:           if (requestCode == MESSAGE_REQUEST_CODE){
35:               if (resultCode== Activity.RESULT_OK){
36:                   String message = data.getStringExtra("MESSAGE_DATA");
37:                   messageTextView.setText(message);
38:               }
39:           }
40:       }
41:   ...
42:   }
```

`MessageActivity` is started from `MainActivity` and has several jobs. `MessageActivity` should include the following:

▶ An `EditText` widget so that the user can enter a message

▶ A `Button` to send the message to `MainActivity`

▶ A `Button` to cancel and send nothing back

The first step is to create `MessageActivity`.

Using StartActivityForResult, Part II: Creating MessageActivity

Use Android Studio to create a new `Activity` called `MessageActivity` and set up what is required to finish this application. You need an `EditText` widget and two `Button` widgets:

1. Create a new `Activity` called `MessageActivity`.

2. When prompted, name the layout **activity_message.xml**.

3. Delete the `TextView` HelloWorld in the activity_message.xml.

4. Add an `EditText` widget with the id `editText`.

5. Add two buttons: one with the id `buttonSend` and the other with the id `buttonCancel`.

6. The result should look similar to the image on the right in Figure 4.1.

At this point, `MainActivity` can start `MessageActivity` and handle a result from `MessageActivity`. You have created a layout file for `MessageActivity` and are ready to add the code to return a result.

As you will recall, the data `MainActivity` expected to handle was an `Intent`. When the user clicks the send message `Button` in `MessageActivity`, an `Intent` must be created. This snippet of code shows what will be done. The value in `EditText` is retrieved as a `String`. An `Intent` called `result` is created. The data to be passed back is added to the `result` `Intent` using the `putExtra()` method. This is where the key `"MESSAGE_DATA"` is used. Check line 36 of Listing 4.2. That is where the `onActivityResult()` method of `MainActivity` checks for the key `"MESSAGE_DATA"`. The `setResult()` method is called with two parameters. The first is the result code. Because this is for the send message `Button`, data is included, and the result code is `Activity.RESULT_OK`. The intent is passed the second parameter. The `finish()` method ends the `Activity`:

```
String message = messageEditText.getText().toString();
Intent result = new Intent();
result.putExtra("MESSAGE_DATA", message );
setResult(Activity.RESULT_OK, result);
finish();
```

That is how data is passed from `MessageActivity` to `MainActivity`. The other possibility is that the user will choose Cancel or click the Back button on the device. For the Cancel case, you send a different result. It will use `Activity.RESULT_CANCELED`, as follows:

```
setResult(Activity.RESULT_CANCELED);
```

Listing 4.3 puts this together for `MessageActivity`.

LISTING 4.3   MessageActivity.java

```
1:   import android.app.Activity;
2:   import android.content.Intent;
3:   import android.support.v7.app.ActionBarActivity;
4:   import android.os.Bundle;
5:   import android.view.Menu;
```

```
 6:   import android.view.MenuItem;
 7:   import android.view.View;
 8:   import android.widget.Button;
 8:   import android.widget.EditText;
10:
11:   public class MessageActivity extends ActionBarActivity {
12:       Button sendMessageButton;
13:       Button cancelButton;
14:       EditText messageEditText;
15:
16:       @Override
18:       protected void onCreate(Bundle savedInstanceState) {
19:           super.onCreate(savedInstanceState);
19:           setContentView(R.layout.activity_message);
20:           messageEditText = (EditText) findViewById(R.id.editText);
21:           sendMessageButton = (Button) findViewById(R.id.buttonSend);
22:           sendMessageButton.setOnClickListener(new View.OnClickListener() {
23:
24:             @Override
25:             public void onClick(View v) {
26:                 String message = messageEditText.getText().toString();
27:                 Intent result = new Intent();
28:                 result.putExtra("MESSAGE_DATA", message );
29:                 setResult(Activity.RESULT_OK, result);
30:                 finish();
31:             }
32:         });
33:         cancelButton = (Button) findViewById(R.id.buttonCancel);
34:         cancelButton.setOnClickListener(new View.OnClickListener() {
35:             @Override
36:             public void onClick(View v) {
37:                 setResult(Activity.RESULT_CANCELED);
38:                 finish();
39:             }
40:         });
21:     }
42: ...
43:
```

Handling Configuration Changes

When you run the Hour4Application, you can request data from MessageActivity and display the result in MainActivity. Something interesting will occur if you change the orientation of your device: The retrieved message is displayed on MainActivity. The message displayed is replaced by the original text "Message to Display." Figure 4.2 shows MainActivity displaying the message result from MessageActivity. The text displayed is "my new message." When the device is rotated, the orientation changes from portrait mode to landscape mode. That is a configuration change that causes the activity to restart. When the activity restarts, the onCreate() method is run again, and the original "Message to Display" text is shown. You can handle configuration changes in several ways to avoid this situation.

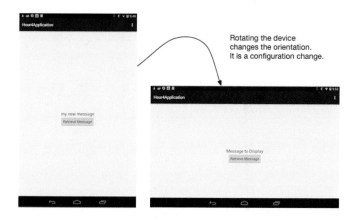

FIGURE 4.2
Changing orientation re-creates the Activity.

Using onSaveInstanceState() for Configuration Changes

One way to handle configuration changes is to save relevant information using the method onSaveInstanceState(). That method is called before an Activity is destroyed and provides a mechanism to save data in a Bundle (android.os.Bundle). If there is a saved Bundle, it is available in the onCreate() method for the Activity. You can address the configuration change issue in MainActivity by saving any data that is being displayed in this way.

To save the text within the messageTextView, you can implement the onSaveInstanceState() method as follows:

```
protected void onSaveInstanceState(Bundle savedInstanceState) {
    super.onSaveInstanceState(savedInstanceState);
    savedInstanceState.putString("saved_message", messageTextView.getText().
toString());
}
```

This method is added to MainActivity. All the work occurs on the saveInstanceState. putString() method. The key "saved_message" is used to save the contents of the messageTextView in the Bundle. For the TextView messageTextView, the contents are retrieved using getText() and converted to a String using toString().

This saves the `Bundle` before the `Activity` is destroyed. If data is saved in this `Bundle`, it is available to you in the `onCreate()` method. Thus far, you have not used the `Bundle` that is passed as a parameter to `onCreate()`. Now you check to see whether there is any data passed in the `Bundle`. If it contains the key `"saved_message"`, you will use the associated `String` to populate the `TextView`.

Listing 4.4 shows the changes to the `onCreate()` method to check whether the passed `Bundle` is null and whether it contains the expected data. Lines 6–9 of Listing 4.4 check to see whether the passed `Bundle` `savedInstanceState` is null. If it is not null, the `"saved_message"` `String` is retrieved and then displayed in the `TextView` `messageTextView`.

LISTING 4.4   MainActivity.java Checking for Saved Data

```
 1:  @Override
 2:  protected void onCreate(Bundle savedInstanceState) {
 3:      super.onCreate(savedInstanceState);
 4:      setContentView(R.layout.activity_main);
 5:      messageTextView = (TextView)findViewById(R.id.textView);
 6:      if (savedInstanceState!=null){
 7:          String savedMessage=savedInstanceState.getString("saved_message");
 8:          messageTextView.setText(savedMessage);
 9:      }
10:      getMessageButton = (Button) findViewById(R.id.button);
11:      getMessageButton.setOnClickListener(new View.OnClickListener() {
12:          @Override
13:          public void onClick(View v) {
14:              Intent getResult = new Intent(getApplicationContext(),
15:                                  MessageActivity.class);
16:              startActivityForResult(getResult, MESSAGE_REQUEST_CODE);
17:          }
18:      });
```

Taking Direct Control of Configuration Changes

There is another way. In many apps, it does not make sense for an `Activity` to restart on an orientation or keyboard change. The Hour 4 application would function properly if a configuration change occurred and `MainActivity` was not re-created. There is a way to accomplish that via a setting in the manifest file. Technically, you are telling the Android system that you are handling configuration changes directly. In the case of orientation and keyboard changes, you will not need to handle the configuration change directly. Essentially, you are indicating that the `Activity` should not be re-created on a configuration change.

This is how `MainActivity` is defined in the AndroidManifest.xml file:

```
<activity
    android:name=".MainActivity"
```

```
        android:label="@string/app_name" >
        <intent-filter>
            <action android:name="android.intent.action.MAIN" />
            <category android:name="android.intent.category.LAUNCHER" />
        </intent-filter>
    </activity>
```

To handle orientation changes directly, you add the following line:

```
Android:configChanges="orientation|KeyboardHidden"
```

That indicates that you will handle these configuration changes in your code. You can do that by implementing the onConfigurationChanged() method of your Activity. If you do not implement the onConfigurationChanged() in the activity, the result will be that the Activity will not restart and there will be no ill effects.

Indicating that you are handling configuration changes in this way is a good way to avoid problems that sometimes arise from configurations changes.

The listing for MainActivity in the AndroidManifest.xml file is as follows:

```
    <activity
        android:name=".MainActivity"
        Android:configChanges="orientation|keyboardHidden"
        android:label="@string/app_name" >
        <intent-filter>
            <action android:name="android.intent.action.MAIN" />
            <category android:name="android.intent.category.LAUNCHER" />
        </intent-filter>
    </activity>
```

Understanding the Activity Lifecycle

In this hour, you learn how to start activities and how activities pass data and work with each other. An activity also has a number of internal states. Activities are created, started, paused, resumed, and destroyed. The states that an activity goes through and the methods that are called when each state occurs is known as the activity lifecycle.

The activity lifecycle is important because each point in the lifecycle provides an opportunity to take an action within the activity. There may be set up work to do when an activity is started and clean up work to do when an activity is paused.

So far, all the activities that we developed have used the onCreate() method to set up the user interface for the app. In onCreate(), we call setContentView() to tie the activity to the layout and defined all the user interface elements like EditText and Buttons.

Consider the states of an `Activity`. When an `Activity` starts, a user interface displays. You started `MainActivity` in your app, and `MainActivity` started `MessageActivity`. When `MessageActivity` started, what happened to `MainActivity`? `MainActivity` is no longer visible to the user, but it did not disappear. `MainActivity` is paused, but running in the background. `MessageActivity` has been created and has started.

Create, Start, Resume, Pause, Stop, and Destroy

The first step in the `Activity` lifecycle is the creation of the `Activity`. When an `Activity` is being created, it is not visible to the user. At the moment that the `Activity` becomes visible to the user, it is considered to have started. The two states of an `Activity` being created and started correspond to the two methods, `onCreate()` and `onStart()`.

An `Activity` can be partially visible. For example, a dialog window may cover an `Activity`. When a dialog window is covering an `Activity`, the user cannot interact with the `Activity`. The `Activity` is paused. There is an `onPause()` callback method for that state.

When an `Activity` comes to the foreground, it is resumed. There is an `onResume()` callback method. Note that `onResume()` is called when the activity is first started and when it is resumed. It is called whenever the activity comes to the foreground.

When an `Activity` is no longer visible to the user, it is stopped. In the Hour 4 application, when `MessageActivity` is displayed, `MainActivity` is no longer visible. When an `Activity` has stopped, the `onStop()` callback method fires.

An `Activity` can be destroyed. In `MessageActivity`, there is an explicit call to the `finish()` method. That ends the `Activity`, and the `Activity` is destroyed. An `Activity` may also be destroyed when the Android system needs additional memory or resources and ends inactive activities. When an `Activity` is destroyed, the `onDestroy()` method is called.

The callback methods for an `Activity` are shown in Figure 4.3. The methods are shown connected to what can be considered their counterparts. You can consider matching methods for creating and cleaning up items. If something is created in `onResume()`, clean it up in `onPause()`. If something is allocated in `onStart()`, clean it up in `onStop()`.

In practice, you may find yourself using `onCreate()`, `onResume()`, and `onPause()` for app initialization and clean up.

In practice, you may find yourself using `onCreate()`, `onResume()`, and `onPause()` for app initialization and cleanup.

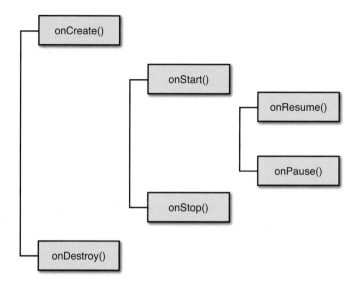

FIGURE 4.3
Callback methods for the `Activity` lifecycle.

Common Tasks in Callback Methods

As you have seen, the `onCreate()` method is used and set up the user interface using `setContentView()` and to initialize any other static parts of the activity. You can write many functional apps just by relying on the `onCreate()` method.

The `onStart()` method runs when an `Activity` comes to the foreground. That makes it a good spot to ensure that any required system resources are still available. For example, if GPS is required for your `Activity`, this is a good place to ensure that it is available. The advantage of checking that in `onStart()` is that `onStart()` is called less often than `onResume()`. So, you will ask the system to perform tasks that negatively affect performance less often.

The `onResume()` method is called both when the activity is first started and when it is resumed. It is called whenever the activity comes to the foreground. That makes it a good place to do things such as call the `getIntent()` method and read extra data that may be passed to the `Activity`.

The `onPause()` method fires when the activity leaves the foreground. That may mean that a dialog window is showing and the activity will resume shortly, or it might mean that it is the first step in the activity being stopped. This makes `onPause()` a good place to do things such as stop animations, save uncommitted data, and release system resources. Anything released with the `onPause()` method should be reset in the `onResume()` method.

The `onStop()` method ensures that the activity is in the background. It is the place to release all resources that are not required for the user to interact with the activity. It is best to kill threads in the `onPause()` or `onStop()` methods. Cleanup may occur in the `onDestroy()` method for any long-running processes that should continue after the activity is stopped.

Table 4.1 shows the key callback methods for activities, with recommendations on the functionality to handle in those methods.

TABLE 4.1   Key Callback Methods of Android Activities

Callback Method	Description	Recommendations
`onCreate()`	Called when an activity is created.	Initialize activity data. Set layout with `setContentView()` and set up the user interface.
`onStart()`	Called when an `Activity` becomes visible.	Check to ensure that resources are enabled.
`onResume()`	Called when the activity is brought to the foreground, including when the activity is first created.	Acquire exclusive resources. Start audio/video. Get intents and extra data.
`onPause()`	Activity is not in the foreground. It may be partially visible, such as when it is covered by a dialog window.	Stop animations, save uncommitted data, and release system resources.
`onStop()`	The activity is completely hidden and not visible to the user. The activity is in the background.	Release all resources not needed for the user to interact with the app. Clean up activity resources.
`onDestroy()`	Called when an application is shutting down.	Most cleanup should be done in `onPause()` and `onStop()`. If there are any long-running threads or processes, kill them here.

Introducing Fragments

A `Fragment (android.app.Fragment)` represents a portion of the user interface within an activity. A `Fragment` can be considered a modular part of an activity that can be added or removed. It is something of a "subactivity." If you consider an `Activity` to include the user interface for your application, you will add widgets like buttons and `textViews` directly to the layout for the `Activity`. A `Fragment` is like a standalone user interface unit that lives within the `Activity`.

Fragments were introduced in Android 3.0 Honeycomb. Honeycomb was created to run on Android tablets. One reason fragments were introduced was to make it easier to create apps that worked well on small devices like phones as well as on larger devices like tablets and televisions.

One advantage of fragments is that they provide a mechanism to develop modular parts of a user interface that can be used in different ways on different devices. Multiple fragments may be combined in either a tablet or phone user interface, but you may develop an app where multiple fragments are shown in the tablet design and only one in the phone design. The same fragments can be used in both devices. You may also find yourself flipping between fragments within a single activity on a phone design.

Like activities, fragments have a lifecycle. They are started, paused, and destroyed. Fragments always live within an activity, and whatever happens in the activity happens in the fragment. If an activity is destroyed, all the fragments within the activity are also destroyed.

Like an activity, you can create a fragment by using a layout file and a single class that defines the fragment and inflates the layout. You can use two techniques to display this fragment in an activity. The fragment can be embedded in the XML layout file for an `Activity,` or it can be added dynamically.

Creating an Activity and Fragment

Android Studio gives you the option to create an `Activity` that includes a `Fragment`. You can create a new project called Hour4ApplicationFragment and specify that the activity to be created should be a Blank Activity with Fragment. Figure 4.4 shows this selection.

FIGURE 4.4
Creating a blank `Activity` with `Fragment`.

When you create a blank `Activity` using Android Studio, an XML layout file is created for the user interface for the `Activity` and a Java source file is created that includes the logic for the `Activity`.

When you create an `Activity` with a fragment, two XML files are created. One file is created for the `Activity` and one for the `Fragment`. Specifically, activity_main.xml is the layout file for the `Activity`, and fragment_main.xml is the file for the `Fragment`.

One Java source file is created. It is MainActivity.java. MainActivity.java includes the initial code for the `Activity`; it also includes a class definition for something called a `PlaceHolderFragment`.

Taking the high-level view, this is how the code and layout files work:

▶ Activity_main.xml is the layout for the activity and a full-screen "shell" for displaying the fragment.

▶ Fragment_main.xml is the layout for the `Fragment`, and all real user interface widgets would go there.

▶ MainActivity.java includes an `onCreate()` method that loads a `Fragment` called `PlaceHolderFragment`.

▶ MainActivity.java defines the `PlaceHolderFragment` class.

Taking a closer look, the activity_main.xml layout file has a single `FrameLayout` with the id of `"container"`. The `layout_width` and `layout_height` are set to `match_parent`, so this single container will fill the available screen space.

The layout for the `Fragment`, fragment_main.xml, includes a `TextView` with the text "Hello World." It is the default layout that you have seen for previous activities.

The `onCreate()` method for `MainActivity` looks quite different. The `setContentView()` method is similar. There is a check for `savedInstanceState` for null. If this is not null, the `Activity` has been created previously, and you would not want to display a `Fragment`. The work of displaying the `Fragment` is in the `getSupportFragmentManager()` call. A `PlaceholderFragment` is added to the container in the layout for the `Activity`:

```
@Override
protected void onCreate(Bundle savedInstanceState) {
    super.onCreate(savedInstanceState);
    setContentView(R.layout.activity_main);
    if (savedInstanceState == null) {
        getSupportFragmentManager().beginTransaction()
                .add(R.id.container, new PlaceholderFragment())
                .commit();
    }
}
```

To complete the picture, the `PlaceholderFragment` must be defined somewhere. It is defined in ActivityMain.java as a static class that extends `Fragment`:

```
public static class PlaceholderFragment extends Fragment {
    public PlaceholderFragment() {
    }
    @Override
    public View onCreateView(LayoutInflater inflater, ViewGroup container,
                             Bundle savedInstanceState) {
        View rootView = inflater.inflate(R.layout.fragment_main, container,
false);
        return rootView;
    }
}
```

The only method implemented in the `PlaceholderFragment` class is the `onCreate View()`. In `onCreateView()`, the fragment layout is inflated and returned as the view for the `Fragment` to display.

The effect is that the `Fragment` user interface is created and displayed within the container `FrameLayout` in the `Activity`.

A `FragmentTransaction` object is created with the method `getSupportFragmentManager()`.

In the `onCreate()` method for the `Activity`, a `FragmentTransaction` is used. The `Fragment` adds the `PlaceHolderFragment` to the `FrameLayout` that is specified by `r.id.container` in the activity_main.xml file:

```
getSupportFragmentManager().beginTransaction()
                .add(R.id.container, new PlaceholderFragment())
                .commit();
```

A `FragmentTransaction` object uses the following methods to manage fragments in a layout:

- **Add()**: Adds a `Fragment` to a layout.
- **Replace()**: Replaces a `Fragment` within a layout.
- **Remove()**: Removes a `Fragment` from a layout.
- **AddToBackStack()**: Adds the set of commands in the transaction to the back stack. The fragment will not be destroyed when it is removed or replaced; it will be stopped. If the user navigates using the Back button, the fragment on the stack is redisplayed.
- **SetTransition()**: Sets an animation for the `FragmentTransaction`.
- **Commit()**: Commits the transaction. This causes the transaction to take effect. The AddToBackStack() method is associated with all the commands that are committed.

Using a Layout for Fragment Display

Fragments can be embedded directly into an XML layout for an activity. Using this approach, the fragment acts as a container for multiple controls. You use the `Fragment` class name to identify the fragment. When the layout is inflated, the `Fragment` class runs, and the user interface displays.

You can modify the code generated by Android Studio to use this method. There are several differences from what was done previously:

▶ Activity_main.xml is the layout for the activity. An element to display the `PlaceholderFragment` is added here.

▶ Fragment_main.xml remains the same.

▶ MainActivity.java includes an `onCreate()` method that just uses `setContentView()` to load the activity_main.xml. No `Fragment` transaction code is included.

▶ MainActivity.java defines the same the `PlaceholderFragment` class.

The biggest change is to activity_main.xml. It now includes a direct reference to the `Fragment` class. It is important to note that the name of the class must be used. The full class name includes the package name. Because the `PlaceholderFragment` class is defined within `MainActivity`, the full class name is `com.talkingandroid.hour4fragmentexample.Main Activity$PlaceholderFragment`:

```
<FrameLayout xmlns:android="http://schemas.android.com/apk/res/android"
    xmlns:tools="http://schemas.android.com/tools" android:id="@+id/container"
    android:layout_width="match_parent" android:layout_height="match_parent"
    tools:context=".MainActivity" tools:ignore="MergeRootFrame">
<fragment android:name=
          "com.talkingandroid.hour4fragmentexample.MainActivity$Placeholder
Fragment"
          android:id="@+id/placeholder"
          android:layout_width="match_parent"
          android:layout_height="match_parent" />
</FrameLayout>
```

As mentioned, the code in the `onCreate()` method for `MainActivity` just uses `setContent-View()` to show this layout. The work of creating and displaying the `PlaceholderFragment` occurs because the `Fragment` is defined directly in the activity_main.xml.

Summary

This hour reviewed some basic information about activities and showed how the method `startActivityForResult()` can be used to retrieve data from an `Activity`. Configuration changes such as changing device orientation cause an `Activity` to restart. Several techniques for handling this were covered. One technique is to save and restore the state of the `Activity` through code. The second technique is to change the manifest file to indicate that the app will handle configuration changes. The `Activity` lifecycle was an important part of this hour. Properly using callback methods within an activity will help you to create robust applications. Fragments were introduced, and two methods to display a simple `Fragment` were implemented.

Q&A

Q. What is the relationship between `Intents` and `Activities`?

A. `Intents` contain a call to action and can carry additional data. The call to action in an `Intent` results in an activity being started. The data provided in the `Intent` is made available to the `Activity`. When `Activities` are started, they are passed `Intents`.

Q. What is the importance of the `Activity` lifecycle?

A. The `Activity` lifecycle provides an opportunity to clean up an app as it is shutting down and to efficiently start and resume apps.

Workshop

Quiz

1. What two methods are used to start `Activities`?

2. When an activity expects a result, what method must be implemented to handle the result?

3. What is the difference between a bundle and extra data?

Answers

1. The two methods are `startActivity` and `StartActivityForResult`. An `Intent` is passed to both. `StartActivityForResult` also takes an integer value to track the request.

2. The method `onActivityResult` must be implemented. It will be passed a result code, a request code, and any data.

3. A `Bundle` is a collection of data. An extra is used to add data to an `Intent`. A `Bundle` can be an extra. That is, a `Bundle` can be defined, populated with data, and then added to an `Intent`.

Exercises

1. Create an `Activity` called `InputActivity`. `InputActivity` should have two `EditText` fields called that accept numbers as input. Add a `Button` to the `Activity` called Add.

When the Add button is clicked, take the data entered in the two `EditText` fields and save the data in a `Bundle`.

2. Create a second `Activity` called `AddActivity` that adds two numbers passed in a bundle and displays the results in a `TextView`.

3. Pass the bundle from the `InputActivity` to the `AddActivity` and verify the results. (This is not a real-world example, but it shows the ability to create activities, design simple layouts, and pass data between activities in a meaningful way.)

HOUR 5

Responsive Apps: Running in the Background

What You'll Learn in This Hour:

▶ Working in the background

▶ Using an `AsyncTask`

▶ Using `IntentServices` and `BroadcastReceivers`

In Hour 4, "Activities and Fragments," you learned about `Activities` and the `Activity` lifecycle. In this hour, you learn more about the UI thread of an `Activity` and how to create responsive apps by using background processes. In a responsive app, the user can still interact with an `Activity` while other tasks are occurring. Topics include the use of the `AsyncTasks`, `IntentServices`, and `BroadcastReceivers`.

Working in the Background

Multiple things are always occurring in an app. Something is displayed, the user taps the screen, or data is retrieved from the Internet and displayed. Some processes work best when they run in the background. Tasks that run in the background do work without interrupting user interaction.

The UI Thread

When an app starts and an `Activity` is launched, the display of widgets on the screen and the interaction with those widgets is handled by the Android operating system. A single thread is used to handle all interactions with the user interface. That means that any action running on that thread will block other user interface interactions. For example, if the user clicks a button for a task that requires 5 seconds to run, the user cannot interact with the user interface during that time. That will lead to a dreaded ANR error: App not responding! If that occurs, the user is given the option to wait or stop the app. Because this single thread handles all the interaction with the Android UI Toolkit, it is known as the *UI thread*.

You should not perform long-running tasks on the UI thread. *Building responsive apps means not blocking the UI thread.*

As you will see, it is possible to run background tasks, but a consequence of having a single UI thread is that the user interface widgets and views cannot be updated directly from those background processes. There are several mechanisms for running a background process and then updating the user interface on the UI thread.

You start learning about the UI thread by creating a nonresponsive app. Don't worry. One goal of this chapter is to learn about turning nonresponsive apps into responsive apps.

To put a delay in your app, use the `SystemClock.sleep()` method. This simulates a time-consuming task. Using sleep puts the focus on methods to address responsiveness. A more typical scenario that would unintentionally create a nonresponsive app would be downloading data or a large image from a network.

You are going to create an app that contains a single activity called MainActivity.java. The user interface will include four `Buttons` and a `TextView`. When the user clicks each `Button`, a 5-second delay will occur, and the `TextView` will be updated. The first `Button`, called `uiThreadButton`, performs the delay on the UI thread. Notice that the user interface is frozen for 5 seconds. Three methods to fix this delay will be implemented.

Listing 5.1 shows the code for the `uiThreadButton` `setOnClickListener()` method. On line 10, a 5-second delay occurs. On line 11, the `TextView` `resultsTextView` is updated with the message "Updated on UI Thread."

LISTING 5.1   Running on UI Thread

```
 1.     @Override
 2.    protected void onCreate(Bundle savedInstanceState) {
 3.        super.onCreate(savedInstanceState);
 4.        setContentView(R.layout.activity_main);
 5.        resultsTextView = (TextView) findViewById(R.id.textView);
 6.        uiThreadButton = (Button) findViewById(R.id.uiThreadButton);
 7.        uiThreadButton.setOnClickListener(new View.OnClickListener() {
 8.            @Override
 9.            public void onClick(View v) {
10.                SystemClock.sleep(5000);
11.                resultsTextView.setText("Updated on UI Thread");
12.            }
13.        }); ...
```

When the user clicks the `uiThreadButton` and this code executes, the app appears to be frozen for 5 seconds before the message is displayed in the `TextView`. When a user clicks a button, the button is highlighted to indicate the pressed state. In this case, the `uiThreadButton` remains in that state as the delay occurs (see Figure 5.1).

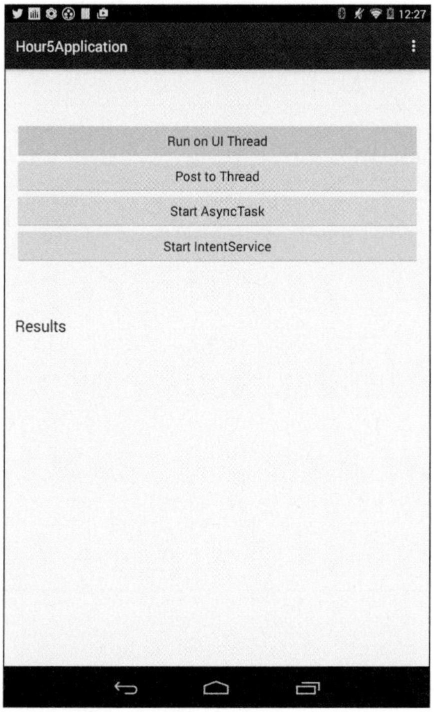

FIGURE 5.1
App frozen with code running on UI thread.

Using a Thread and View.post()

The first approach to fixing this is to move the processing for the 5-second delay to another thread. Threads other than the UI thread are known as *worker threads*.

You can create a worker thread to ensure that any delay will occur in the background (although that will present a new issue because it is not possible to update the user interface from a worker thread). There needs to be a mechanism to initiate an update to the user interface. The post() method is the most direct way to initiate an update from a worker thread. The post() method is available to any View(android.view.View). Each widget, such as a button or TextView, is a View. Listing 5.2 prevents the app from freezing by creating a worker thread for the delay.

In line 5 of Listing 5.2, a new Thread(java.lang.Thread) is defined. That thread contains a Runnable(java.lang.Runnable). On line 7, the 5-second delay occurs within the run() method of the Runnable. That delay is occurring on the worker thread. On line 8, the post() method is called for the TextView resultTextView. By calling post(), you are executing code that will run on the UI thread. On line 10, the setText() method is called, and the user interface is updated.

The effect of this is that when the user clicks the `postButton`, the app is not frozen.

LISTING 5.2   Using View.post()

```
1.      postButton = (Button) findViewById(R.id.postButton);
2.      postButton.setOnClickListener(new View.OnClickListener() {
3.          @Override
4.          public void onClick(View v) {
5.              new Thread(new Runnable() {
6.                  public void run() {
7.                      SystemClock.sleep(5000);
8.                      resultsTextView.post(new Runnable() {
9.                          public void run() {
10.                             resultsTextView.setText("Updated using post ");
11.                         }
12.                     });
13.                 }
14.             }).start();
15.         }
16.     });
```

Using `post()` is direct, but can become complicated. There are several other techniques to create responsive apps and to run intense processes in the background. You'll continue to use this simple example of a 5-second delay as you learn these techniques.

Using an AsyncTask

The `AsyncTask` class is used to manage background operations that will eventually post back to the UI thread.

To use an `AsyncTask`, you must create a subclass of the `AsyncTask` class and implement the appropriate callback methods:

▶ **onPreExecute()**: This method runs on the UI thread before background processing begins.

▶ **doInBackground()**: This method runs in the background and is where all the real work is done.

▶ **publishProgress()**: This method, called from the `doInBackground()` method, periodically informs the UI thread about the background process progress. This method sends information to the UI process. Use this opportunity to send updated progress for a progress bar that the user can see.

▶ **onProgressUpdate():** This method runs on the UI thread whenever the `doInBack-ground()` method calls `publishProgress()`. This method receives information from the background process. Use this opportunity to update a `ProgressBar` control that the user can see.

▶ **onPostExecute():** This method runs on the UI thread once the background processing is completed.

When launched with the `execute()` method, the `AsyncTask` class handles processing in a background thread without blocking the UI thread.

Three generic types are used with an `AsyncTask`. These represent the parameters passed to the task, the progress values used, and the final return value of the task. The class is defined with these generic types, as follows:

```
android.os.AsyncTask<Params, Progress, Result>
```

It is not required to use all types. `Void` indicates that the generic type is not used. The following defines `MyTask` with no parameters, progress types, or return values:

```
class MyTask extends AsyncTask<Void, Void, Void> { ... }
```

In the simple case of updating a `TextView` from an `AsyncTask`, you will use the `preExecute()`, `postExecute()`, and `doInBackground()` methods. In `preExecute()`, the `resultsTextView` will be updated to indicate that the `AsyncTask` has started. The 5-second delay will occur in the `doInBackground()` method. In the `postExecute()` method, the user interface will be updated. That occurs after the 5-second delay.

In this case, the `AsyncTask` can be defined completely within the `MainActivity.java` class.

Listing 5.3 shows the code for an `AsyncTask` called `DelayTask`.

LISTING 5.3   Update the User Interface from an AsyncTask

```
 1:     class DelayTask extends AsyncTask<Integer, Integer, Integer> {
 2:        @Override
 3:        protected void onPreExecute() {
 4:            resultsTextView.setText("Starting AsyncTask");
 5:        }
 6:        @Override
 7:        protected void onPostExecute(Integer result) {
 8:            if (result==0){
 9:                resultsTextView.setText("Updated via AsyncTask");
10:            }
11:        }
12:        @Override
13:        protected Integer doInBackground(Integer... params) {
```

```
14:                 SystemClock.sleep(5000);
15:                 return 0;
16:             }
17:         }
```

In the `onPreExecute()` method on line 4, the `TextView` `resultsTextView` is updated to display "Starting AsyncTask". The methods `onPreExecute()` and `onPostExecute()` both run on the UI thread and have access to the views defined in the activity.

The delay that has been implemented occurs in the `doInBackground()` method on line 14. In this case, the `doInBackground()` method always returns 0. The result returned on line 15 is passed as a parameter to the `onPostExecute()` method on line 7. If your code app requires different results to display based on what occurs in the background, you could use the result from `doInBackground()` to determine different actions in `onPostExecute()`.

In Listing 5.3, the `onPostExecute()` method updates the `resultTextView`.

In other apps, you might use the `onPreExecute()` method to show a `ProgressBar` to indicate that some work is being performed. That `ProgressBar` would be hidden in the `onPostExecute()` method.

The `publishProgress()` and `onProgressUpdate()` methods work in tandem to send updates from the `doInBackground()` method and to publish show updates on the UI thread. When the `publishProgress()` method is called from `doInBackground()`, `onProgress Update()` runs on the UI thread.

The `AsyncTask` class is ideal for short operations that interact with the user interface.

▼ TRY IT YOURSELF

Showing a ProgressBar While a Background Task Is Running

It is important to show the user visual feedback. Sometimes that means showing a `ProgressBar` while a task is running. Follow these steps to add a `ProgressBar` to an AsyncTask:

1. Use the `AsyncTask` code in Hour 5 as a starting point.

2. Add a `ProgressBar` to the layout for your activity.

3. Show the `ProgressBar` while the `AsyncTask` runs (use `onPreExecute()`).

4. Remove the `ProgressBar` when the `AsyncTask` completes (use `onPoseExecute()`).

Service and IntentService

An Android `Service` is a background process that runs independently of an `Activity`. Services are very powerful. A `Service` object is created by extending the `Service` (`android.app.Service`). Like an `Activity`, the `Service` must be defined in the AndroidManifest.xml file. A `Service` has a lifecycle that includes an `onCreate()` method. Other methods such as `onStartCommand()`, `onBind()`, and `onDestroy()` are part of the `Service` class.

An `IntentService` is a simplified version of a service.

You will create an `IntentService` using the same 5-second delay method used for other examples in this chapter. Typically, an `IntentService` is used for more complex tasks.

Using an IntentService

An `IntentService` (`android.app.IntentService`) provides a simplified way to implement a `Service`. An `IntentService` requires the implementation of a method called `onHandleIntent()`.

By using an `IntentService`, you can initiate a background process that handles some work and that can occur while the user in still interacting with the application. An `IntentService` is completely independent of an `Activity`. An `IntentService` will continue to run as the user interacts with various activities within the app. The `IntentService` you create will broadcast a message after a 5-second delay. You will use a `BroadcastReceiver` to handle the message from the `IntentService`.

Figure 5.2 shows a basic interaction between an `Activity` and an `IntentService`.

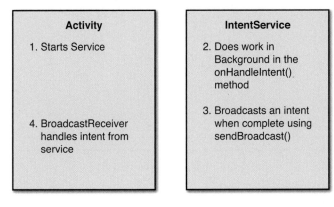

FIGURE 5.2
Interaction between an `Activity` and an `IntentService`.

Defining an IntentService

To develop an `IntentService`, you must implement the `onHandleIntent()` method. An `IntentService` also requires an empty constructor.

Listing 5.4 shows the entire code for the `IntentService` DelayService.java code for this project.

The empty constructor is included in lines 11–13. The `onHandleIntent()` method is in lines 15–21. The "work" done in this service is to call `SystemClock.sleep()` on line 16 to have the service sleep for 5 seconds.

Lines 17–20 of Listing 5.4 creates an `Intent` that includes an extra that specifies the message to be broadcast. The `Intent` is sent when the work is complete. The `Intent` created in this `IntentService` is handled when you define your `BroadcastReceiver`.

LISTING 5.4   DelayService.java: An IntentService Class

```
 1:   package com.talkingandroid.hour5application;
 2:   import android.app.IntentService;
 3:   import android.content.Intent ;
 4:   import android.content.Context;
 5:   import android.os.SystemClock;
 6:   public class DelayIntentService extends IntentService {
 7:       public static final String ACTION_DELAY =
 8:                 "com.talkingandroid.hour5application.action.DELAY";
 9:       public static final String EXTRA_MESSAGE =
10:                 "com.talkingandroid.hour5application.extra.MESSAGE";
11:         public DelayIntentService() {
12:             super("DelayIntentService");
13:         }
14:         @Override
15:         protected void onHandleIntent (Intent  intent) {
16:             SystemClock.sleep(5000);
17:             Intent  broadcastIntent  = new Intent ();
18:             broadcastIntent .setAction(ACTION_DELAY);
19:             broadcastIntent .putExtra(EXTRA_MESSAGE, "UPDATE:  USING INTENT
SERVICE");
20:             sendBroadcast(broadcastIntent );
21:           }
22:   }
```

Updating the Manifest for an IntentService

An `IntentService` must be defined in the AndroidManifest.xml file. The definition for a service is like that of an `Activity`. In this case, our service is the `DelayService` class, and the AndroidManifest.xml includes the following:

```
<service
    android:name="com.talkingandroid.hour5application.DelayService">
</service>
```

Starting the IntentService from an Activity

In MainActivity.java, you will define an `Intent` for the `DelayService` class and then call `startService()` to start the service. This is the similar to creating an `Intent` for an `Activity` and then starting that `Activity`. You can implement this code within a `Button`'s `onClick()` method.

Listing 5.5 shows the button definition and the implementation for calling the `DelayService`. The `delayIntent` is defined on lines 5 and 6, and the `startService()` method is called on line 9.

LISTING 5.5 Starting an IntentService

```
1:      intentServiceButton = (Button) findViewById(R.id.intentServiceButton);
2:      intentServiceButton.setOnClickListener(new View.OnClickListener() {
3:          @Override
4:          public void onClick(View v) {
5:              Intent  delayIntent  = new Intent (getApplicationContext(),
6:                                      DelayIntentService.class);
7:              startService(delayIntent );
8:          }
9:      });
```

That's it. You've created the `DelayService` and launched it from your `Activity`. You have one more step to complete the implementation. The goal is to have a 5-second delay and to update the user interface. This code starts the `DelayService`. The `onHandleIntent()` code will run, and the 5-second delay will occur. To update the user interface when the `DelayService` completes, you must implement a `BroadcastReceiver`. Typically, you want something to happen when an `IntentService` completes. The `IntentService` can send a broadcast, and the required work will be done in the `BroadcastReceiver`.

Referring to Figure 5.2, you have implemented the code for steps 1, 2, and 3. The code for step 4 must be done.

Adding a BroadcastReceiver

When the `DelayService` `onHandleIntent()` method finishes, we want to relay that information to the `MainActivity`. To do that, the service will broadcast an `Intent` using the `sendBroadcast()` method, and `MainActivity` will handle the `Intent` with a `BroadcastReceiver`.

In Listing 5.5, you saw how to start an `IntentService` in MainActivity.java.

Listing 5.4 is the complete `DelayService` code, and it includes creating an `Intent` and the call to the `sendBroadcast()` method. On line 18 of Listing 5.4, the `setAction()` method is called on the `Intent` with the parameter `ACTION_DELAY` that was defined as `"com.talkingandroid.hour5application.action.DELAY"` on lines 7 and 8. That action identifies the `Intent`. The extra data is added to the `Intent` with the `putExtra()` method:

```
Intent  broadcastIntent  = new Intent ();
broadcastIntent .setAction(ACTION_DELAY);
broadcastIntent .putExtra(EXTRA_MESSAGE, "UPDATE:  USING INTENT SERVICE");
sendBroadcast(broadcastIntent );
```

The remaining step is to implement a `BroadcastReceiver` in MainActivity.java.

You will create a `BroadcastReceiver` class called `DelayReceiver` within MainActivity.java. The `DelayReceiver` will be passed the `Intent` that was created in the service. That `Intent` includes a message as extra data. You can then display that data in the `resultTextView`.

After you create a `DelayReceiver`, it must be registered in the `Activity` `onResume()` method and unregistered in the `Activity` `onPause()` method.

Listing 5.6 shows the `DelayReceiver` class.

LISTING 5.6   BroadcastReceiver Implementation (MainActivity.java)

```
 1:  public class DelayReceiver extends BroadcastReceiver {
 2:     @Override
 3:     public void onReceive(Context context, Intent  intent) {
 4:         if (intent.getAction().equals(DelayIntentService.ACTION_DELAY)){
 5:             String message = intent.getExtras().
 6:                             getString(DelayIntentService.EXTRA_MESSAGE);
 7:             resultsTextView.setText( message);
 8:         }
 9:     }
10:  }
```

The `DelayReceiver` class extends `BroadcastReceiver` and implements the `onReceive()` method. The `onReceive()` method is passed an `Intent`. You need to verify that `Intent` passed as a parameter is one that you should act on. On line 4 of Listing 5.6, a comparison is made between the action for the parameter `intent` and `DelayIntentService.ACTION_DELAY`. If these actions match, the code to display the message is run. On lines 5 and 6, the `message` string is populated by reading the `Intent` extra data. (See line 19 of Listing 5.4 to see how this extra was added to the intent.)

On line 7 of Listing 5.6, the `String` message from the intent is displayed in the `resultsTextView`.

A `BroadcastReceiver` must be registered and unregistered. The `registerReceiver()` and `unregisterReceiver()` methods are used for this. When the `registerReceiver()` method is called, it specifies which `BroadcastReceiver` should run based on an `Intent` filter.

The `registerReceiver()` method is called in the `Activity onResume()` method. The field `delayReceiver` is of type `DelayReceiver`. The `Intent Filter` parameter passed to the `registerReceiver()` method filters based on the action associated with the intent.

The `BroadcastReceiver` is unregistered in the `Activity onPause()` method.

The `onResume()` and `onPause()` methods are shown:

```
@Override
    protected void onResume (){
        super.onResume();
        registerReceiver(delayReceiver, new Intent Filter(DelayIntentService.
ACTION_DELAY));
    }

    protected void onPause (){
        super.onPause();
        unregisterReceiver(delayReceiver);
    }
```

Using an `IntentService` and a `BroadcastReceiver` in tandem is a powerful way to invoke a background task and have a notification sent when that task is complete. As you have seen, there are a number of steps to creating an `IntentService` and `BroadcastReceiver`. The 5-second delay was used only as an example to show the implementation steps. `IntentServices` and `BroadcastReceivers` can be powerful tools that you can use to create sophisticated applications.

NOTE

IntentServices and BroadcastReceivers

In the example in this hour, an `IntentService` and a `BroadcastReceiver` were implemented in the same `Activity`. That does not need to be the case. A `Service` runs in the background and is completely independent of an `Activity`.

Listing 5.7 is the full code listing for MainActivity.java. It includes all the examples from this chapter. The associated layout file has four `Buttons` and a `TextView`. Listing 5.4 includes the full code for DelayService.java, so the full Java listings referred to in this chapter are included in their entirety.

LISTING 5.7 Full Listing of MainActivity.java

```
 1:   package com.talkingandroid.hour5application;
 2:   import android.content.BroadcastReceiver;
 3:   import android.content.Context;
 4:   import android.content.Intent ;
 5:   import android.content.Intent Filter;
 6:   import android.os.AsyncTask;
 7:   import android.os.SystemClock;
 8:   import android.support.v7.app.ActionBarActivity ;
 9:   import android.os.Bundle;
10:   import android.view.View;
11:   import android.widget.Button;
12:   import android.widget.TextView;
13:
14:   public class MainActivity  extends ActionBarActivity  {
15:
16:       Button uiThreadButton;
17:       Button postButton;
18:       Button asyncTaskButton;
19:       Button intentServiceButton;
11:       TextView resultsTextView;
12:       DelayReceiver delayReceiver = new DelayReceiver();
13:
14:       @Override
15:       protected void onCreate(Bundle savedInstanceState) {
16:           super.onCreate(savedInstanceState);
17:           setContentView(R.layout.activity_main);
18:           resultsTextView = (TextView) findViewById(R.id.textView);
19:           uiThreadButton = (Button) findViewById(R.id.uiThreadButton);
20:           uiThreadButton.setOnClickListener(new View.OnClickListener() {
21:               @Override
22:               public void onClick(View v) {
23:                   SystemClock.sleep(5000);
24:                   resultsTextView.setText("Updated on UI Thread");
25:               }
26:           });
27:
28:           postButton = (Button) findViewById(R.id.postButton);
29:           postButton.setOnClickListener(new View.OnClickListener() {
30:               @Override
31:               public void onClick(View v) {
32:                   new Thread(new Runnable() {
33:                       public void run() {
34:                           SystemClock.sleep(5000);
35:                           resultsTextView.post(new Runnable() {
36:                               public void run() {
37:                                   resultsTextView.setText("Updated using post ");
```

```
38:                                    }
39:                              });
40:                         }
41:                    }).start();
42:
43:               }
44:          });
45:
46:          asyncTaskButton = (Button) findViewById(R.id.asyncTaskButton);
47:          asyncTaskButton.setOnClickListener(new View.OnClickListener() {
48:               @Override
49:               public void onClick(View v) {
50:                    new DelayTask().execute();
51:               }
52:          });
53:
54:          intentServiceButton = (Button) findViewById(R.id.intentServiceButton);
55:          intentServiceButton.setOnClickListener(new View.OnClickListener() {
56:               @Override
57:               public void onClick(View v) {
58:                    Intent  delayIntent  = new Intent (getApplicationContext(),
59:                                          DelayIntentService.class);
60:                    startService(delayIntent );
61:               }
62:          });
63:     }
64:
65:     @Override
66:     protected void onResume (){
67:          super.onResume();
68:          registerReceiver(delayReceiver,
69:                    new Intent Filter(DelayIntentService.ACTION_DELAY));
70:     }
71:
72:     protected void onPause (){
73:          super.onPause();
74:          unregisterReceiver(delayReceiver);
75:     }
76:
77:     class DelayTask extends AsyncTask<Integer, Integer, Integer> {
78:
79:          @Override
80:          protected void onPreExecute() {
81:               resultsTextView.setText("Starting AsyncTask");
82:          }
83:
84:          @Override
```

```
85:            protected void onPostExecute(Integer result) {
86:                if (result==0){
87:                    resultsTextView.setText("Updated via AsyncTask");
88:                }
89:            }
90:
91:            @Override
92:            protected Integer doInBackground(Integer... params) {
93:                SystemClock.sleep(5000);
94:                return 0;
95:            }
96:        }
97:
98:        public class DelayReceiver extends BroadcastReceiver {
99:            @Override
100:           public void onReceive(Context context, Intent  intent) {
101:               if (intent.getAction().equals(DelayIntentService.ACTION_DELAY)){
102:                   String message = intent.getExtras().
103:                                       getString(DelayIntentService.EXTRA_MESSAGE);
104:                   resultsTextView.setText( message);
105:               }
106:           }
107:        }
108: }
```

Using Android Studio for IntentServices

Android Studio provides a wizard to generate both `IntentService` and `BroadcastReceiver` code. The process is similar to using Android Studio to create a new `Activity`. One advantage of using Android Studio is that the AndroidManifest.xml file is updated automatically. The code generated for both an `IntentService` and `BroadcastReceiver` is more complicated than the code that was implemented in this hour, but the concepts of starting the service, broadcasting an `Intent`, and having the `BroadcastReceiver` handle the `Intent` are the same.

Figure 5.3 shows the menu options to add a new `IntentService` in Android Studio.

▼ TRY IT YOURSELF

Creating an IntentService Using Android Studio

Android Studio provides a starting point for `IntentServices`. You should understand what is there, so follow these steps to generate an `IntentService`:

1. Create a new `IntentService` class using Android Studio (New, Service, IntentService).

2. Open the code for the `IntentService`.

3. Note the methods implemented and the style and structure of the generated code.

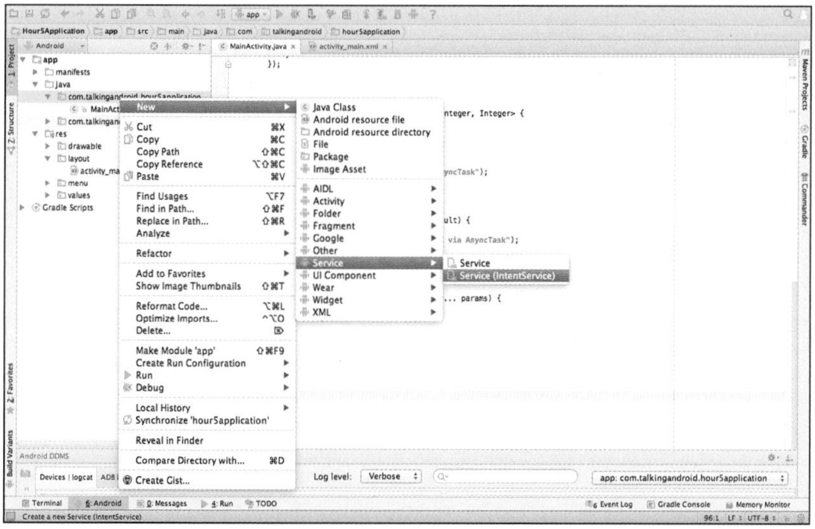

FIGURE 5.3
Using Android Studio to generate `IntentService` code.

Summary

This hour highlighted the importance of running code in the background in order to create responsive apps. Three methods for running processes in the background were demonstrated: to use `View.post()`, to use an `AsyncTask`, and to use an `IntentService`. The interaction between an `IntentService` and a `BroadcastReceiver` was demonstrated.

Q&A

Q. When should I use an `AsyncTask` or `IntentService`?

A. An `AsyncTask` provides background processing and mechanisms to make updates on the UI thread. It is ideal for short-lived tasks in an `Activity` that are used to update the user interface. An `IntentService` can be used for tasks that run longer and are not necessarily tied to one `Activity`.

Q. Is a `BroadcastReceiver` required when I use an `IntentService`?

A. No, sending an `Intent` and using a `BroadcastReceiver` is a way to indicate that the `IntentService` has completed and an action should occur. That fit the example and goal of this chapter. You could use an `IntentService` for any background task. For example, you might retrieve data and store data in the background using an `IntentServices`. Your app would show those updates the next time the local data is accessed.

Workshop

Quiz

1. What methods in an `AsyncTask` can make updates on the UI thread?

2. What method must be implemented in an `IntentService`?

Answers

1. In the example, you implemented `onPreExecute()` and `onPostExecute()` to update the user interface on the UI thread. In addition, you can use `onProgressUpdate()`.

2. To use an `IntentService`, you must implement `onHandleIntent()`.

Exercise

Starting with the `AsyncTask` code in this hour, implement an `AsyncTask` that uses `publishProgress()` and `onProgressUpdate()` to make periodic updates to the user interface. For a basic approach example, update the user interface when the `AsyncTask` starts, update the user interface after 2 seconds using `publishProgress`, and then update the user interface when another 3 seconds pass and the background task completes.

PART II

Creating the User Interface

HOUR 6
Using Basic UI Controls

What You'll Learn in This Hour:

▶ Using the Android Studio palette

▶ Handling user input

▶ Using Buttons for user actions

In this hour, you look at three common controls in close detail. By using a Button, EditText, and TextView with different properties, you'll see that you can create a variety of user interfaces. The functionality and tone of the apps can change, even when using the same views.

Using the Android Studio Palette

When you create a user interface using the visual editor in Android Studio, you select items from the palette. The palette organizes these items into categories that include Layouts, Widgets, Text Fields, Containers, and more. The Widget category includes TextView, Button, and ImageView components. The Text Fields category includes Plain Text, Passwords, and more. You'll examine these items individually and see how you can use them to create user interfaces with different functionality and styles.

You've already used the Android Studio palette for the activities and layouts in earlier chapters. The process now is the same. Create a new project with a blank activity. The examples in this chapter use API level 21 Lollipop, so select that when you create the activity.

As you've seen before, a layout file called activity_main.xml will be created. The work involved in this chapter is to modify that layout file. Start by deleting the TextView with the string "Hello World".

Note that you can move between design and TextView components when editing the layout file. In the TextView, you can directly edit the XML. That proves helpful in certain situations.

You will be creating a layout file that looks like Figure 6.1. As you can see in the figure, when a layout is highlighted, you are presented with the palette, a design view of the form, a Component Tree section, and a Properties section.

FIGURE 6.1
Layout with `TextView` and `EditText`.

You can modify the properties of a control in the Properties section. You can click a control within the design view to edit common properties.

NOTE

Views, Widgets, and Input Controls

A `View` (`android.view.View`) is the basic user interface element in Android. A `View` represents a rectangle that is displayed on the screen and has event handling. Widgets like `TextView` (`android.widget.TextView`) and `Button` (`android.widget.Button`) are extended from the `View` base class. Every widget is a `View`. As a whole, these interactive parts of your app are called *input controls*.

Handling User Input

In many apps, there is a need to collect basic information from the user. The most basic data entry field to use on a layout is an `EditText`. You used an `EditText` in previous examples. As you design layouts, you can use `TextViews` as labels for clarity and perhaps to add instructions. Buttons are used to initiate an action.

A `TextView` component displays text that the user cannot change. An `EditText` view is intended for user input. Like other controls, it is possible to change the `size`, `color`, and `background` properties of both a `TextView` component and an `EditText` view.

Adding a TextView

Start with the apparently simple `TextView` component. You can change the text color and size, you can create a resource to hold the text to be displayed in the `TextView`, and you can do all of that through Android Studio.

Positioning a TextView

In design view, you can drag and drop a `TextView` component to position it where you want in the user interface for the current layout. Choose Plain TextView from the palette and position it on the top and left side layout. Figure 6.2 shows the Android Studio palette when specifying a `TextView`.

FIGURE 6.2
Position the `TextView`.

You can do that visually. The options for position controls have a relationship to the layout being used. When you create an `Activity` using Android Studio, a `RelativeLayout` is used in the XML layout file. A `RelativeLayout` provides flexibility and provides the ability for controls to be positioned relative to each other. For example, one control can be specified to be positioned below another control.

GO TO ▶ CHAPTER 7, "USING LAYOUTS," to learn more about layouts.

Examine the layout in Android Studio, and you should see something like the following:

```
<TextView
        android:layout_width="wrap_content"
        android:layout_height="wrap_content"
        android:text="new text"
        android:id="@+id/textView"
        android:layout_alignParentStart="true"
        android:layout_alignParentTop="true" />
```

The attribute `android:layout_alignParentTop` positions the `TextView` at the top of the interface. The parent of this control is the relative layout. The attribute `android:layout_alignParentStart` puts the `TextView` at the start of the parent. These two attributes put the view in the top left of the user interface.

Using a String Resource to Change Text

You learned about string resource files in Hour 3, "Understanding Resources." You should always use a resource for any text that is displayed in the user interface. The text is easy to modify, and by using resource files, you are well positioned to internationalize your app by creating alternative language-specific resources.

TIP

Always Use a Resource File for String Values

By putting string values in resource files, you can separate the text content from your code. The `String` values are all in one logical place. You can easily reuse the same value in different parts of your code. This method prepares your app for internationalization. You can provide alternative resource files for different languages.

▼ TRY IT YOURSELF

Adding a String Resource to Display in the TextView

Using the properties editor in Android Studio, you can create a new resource to display content in the TextView:

1. Select the `TextView` in Android Studio.

2. Find the `Text` property and open the resource editor. (You can also double-click the `TextView` and open the resource editor there.)

3. Choose New Resource.

4. Select New String Value.

5. Enter a resource name and value for display in the `TextView` (see Figure 6.3).

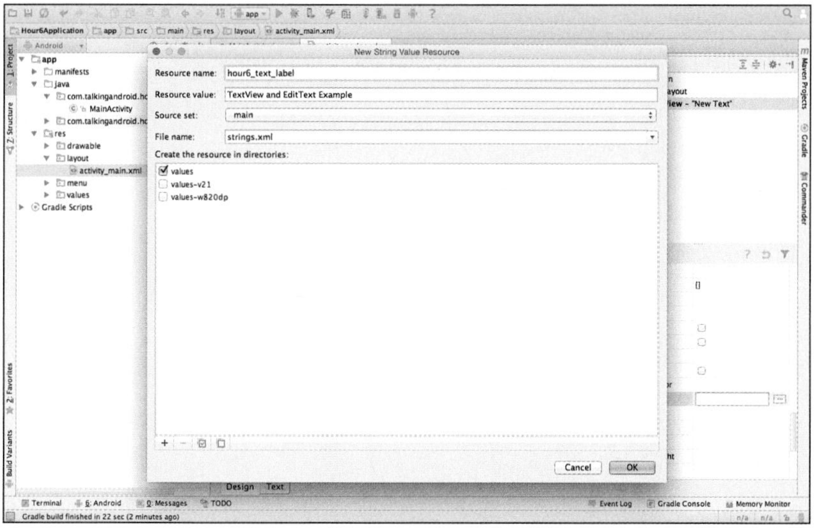

FIGURE 6.3
Adding a string resource.

Changing Text Color

To change the color of the text in the `TextView`, find `textColor` property and open the color dialog (see Figure 6.4). The basics of using color were covered in Hour 3.

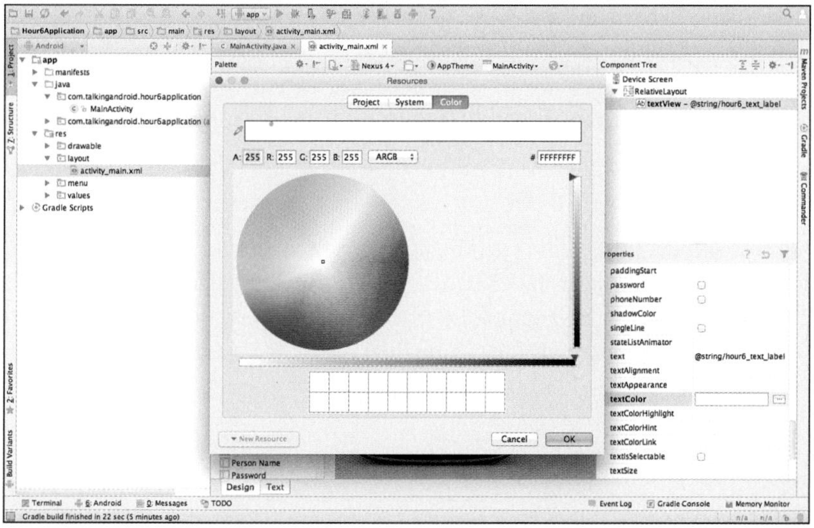

FIGURE 6.4
Changing color.

Text Size and Style

Remember text size is set using sp units. Style refers to bold, italic, or normal.

With the `textSize` set to 24sp and the `textStyle` set to bold, the layout XML file for the `TextField` shows the following:

```
<TextView
    android:layout_width="match_parent"
    android:layout_height="wrap_content"
    android:text="@string/hour6_text_label"
    android:id="@+id/textView"
    android:layout_alignParentStart="true"
    android:layout_alignParentTop="true"
    android:textColor="#ff2d1dff"
    android:textSize="24sp"
    android:textStyle="bold" />
```

Using EditText

An `EditText` is used for data entry. There are two properties for an `EditText` that help the user enter valid data. The first is the `hint` property, and the second is the `inputType`. A hint is displayed in the contents of an unedited `EditText`.

Adding a Hint

In Figure 6.1, the hint for `editText` says, "Enter a name," and the hint for `editText2` says, "Enter a number."

The `hint` property should be added as a new `String` resource.

Understanding InputType and Keyboard Display

For an `EditText`, there is a long list of `inputType` properties. See Figure 6.5 for some of the values that you can select.

The `inputType` property has a long list of choices. The purpose of the `inputType` property is to show the appropriate keyboard for use with the `EditText` view. If the intended input is a number, the keyboard will show numbers. If the input value is an email address, the keyboard will show text and an @ symbol. An `EditText` view has a method called `getText()` to access the current value in the view.

FIGURE 6.5
Options for InputType in Android Studio.

Using Buttons for User Actions

You have used buttons in previous examples. You can create buttons with a variety of styles and attributes.

First, there are two controls that are buttons. One is a Button, and the other is an ImageButton. A Button contains a text label, and an ImageButton contains an image. In Android Studio, both Button and ImageButton components are listed in the Widgets section of the palette.

Button Properties

You can add a Button and an ImageButton to the layout. Similar to the TextView, you can change properties like text and textColor.

To add an image to the ImageButton, select the src property, and then choose a drawable. You can use ic_launcher.png. The result should look like Figure 6.6.

The XML layout for the Button and ImageButton components is shown here. For the drawables, you can use the ic_launcher.png file. That default image is used for an app icon and provided when you create an Activity:

```
<Button
      android:layout_width="wrap_content"
      android:layout_height="wrap_content"
      android:text="New Button"
      android:id="@+id/button"
      android:layout_below="@+id/editText2"
      android:layout_alignParentStart="true" />

  <ImageButton
      android:layout_width="wrap_content"
      android:layout_height="wrap_content"
      android:id="@+id/imageButton"
      android:layout_alignParentStart="true"
      android:src="@drawable/ic_launcher"
      android:layout_below="@+id/button" />
```

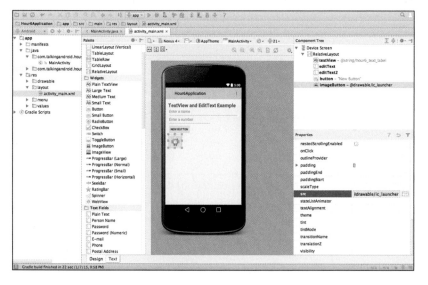

FIGURE 6.6
Adding an image to an `ImageButton`.

You can programmatically change the contents and properties of a button. As an example, you'll swap the image in the `ImageButton` in this layout. That will show how to code for the button being clicked, how to add a new image resource, and how to update the image in an `ImageButton`.

Handling a Button Click

You've added an `onClickListener()` into the Java code of previous examples. You might have noticed in the properties for a `Button` a property called `onClick`. By using the `onClick` property, you can tie the button click to a specific method in your activity.

TIP

Learning More About a Property

In Android Studio, you can get help for a particular property for an input control by selecting the property and then choosing the question mark (?) icon. For example, choosing help for the `onClick` property displays the following:

onClick - Name of the method in this View's context to invoke when the view is clicked. This name must correspond to a public method that takes exactly one parameter of type View. For instance, if you specify android:onClick="sayHello", you must declare a public void sayHello(View v) method of your context (typically, your Activity).

The app is simple, but it is worthwhile to plan what will happen. That way, you can determine what resources are required. The goal is to change the image in the `ImageButton` when the `Button` is clicked. These are the items that the user sees in the app and how they change:

▶ Show Icon in `ImageButton`

▶ Display text "Show Skateboarder" in `Button`

▶ When user clicks `Button`

▶ Show skateboarder image in `ImageButton`

▶ Change text to "Show Icon" in `Button`

There are two text messages to display. Those should be stored as string resources. There is a new image of an Android robot on a skateboard that displays. That image file needs to be added to the Drawable folder.

You can place the image into the Drawable folder using the file system. On an OS X system, you use Finder. On a Windows system, you use Windows Explorer. The full path to the folder is something like this: AndroidStudioProjects/Hour6Application/app/src/main/res/drawable.

The skateboard filename is robot_skateboarding.png, so that file should be moved into the drawable folder. It is then available as a resource in your code by referencing the resource `R.drawable.robot_skateboarding`.

You can create the `String` resource with the text "Show Icon," but creating a new string resource through the `Text` property of the `Button` component in the layout. The process is the same that you used with the `TextView`.

You can create an additional `String` resource with the text "Show Skateboarder" in two ways. You can modify the strings.xml file in the values folder directly, or you can use the associated editor as shown in Figure 6.7. You access that editor by selecting Open Editor when the strings.xml file is selected. Choose the plus sign (+) to add a new entry.

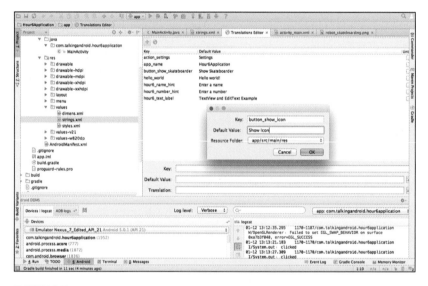

FIGURE 6.7
Adding a new string resource.

The strings.xml file will now have entries that include the following:

```
<string name="button_show_skateboarder">Show Skateboarder</string>
<string name="button_show_icon">Show Icon</string>
```

The `Button` and `ImageButton` components are defined in the activity_main.xml file as follows:

```
<Button
    android:layout_width="wrap_content"
    android:layout_height="wrap_content"
    android:text="@string/button_show_skateboarder"
    android:id="@+id/button"
    android:layout_below="@+id/editText2"
    android:layout_alignParentStart="true"
    android:onClick="changeImage" />
```

```
<ImageButton
    android:layout_width="wrap_content"
    android:layout_height="wrap_content"
    android:id="@+id/imageButton"
    android:layout_alignParentStart="true"
    android:src="@drawable/ic_launcher"
    android:layout_below="@+id/button" /
```

The Button with id of button has an android:onClick property set to "changeImage".

You need to add a changeImage() method to mainActivity. That method is passed a View component. That View will be the clicked Button. The first thing you should do in the code is to cast the view to a Button.

Listing 6.1 shows the changeImage() method associated with the onClick property for the button. On line 1, a View v is passed to the method. That View is the Button that is clicked, and on line 2, it is cast to type Button and placed in the variable button.

The ImageButton is assigned to the variable imageButton on line 3 using the familiar findViewById() method.

The logic is to check the label on the button to determine what action to take. The if statement is on lines 4–5 and compares the text in the button to the text in the resource R.string. button_show_skateboarder. That text says, "Show Skateboarder." If there is a match, the image for the imageButton is set on lines 6–7. The button text is set on line 8. Because the text was set to "Show Skateboarder," it is not set to say "Show Icon." That is all done using references to resource files.

The getText() and setText() methods check the text value and change contents. To change the image, the method setImageDrawable() is used on line 6.

The skateboarding robot image was imported into the drawables resource folder.

If the text does not match "Show Skateboarder," it must say "Show Icon," and the code that executes is shown in lines 10–14 of Listing 6.1.

LISTING 6.1   Code Associated with the Button onClick Property

```
1: public void changeImage(View v){
2:    Button = (Button) v;
3:    ImageButton imageButton = (ImageButton) findViewById(R.id.imageButton);
4:    if (button.getText().toString().equals
5:        (getResources().getString(R.string.button_show_skateboarder))){
6:           imageButton.setImageDrawable(
7:                      getResources().getDrawable(R.drawable.robot_skateboarding));
8:           button.setText(getResources().getString(R.string.button_show_icon));
9:    } else {
```

```
10:             imageButton.setImageDrawable(
11:                   getResources().getDrawable(R.drawable.ic_launcher));
12:         button.setText
13:               (getResources().getString(R.string.button_show_skateboarder));
14:     }
15: }
```

Figure 6.8 shows the two states of the app.

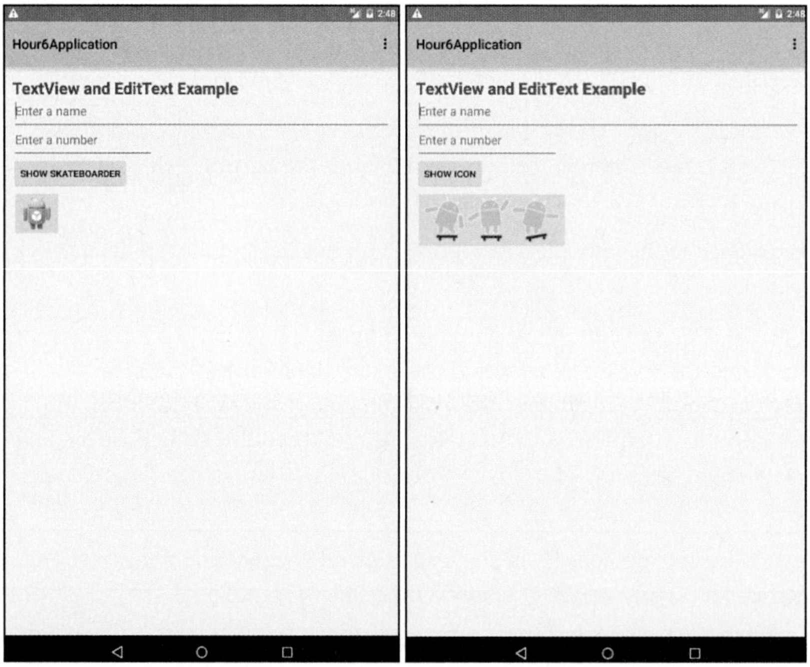

FIGURE 6.8
Switching between images.

Summary

This hour covered `TextView`, `EditText`, and `Button` components in detail. You modified the properties of a `TextView` through Android Studio. `EditText` is used to accept user input. A hint can be set for the `EditText` and the `inputType` to determine the keyboards that display to the user. You can use the `setText()` and `getText()` methods to set and retrieve the text in an `EditText`. `Button` and `ImageButton` components were introduced, as was the `onClick` property.

Q&A

Q. Should I use the `onClick` property for handling all click events?

A. You've used `setOnClickListener()`, and you have used the `onClick` property. Both are reasonable approaches, and the design of your app may drive the choice. Using the `onClick` property does restrict you to defining a public method in the `Activity`.

Q. Is there an advantage to directly editing XML layout and resource files instead of using the design tools and wizards?

A. The potential advantage of directly editing XML layouts and even resource files is the fine-grained control that you have. When using a `RelativeLayout` and placing one control below another, it can be easier to directly edit the XML. The disadvantage is that this approach can be more error prone. It is typical to use both visual editing and direct text editing to get things just right in your app.

Workshop

Quiz

1. What does a hint do in an `EditText`?

2. How would you specify that an `EditText` should display a keyboard for a telephone number format?

3. What does the `getResources()` method do?

Answers

1. The hint is displayed in the `EditText` view as a prompt for the user. It is overwritten by user input.

2. To display a keyboard, the `inputType` property must be set. In this case, the `inputType` is set to `phone`.

3. The `getResources()` method makes resources available for use. This was covered in Hour 3 when you learned about properties. In this hour, `getResources()` is used to get string and image resources.

Exercise

Implement a sample app with `EditView`, `Button`, and `TextView` components. Use the `EditView` to request that the user to enter a word. The `Button` should have the text "Add Word." When the user clicks the `Button`, update the `TextView` by appending the new word to what is in the `TextView`. Initially, set the text in the `TextView` to "Words:". As a hint, you need to retrieve the contents of the `TextView` and then append the entered word.

HOUR 7
Using Layouts

What You'll Learn in This Hour:

- ▶ Getting started with layouts
- ▶ Using `RelativeLayout`
- ▶ Using different types of layouts
- ▶ Creating useful layouts

The Android system uses layouts to properly display the user interface on different devices. Each `Activity` that you have created includes an XML layout file that uses a `RelativeLayout` component. The XML layout files are the templates for what the screen will look like. In this hour, you learn about different types of layouts and how to use them.

Getting Started with Layouts

Layout XML files are used to define what a screen (or portion of the screen) will look like in your Android apps. Layout XML files define the look of a user interface. The layout contains different types of view controls, such as `EditText` and `Button` controls. These view controls may reference other resources, such as strings, colors, dimensions, and drawables.

You learned in Hour 6, "Using Basic UI Controls," that a `View` is the most basic component for building a user interface in Android. Every `Button`, `TextView`, or `Layout` is a type of view. A `ViewGroup` is a container for other views. When you place a `Button` on the user interface using Android Studio, you are adding the `Button` to the `RelativeLayout`. In that case, the `Button` is considered a view of the `RelativeLayout`.

There are several types of layouts in addition to `RelativeLayout`. They include `LinearLayout`, `FrameLayout`, `TableLayout`, and `GridLayout`.

Each layout class is a container for other views. Different layout class types apply different rules for how child views are added. The child views can have different properties set based on the layout. For example, when you are using a `RelativeLayout`, one `Button` may be placed below another using the attribute `android:layout_below`. That attribute is not used in `LinearLayout` or `FrameLayout`.

It is common practice to use an XML layout file to define the views for the user interface. You can also create any view programmatically. A layout is a container for other views, whether the layout is defined in an XML file or is created on the fly.

As you have seen, layout resource files are stored in the /res/layout directory hierarchy.

NOTE

Using an `include` in a Layout XML File

The XML layout includes support for an `<include/>` element. To use an `include`, create a layout file to be embedded in other layouts. Then reference it as a resource. The layout named basicHeader.xml can be referenced in other layout files by using `<include layout="@layout/basicHeader "/>`.

Designing Layouts Using the Android Studio

When you create a new `Activity` using Android Studio, an activity_main.xml file is created. That layout file uses a `RelativeLayout` as the container. The layout includes a single `TextView` that is the child of the `RelativeLayout`.

Listing 7.1 shows an initial activity_main.xml file. The `TextView` is contained within the definition of the `RelativeLayout`. No information is included to indicate where the `TextView` should be placed. In a `RelativeLayout`, the default position for a child view is at the top and leftmost position in the layout. Figure 7.1 shows the `TextView` in that position.

LISTING 7.1   RelativeLayout in XML File (activity_main.xml)

```
 1: <RelativeLayout xmlns:android="http://schemas.android.com/apk/res/android"
 2:                 xmlns:tools="http://schemas.android.com/tools"
 3:                 android:layout_width="match_parent"
 4:                 android:layout_height="match_parent"
 5:                 android:paddingLeft="@dimen/activity_horizontal_margin"
 6:                 android:paddingRight="@dimen/activity_horizontal_margin"
 7:                 android:paddingTop="@dimen/activity_vertical_margin"
 8:                 android:paddingBottom="@dimen/activity_vertical_margin"
 9:                 tools:context=".MainActivity">
10:
11:     <TextView android:text="@string/hello_world"
12:                 android:layout_width="wrap_content"
13:                 android:layout_height="wrap_content" />
14:
15: </RelativeLayout>
```

FIGURE 7.1
`RelativeLayout` in Android Studio.

In Android Studio, you can switch between design and text modes. Figure 7.1 is in design mode. Notice the Design and Text tabs near the bottom of the image.

Editing in text mode can be useful. When you use a `RelativeLayout`, you position child views relative to other views. A view can be above, below, to the left of, or to the right of another view. It is often easier to do that positioning directly to the XML in text mode rather than in design mode.

You may find yourself switching back and forth between the design and text modes frequently.

Editing Layouts Using XML

You can edit the raw XML of a layout file. As you create more apps, it will become natural to edit the XML layout file directly. By switching to the XML view frequently, you will gain an understanding of XML generated by each type of control. As you change properties using the visual editor, they are also changed in the XML. Over time, it may become faster for you to make certain changes directly in the XML file.

Because you can edit the XML file as a text file, it can be useful to search for certain terms or make other changes directly.

Using Layout Resources Programmatically

In Hour 6, you created `Text`, `Button`, and `EditText` controls. Those input controls were defined in the activity_main.xml file in the/res/layout directory. They were defined in the XML within a `RelativeLayout` element.

To use this XML layout file in an `Activity`, you called the method `setContentView()`. This is the line of code that is included when the project is generated:

```
setContentView(R.layout.activity_main);
```

An `Activity` uses the `setContentView()` method to associate the `Activity` with the `View`. When you want to access the controls defined in the layout, you used `findViewById()`. To create a new `Button` from an `id` in the layout file and assign it to the variable `myButton`, use the following:

```
Button myButton =  (Button)findViewById(R.id.button1);
```

The `findViewById()` method is available within an `Activity`. It is also available from any `View`. You can create views on the fly from XML layouts. You *inflate* the layout file into a `View` object using the `LayoutInflater` class. Then you use the new `View` to access controls like `Buttons`. The following listing shows an example of using a `LayoutInflater` and to create a `View`:

```
LayoutInflater inflater = LayoutInflater.from(context);
View exampleView = inflater.inflate(R.layout.example, container, false);
Button myExampleButton =  (Button)exampleView.findViewById(R.id.button1);
```

Becoming a RelativeLayout Expert

A `RelativeLayout` provides accurate control for placing child views and flexibility for the layout to work well on devices with different screen sizes.

In a `RelativeLayout`, each child view is placed in relation to the other views in the layout, or relative to the edges of the parent.

Aligning to Parent

When a child view is placed relative to the parent, the view can be centered, in relation to the sides of the parent or in relation to the start or end of the parent.

When a view is placed in relation to the side of a parent, you can use attributes such as `layout_alignParentLeft` and `layoutAlignParentBottom`. The difference between `layout_alignParentLeft` and `layout_AlignParentStart` is to account for right-to-left (RTL) languages. In an RTL language, text starts on the right. When you use `layout_AlignParentStart` for an RTL language, the view is placed on the right side of the screen.

The following attributes are used to position child views relative to the sides of the parent:

- ▶ `android:layout_alignParentStart`
- ▶ `android:layout_alignParentEnd`
- ▶ `android:layout_alignParentBottom`
- ▶ `android:layout_alignParentRight`
- ▶ `android:layout_alignParentTop`
- ▶ `android:layout_alignParentLeft`

The following attributes are used to position child views relative to the center of the parent:

- ▶ `android:layout_centerInParent`
- ▶ `android:layout_centerVertical`
- ▶ `android:layout_centerHorizontal`

Figure 7.2 shows `TextView` aligned to parent top and left. The layout file includes this `TextView` element:

```
<TextView android:text="@string/hello_world"
    android:layout_width="wrap_content"
    android:layout_height="wrap_content"
    android:layout_alignParentTop="true"
    android:layout_alignParentLeft="true" />
```

Aligning Views Relative to Each Other

Child views can be set above, below, to the right of, and to the left of other views. At least one view must be placed on the screen as a starting point. It is likely that one or more views will be aligned to the parent. Then other views can be placed relative to those views.

Like aligning to the parent, the `RelativeLayout` class also provides the corresponding layout attributes to replace left/right positions for RTL languages. For example, you can use `android:layout_toStartOf` instead of `android:layout_toLeftOf`.

In Figure 7.3, two views are aligned to the parent. The top-left and centered `TextViews` are aligned to the parent. The other `TextViews` are set relative to these views.

FIGURE 7.2
Aligning `TextView` to parent.

FIGURE 7.3
Aligning `TextViews` relative to each other.

The layout file that corresponds to Figure 7.3 is as follows:

```
<RelativeLayout xmlns:android="http://schemas.android.com/apk/res/android"
    xmlns:tools="http://schemas.android.com/tools"
    android:layout_width="match_parent"
    android:layout_height="match_parent"
    android:paddingLeft="@dimen/activity_horizontal_margin"
    android:paddingRight="@dimen/activity_horizontal_margin"
    android:paddingTop="@dimen/activity_vertical_margin"
    android:paddingBottom="@dimen/activity_vertical_margin"
    tools:context=".MainActivity">

    <TextView android:text="@string/center" android:layout_width="wrap_content"
        android:layout_height="wrap_content"
        android:textAppearance="?android:attr/textAppearanceLarge"
        android:layout_centerInParent="true"
        android:id="@+id/textViewCenter" />

    <TextView
        android:layout_width="wrap_content"
        android:layout_height="wrap_content"
        android:textAppearance="?android:attr/textAppearanceLarge"
        android:text="@string/top_left"
        android:id="@+id/textViewTopLeft"
        android:layout_alignParentTop="true"
        android:layout_alignParentStart="true" />

    <TextView
        android:layout_width="wrap_content"
        android:layout_height="wrap_content"
        android:textAppearance="?android:attr/textAppearanceLarge"
        android:text="@string/below_top_left"
        android:id="@+id/textViewBelowTopLeft"
        android:layout_below="@+id/textViewTopLeft"
    />

    <TextView
        android:layout_width="wrap_content"
        android:layout_height="wrap_content"
        android:textAppearance="?android:attr/textAppearanceLarge"
        android:text="@string/below_center"
        android:id="@+id/textViewBelowCenter"
        android:layout_below="@+id/textViewCenter"
        android:layout_alignStart="@+id/textViewCenter" />

</RelativeLayout>
```

One way to use a `RelativeLayout` is to put a view in the middle of the design that references something above it and below it. Figure 7.4 shows a layout in Android Studio that has:

- ▶ A `Button` aligned with the bottom of the parent:
  `android:layout_alignParentBottom="true"`

- ▶ A `TextView` that is in the top-left corner

- ▶ A `VideoView` that is below the `TextView` and above the `Button`

FIGURE 7.4
`RelativeLayout` design.

To set the position of the `VideoView`, you use these properties:

```
android:layout_below="@+id/textView1"
android:layout_above="@+id/loadPhotosButton"
```

Common Attributes

Certain attributes are common across layouts and the child views within layouts. For example, all layouts share the attributes `android:layout_width` and `android:layout_height` for controlling how wide and high an item is. These attribute values can be specified in units like density independent pixels (20dp), or they be specified as constant values that have a specific meaning. Possible values are `match_parent` and `wrap_content`.

Using `match_parent` instructs a layout to scale to the size of the parent layout, and using `wrap_content` wraps the child `View` control.

Layout Margins

Layout margins define the amount of space between a child view and the side of a parent container. To "push" a button down and to the right, you set the margin from the top and the left side of the layout. By adding these two lines to the layout for the first `Button`, you push the button down 40 pixels and to the right 120 pixels:

```
android:layout_marginTop="40dp"
android:layout_marginLeft="120dp"
```

Padding

Padding is the amount of space that is added to a side of a widget to give it more space on the screen. Padding refers to the internal padding. For a standard `Button`, it is the space added between the button's text and sides of the button. Padding may be set for the whole widget or set specifically for the top, bottom, left, and right sides.

Figure 7.5 shows a new XML layout file with three buttons to show the effect of padding.

The first button has no `padding` property specified. The second button has its `padding` set to 40dp on all sides by setting `android:padding="40dp"`. All sides of the button are padded with 40 device pixels. The third button has its padding set to 40dp for the right and left. The right padding is set using `android:paddingRight="40dp"`, and the left padding is set using `android:paddingRight="40dp"`.

FIGURE 7.5
Using padding.

More Layout Types

It is common for a screen to be encapsulated in one large parent layout. RelativeLayout and LinearLayout are often used. Table 7.1 lists the most common Layout controls.

TABLE 7.1 Common Layout Controls

Layout Control Name	Description	Key Attributes/Elements
LinearLayout	Each child view is placed after the previous one, in a single row or column.	Orientation (vertical or horizontal).
RelativeLayout	Each child view is placed in relation to the other views in the layout, or relative to the edges of the parent layout.	Many alignment attributes to control where a child view is positioned relative to other child View controls.
FrameLayout	Each child view is stacked within the frame, relative to the top-left corner.	The order of placement of child View controls is important, when used with appropriate gravity settings. Controls may overlap.

Layout Control Name	Description	Key Attributes/Elements
`TableLayout`	Each child view is a cell in a grid of rows and columns.	Each row requires a `TableRow` element.
`GridLayout`	Each child view is placed in a rectangular grid.	Rows and columns using `RowSpec` and `ColumnSpec` are key attributes.

Using LinearLayout

A `LinearLayout` positions views in either a column or a row. The `LinearLayout`'s orientation property determines the direction. If the orientation is vertical, the child views are stacked in a column. If the orientation is horizontal, the child views are placed in a row. Although there are many common attributes across layouts, the difference between different types of layouts is the order and rules they use for drawing widgets on the screen. Orientation is unique to `LinearLayout`s:

```
android:orientation="vertical"
```

Gravity

The property `layout_gravity` applies to child views. The `layout_gravity` property can be set to values like left, right, center, and so on:

```
android:layout_gravity="right"
```

The property `layout_gravity` applies to the child views. Android gravity can apply to the entire layout. By setting gravity to right for a `LinearLayout`, all child views are moved to the right:

```
android:gravity="right"
```

Weight

The Android `layout_weight` property gives more space on the screen to the view with the higher weight. You can see this most easily when creating a `LinearLayout` with horizontal orientation.

▼ TRY IT YOURSELF

Throwing Weight Around in a Layout

Follow these steps to see a good example of how the `layout_weight` attribute works and can be used in your designs:

1. Create a new XML layout file called weight_example.xml in the res/layout folder.

2. Use a `LinearLayout` with the orientation set to horizontal for the layout.

3. Add two buttons to the layout. Their width should be set to `match_parent`.

4. Set the `layout_weight` attribute for both buttons to 1. They should share the available space.

5. Change the weight of only one of the buttons and check the result visually using Android Studio.

FrameLayout

A `FrameLayout` is a container that has no special rules for drawing widgets. By default, all widgets are drawn in the upper-left corner of the screen. That might not sound useful, but by using the layout margin, you can place widgets anywhere. The `FrameLayout` is helpful when two widgets should be drawn on top of each other. For example, we might put a `TextView` on top of an image or use several images to draw shadows and highlights within the UI.

You can use `layout_margins` within a `FrameLayout` to create interesting and useful designs.

When `LinearLayouts` and `RelativeLayouts` are used, the Android operating system takes the physical screen dimension into consideration when rendering the user interface. Because these layouts use components that are relative to each other, there is more opportunity for the system to optimize the experience. For that reason, `LinearLayouts` and `RelativeLayouts` are generally recommended. Using `RelativeLayouts` is highly recommended in most cases.

Summary

In this hour, you reviewed what layouts are and how they worked. You examined `LinearLayout` and `RelativeLayout` in more detail as a way to understand how layouts work. XML layouts are used to create user interfaces in Android by positioning child views on the screen. Using padding, margins, and other attributes, you have significant control over the user interface.

Q&A

Q. With a `LinearLayout`, what is meant by orientation?

A. Orientation defined the direction of the `LinearLayout`. Vertical creates a column, and horizontal creates a row. Orientation is not used in `FrameLayouts` or `RelativeLayouts`. Different layouts have different rules for laying out child views. That means they may have different attributes.

Q. What is the difference between a `FrameLayout` and a `RelativeLayout`?

A. In a `RelativeLayout`, it is possible to position widgets relative to one another. That cannot be done in `FrameLayout`.

Workshop

Quiz

1. What is the difference between setting a layout margin and layout padding?

2. What is the relationship between a `LinearLayout` and a `ViewGroup`?

3. How would you position a `Button` 100 pixels from the top of the device screen? Use density-independent pixels.

Answers

1. Layout margins define the distance between a component and the edge of the layout. Padding pads the size of the component. Depending on the component, this can have different effects.

2. A `LinearLayout` extends the `ViewGroup` class. A `ViewGroup` is a `View` in Android that contains other views.

3. Set the margin to be 100 device pixels from the top of the screen using `android:layout_marginTop="100 dp"`.

Exercises

1. Using `FrameLayout`, implement a user interface with a button in each corner of the screen. Do the same with a `RelativeLayout`.

   To do this using a `FrameLayout`, follow these steps:

   1. Create a layout file using `FrameLayout`.

   2. reate four buttons.

3. Set the `topMargin` and `leftMargin` of each `Button` so that the `Buttons` are placed in corners.

2. Try using one layout within another; specifically, create a `LinearLayout` with vertical orientation. Add a `FrameLayout` and a `Button`. Then add an `ImageView` to the `FrameLayout`.

3. Create an XML layout that uses `RelativeLayout`. Place an `ImageView` and `TextView` in the layout. Now, use that layout as an `include` in another layout.

ListViews and Adapters

What You'll Learn in This Hour:

▶ Getting started with `ListViews`

▶ Extending `BaseAdapter`

▶ Introducing the view holder pattern

Showing a list of relevant information is key to many Android apps. In the installed apps on any Android device, there are lists of text messages, contacts, and emails. In this hour, you learn about displaying information in a `ListView`. `ListViews` use adapters to make the connection between the data to use and how it is displayed.

Getting Started with ListViews

A `ListView(android.widget.ListView)` is a container that shows child views in a vertical list. Using Android Studio, you can add a `ListView` container to a layout. Figure 8.1 shows a `ListView` within Android Studio being displayed with width set to `match_parent` and height set to `wrap_content`. The `ListView` is positioned at the top and start of the parent.

`ListViews` display a set of data. When using a `ListView`, you specify a layout to display a single item from that set of data. That single layout will be used to populate multiple child views within the `ListView`. Android provides some predefined values that can be used in simple cases.

An adapter handles the relationship between the data and the view that displays that data.

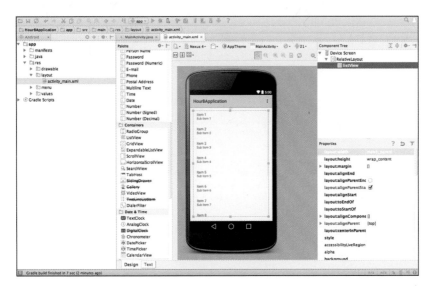

FIGURE 8.1
A `ListView` shown in Android Studio.

Using ArrayAdapters

When a view requires data to function, an `Adapter` is used to bind the data to the view. An `Adapter` makes the handshake between the view and the data. The `ArrayAdapter` (`android.widget.ArrayAdapter`) class is used for connecting data that is stored in an array to `ListView`.

To create an array, you start with a `String Array` that is defined as a resource.

In the Strings.xml file in the res/values/ folder, create an array called `pie_array`, as follows:

```
<string-array name="pie_array">
    <item>apple</item>
    <item>blueberry</item>
    <item>cherry</item>
    <item>coconut cream</item>
</string-array>
```

That is the data that you use to display the list of pies in a `ListView`. You have a layout file called activity_main.xml with a single `ListView` defined, and you have the data to display defined as a resource.

The next step is to retrieve the data from the resource and display it in the `ListView`. That is done in Listing 8.1 using an `ArrayAdapter`.

LISTING 8.1 An Activity with a ListView

```
 1: package com.bffmedia.hour8application;
 2: import android.app.Activity;
 3: import android.content.res.Resources;
 4: import android.os.Bundle;
 5: import android.view.Menu;
 6: import android.view.MenuItem;
 7: import android.view.View;
 8: import android.widget.AdapterView;
 9: import android.widget.ArrayAdapter;
10: import android.widget.ListView;
11: import android.widget.Toast;
12:
13: public class MainActivity extends Activity {
14:     ListView pieListView;
15:     String[] pies;
16:
17:     @Override
18:     protected void onCreate(Bundle savedInstanceState) {
19:         super.onCreate(savedInstanceState);
20:         setContentView(R.layout.activity_main);
21:         Resources resources = getResources();
22:         pies = resources.getStringArray(R.array.pie_array);
23:         pieListView = (ListView) findViewById(R.id.listView);
24:         pieListView.setAdapter(new ArrayAdapter<String>(this,
25:                             android.R.layout.simple_list_item_1, pies));
26:         pieListView.setOnItemClickListener(new AdapterView.OnItemClickListener() {
27:             @Override
28:             public void onItemClick(AdapterView<?> parent, View view, int position,
29:                             long id) {
30:                 Toast.makeText(getApplicationContext(),
31:                             pies[position], Toast.LENGTH_SHORT).show();
32:             }
33:         });
34:     }
35: }
```

You can think of the code in Listing 8.1 as having three distinct sections:

▶ The array pies and the ListView pieListView are defined on lines 21–23.

▶ The pieListView Adapter is set on lines 24–25.

▶ An action is specified for what happens when the user clicks an item in the list on lines 26–34.

Displaying Data

Take a closer look at lines 24 and 25. The `pieListView` calls the `setAdapter()` method. That method specifies the adapter to use when populating the `ListView`. In this case, a new `ArrayAdapter` is defined with three parameters: `this`, `android.R.layout.simple_list_item_1`, and `pies`. The parameters correspond to a context, a resource id, and an array.

The context passed is the current activity. The array `pies` is defined on line 15. The values for `pies` come from a resource file. On lines 21 and 22, the resource values are loaded into `pies`.

The resource id `android.R.layout.simple_list_item_1` was not defined in your resources or Java code. It is one of the predefined Android resources that you can use in your apps. It is a single `TextView` component defined in a resource file.

The association of the data in the array with the resource file is used by the `ListView` to display the data.

Using OnItemClickListener

You use an `OnItemClickListener` to detect that an item in the list has been clicked. When the click is detected, several parameters are passed to the `onItemClick()` method. You overwrite the `onItemClick()` method to react to the click.

In lines 28 and 29, you can see that the parameters passed are an `AdapterView`, a view, an integer-indicated position, and a long for id. The `AdapterView` is the `ListView` itself. The `View` is the child view that was clicked. You will see later in this hour that it can be useful to use the child view itself to pass additional data. The position and id tell you about the data being displayed.

Because you are using an `ArrayAdapter`, you can use the `position` in the original array to retrieve your data. On line 31, `pies[position]` indicates the array element specified by `position`. Lines 30 and 31 show the selected value in a `Toast` message.

Figure 8.2 shows the result of selecting coconut cream.

▼ TRY IT YOURSELF

Adding Data to a Resource Array

You can use resource files for creating `String` arrays. That can prove useful if you have a set list or fixed list of items for the user to work with. Follow these steps to show more data in the app by adding more items to the array in the resource file:

1. Listing 8.1 uses an `ArrayAdapter` to display a list of pies in a `ListView`.

2. The pies are defined in a resource array.

3. Add two more pie types to the array.

4. Check the resulting data displayed in the `ListView`.

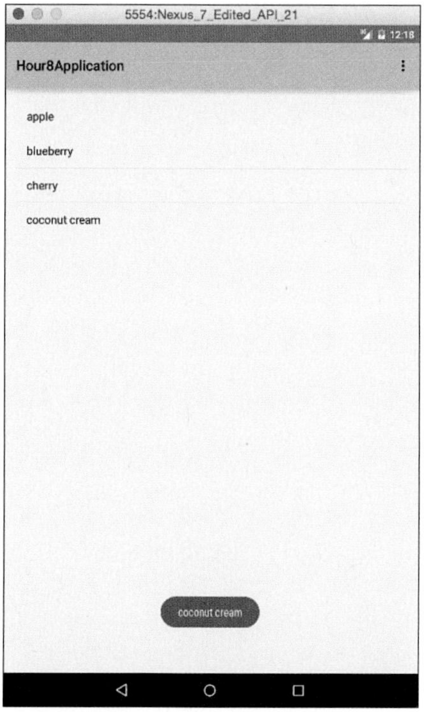

FIGURE 8.2
ListView using ArrayAdapter.

Changing the Child View

You can define your own resource for displaying the data when using an ArrayAdapter. You would define a TextView in a layout file and use it with the adapter. A TextView is defined in a file called text_view_item.xml in the Layout folder. The textSize is 24sp, and the textColor is blue:

```xml
<?xml version="1.0" encoding="utf-8"?>
<TextView xmlns:android="http://schemas.android.com/apk/res/android"
    android:layout_width="match_parent" android:layout_height="wrap_content"
    android:textStyle="bold"
    android:text="This is a Test"
    android:textSize="24sp"
    android:textColor="#0000ff">
</TextView>
```

To associate this resource with the ArrayAdapter, a single change is made in your code. The resource android.R.layout.simple_list_item_1 is replaced by R.layout.text_view_item in the setAdapter() method, as follows:

```
pieListView.setAdapter(new ArrayAdapter<String>(this,
                 R.layout.text_view_item, pies));
```

You are no longer using a predefined Android resource. You are using a resource that you defined that is specific to your app. Figure 8.3 shows the result.

FIGURE 8.3
ListView using a custom resource.

Extending Base Adapters

An ArrayAdapter is useful in simple cases and helpful in explaining how adapters work. Android provides several additional types of adapters. They include a BaseAdapter and CursorAdapters. Material design and Android 5.0 Lollipop introduced the RecyclerView. Adapter to be used with RecyclerViews. You examine the RecyclerView in more detail in Hour 9, "Material Design," and the CursorAdapter in Hour 16, "Using SQLite and File Storage."

You can customize the BaseAdapter class to work with different data and more complex objects. As a first step, you re-create the functionality of displaying a list of pies using a

`BaseAdapter` instead of an `ArrayAdapter`. That will provide you with the concepts required for making a more complex adapter.

The goal is to show how the `BaseAdapter` can be extended.

To use a `BaseAdapter`, you must implement four methods: `getCount()`, `getItem()`, `getItemId()`, and `getView()`. As with the `ArrayAdapter`, you are working with a set of individual items. In this case, you create the `PieAdapter` class as an extension of `BaseAdapter`. `PieAdapter` will work with precisely the same string array that you used with the `ArrayAdapter` in Listing 8.1. For this example, the `PieAdapter` class will be defined within MainActivity.java.

The methods you must implement in `BaseAdapter` are as follows:

- ▶ **`getCount()`**: Return the number of items in the underlying data.

- ▶ **`getItem()`**: Return a specific item in the list.

- ▶ **`getItemId()`**: Return the `id` of a specific item in the list.

- ▶ **`getView()`**: Return a view that displays the contents of a specific item in the list.

By creating the view you desire and returning it using `getView()`, you can customize how the item is displayed within the list.

Creating a BaseAdapter

Listing 8.2 is a simple version of a `BaseAdapter` that illustrates these methods.

LISTING 8.2   **Extending BaseAdapter**

```
 1:    public class PieAdapter extends BaseAdapter {
 2:       Context mContext;
 3:       String mPies[];
 4:       LayoutInflater mInflater;
 5:       public PieAdapter(Context c, String[] pies) {
 6:            mContext = c;
 7:            mPies = pies;
 8:            mInflater = (LayoutInflater) mContext.getSystemService
 9:                                    (Context.LAYOUT_INFLATER_SERVICE);
10:       }
11:       public int getCount() {
12:            return  mPies.length;
13:       }
14:       public Object getItem(int position) {
15:            return mPies[position];
16:       }
17:       public long getItemId(int position) {
```

```
18:            return position;
19:        }
20:        public View getView(int position, View convertView, ViewGroup parent) {
21:          TextView textView = (TextView) mInflater.inflate(
22:                                 R.layout.text_view_item, null);
23:          textView.setText(mPies[position]);
24:          return view;
25:        }
26:    }
```

The `PieAdapter` in Listing 8.2 uses a `String Array` as the set of items. The `getCount()` method of line 11 uses the length of the array to determine the number of available items. The `getItem()` and `getItemId()` methods are both passed the position in the list. For `getItem()`, `position` is used to get the item in that position in the array. For `getItemId()`, `position` itself is used as the `id`.

Recall that when you set the `pieListView` using an `ArrayAdapter`, you used `R.layout.text_view_item` as the resource. Using a `BaseAdapter`, you inflate the `R.layout.text_view_item` resource in your `getView()` method. On line 21, a `TextView` is created using the resource. On line 23, the `TextView` is set to have the text value from the `pie` array. The `TextView` is returned on line 24. That `TextView` is the custom view created in your `BaseAdapter`.

When you associated an `ArrayAdapter` with a `ListView`, you used the following:

```
pieListView.setAdapter(new ArrayAdapter<String>(this,
              R.layout.text_view_item, pies));
```

To use your new `PieAdapter` class, you instantiate it and set the list adapter as follows:

```
PieAdapter adapter = new PieAdapter(this, pies);
setListAdapter(adapter);
```

The result is precisely the same as using the `ArrayAdapter`. Because the same resource file and the same data is used, the look of each item in the list is the same. In this section, you learned about the methods required to create a `BaseAdapter`. The next step is to create a more complex child view to be displayed in the list.

Adding a Complex Child View to a ListView

Implementing a `BaseAdapter` like the `PieAdapter` of Listing 8.2 is fairly straightforward. You have a set of items, and the `BaseAdapter` is the mechanism for tying the data in those items to a particular view.

As a next step, you use and display data with multiple attributes. Keeping with the pie theme, you create a pie object that has name, description, and price. The objective is to display each pie in the list using these attributes.

The class `Pie` has two member fields and a constructor:

```
private class Pie {
    String mName;
    String mDescription;
    double mPrice;
    public Pie (String name, String description, double price){
        this.mName = name;
        this.mDescription = description;
        this.mPrice = price;
    }
}
```

To create an `ArrayList` of `Pie` objects, create the `makePies()` method. For simplicity, the `makePies()` method is part of the `Activity`, and the `Pie` class is defined within the `Activity`.

The `makePies()` method returns an `ArrayList` of `Pie` objects:

```
private ArrayList<Pie> makePies(){
    ArrayList<Pie> pies = new ArrayList<Pie>();
    pies.add(new Pie("Apple", "An old-fashioned favorite.", 1.5));
    pies.add(new Pie("Blueberry", "Made with fresh Maine blueberries.", 1.5));
    pies.add(new Pie("Cherry", "Delicious and fresh made daily.", 2.0));
    pies.add(new Pie("Coconut Cream", "A customer favorite." 2.5));
    return pies;
}
```

Implementing a `ListView` that displays this collection of pies requires two things:

▶ You need to create a layout to be used to display a single pie. For that, you use a `RelativeLayout` that contains three `TextViews`.

▶ You need to create an adapter to handle this new data. To do that, you create a new adapter class that extends `BaseAdapter` and can handle displaying an `ArrayList` of `Pie` objects.

Start with the layout file.

▼ TRY IT YOURSELF

Creating a Layout to Display Information in a ListView

Your goal is to create a layout file that you can use to display the data in a single `Pie` object. That layout file will be used for each child view displayed in the `ListView`:

1. Create a new XML layout file called pie_view_item.xml in the res/layout folder.

2. Use a `RelativeLayout`.

3. Add a `TextView` called `textViewName` in the upper-left corner.

4. Add a `TextView` called `textViewPrice` in the upper-right corner.

5. Add a `TextView` called `textViewDescription` below `textViewName`.

The design view for your pie_view_item.xml should look like Figure 8.4.

FIGURE 8.4
Design `View` for child view.

The XML for your pie_view_item.xml should look something like this:

```
<?xml version="1.0" encoding="utf-8"?>
<RelativeLayout xmlns:android="http://schemas.android.com/apk/res/android"
    android:layout_width="match_parent" android:layout_height="match_parent">

    <TextView
        android:layout_width="wrap_content"
```

```
        android:layout_height="wrap_content"
        android:textAppearance="?android:attr/textAppearanceLarge"
        android:text="Large Text"
        android:id="@+id/textViewName"
        android:layout_alignParentTop="true"
        android:layout_alignParentStart="true"
        android:paddingStart="10dp" />

    <TextView
        android:layout_width="wrap_content"
        android:layout_height="wrap_content"
        android:textAppearance="?android:attr/textAppearanceMedium"
        android:text="Medium Text"
        android:id="@+id/textViewDescription"
        android:layout_below="@+id/textViewName"
        android:layout_alignParentStart="true"
        android:paddingStart="10dp" />

    <TextView
        android:layout_width="wrap_content"
        android:layout_height="wrap_content"
        android:textAppearance="?android:attr/textAppearanceLarge"
        android:text="Large Text"
        android:id="@+id/textViewPrice"
        android:layout_alignParentTop="true"
        android:layout_alignParentEnd="true"
        android:paddingEnd="10dp" />
</RelativeLayout>
```

After you have the created the XML layout file, you can make changes to the `BaseAdapter` to display all three values within a `Pie` object.

Because you are now using an `ArrayList` for the data, there are small changes in the constructor, the `getCount()` method, and the `getObject()` method. You can see those in Listing 8.3.

The most significant changes are to the `getView()` method. The `pie_view_item` resource is inflated into a `View` object. From that `View`, the three `TextViews` that are to be used for name, description, and price are retrieved.

You can think of the `getView()` method as having two distinct parts. In the first part, the `TextViews` are created. In Listing 8.3, that occurs in lines 21–27.

In the second part, the `TextViews` are populated with data. The data comes from a single `Pie` object called `currentPie`. The `currentPie` is populated on line 28 using the position in the

`ArrayList` to get the data. Lines 29–33 load the `TextViews` with data. The price, which is stored as a double, is converted to a currency string to display.

Figure 8.5 shows the resulting app display.

LISTING 8.3   BaseAdapter with Complex Child View

```
1:     public class PieAdapter extends BaseAdapter {
2:         Context mContext;
3:         ArrayList<Pie>  mPies;
4:         LayoutInflater mInflater;
5:         public PieAdapter(Context c, ArrayList<Pie> pies) {
6:             mContext = c;
7:             mPies = pies;
8:             mInflater = (LayoutInflater) mContext.getSystemService(
9:                     Context.LAYOUT_INFLATER_SERVICE);
10:        }
11:        public int getCount() {
12:            return  mPies.size();
13:        }
14:        public Object getItem(int position) {
15:            return mPies.get(position);
16:        }
17:        public long getItemId(int position) {
18:            return position;
19:        }
20:        public View getView(int position, View convertView, ViewGroup parent) {
21:            View view =  mInflater.inflate(R.layout.pie_view_item, null);
22:            TextView textViewName = (TextView)
23:                                    view.findViewById(R.id.textViewName);
24:            TextView textViewDescription = (TextView)
25:                                    view.findViewById(R.id.textViewDescription);
26:            TextView textViewPrice = (TextView)
27:                                    view.findViewById(R.id.textViewPrice);
28:            Pie currentPie = mPies.get(position);
29:            textViewName.setText(currentPie.mName);
30:            textViewDescription.setText(currentPie.mDescription);
31:            NumberFormat formatter = NumberFormat.getCurrencyInstance();
32:            String price = formatter.format(currentPie.mPrice);
33:            textViewPrice.setText(price);
34:            return view;
35:        }
36:    }
```

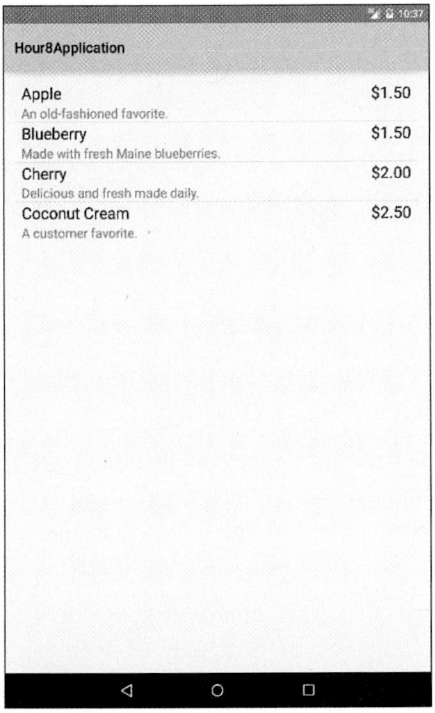

FIGURE 8.5
Displaying objects in a `ListView`.

Introducing the View Holder Pattern

There is a way to make a `BaseAdapter` more efficient. You implement the view holder pattern with the `PieAdapter`. Doing so will also help you understand how Android deals with views when they are used in a list.

The expensive operations in Android are creating a new view and finding the view by ID. If you avoid those operations, the adapter is more efficient. In Listing 8.3, you can see that the methods to inflate a `View` and to create new `TextViews` are used in lines 21–28. Each time a row in the `ListView` is displayed, these methods are called.

The opportunity for efficiency comes because Android reuses views that have been shown in the `ListView`. On line 20 of Listing 8.3, the `getView()` method is passed a `View` named `convertView`. If `convertView` is not null, it is a `View` that is being reused. You can use it directly to avoid recreating new `View` objects. You will not want the contents of the passed `View`, but by reusing it, you avoid the expensive operations of creating new `View` objects.

The pattern to implement this is known as the *view holder pattern*.

To use the view holder pattern, you create an object that contains fields for each view you intend to use. In this case, you can define a `ViewHolder` object as follows:

```
private static class ViewHolder {
    public TextView textViewName;
    public TextView textViewDescription;
    public TextView textViewPrice;
}
```

Listing 8.4 shows the changes to the `getView()` method to implement the view holder pattern.

The logic for reuse begins on line 3. Remember that `convertView` can be null or it can contain a `View` that can be reused. Line 3 checks to see whether it is null.

If `convertView` is null, a new `View` must be created. Line 4 creates a new `View` by inflating the XML layout. The inflated `View` is assigned to `convertView`. On line 5, a new `ViewHolder` is created. On Line 6, `findViewById()` for the resource `R.id.textViewName` is used to assign the `textViewName` field within `viewHolder`.

This is essentially the same process that you used previously. You are creating new `TextViews` for the app, but instead of using them directly, you are storing them in the `ViewHolder` object. Lines 6–11 create new `TextViews`.

Remember, this is still the case where `convertView` was null. The code in lines 5–12 has created a new `ViewHolder` object and created new `TextViews` for that object.

Line 12 takes the `ViewHolder` object named `viewHolder` and associates it with the `View` `convertView`. That is done with the `setTag()` method. Using `setTag()` is powerful. It enables you to associate any object with a view. In this case, the `viewHolder` object is tied to `View` `convertView`.

Continuing the case where `convertView` is null, after setting the tag on line 23, the text value for all the `TextViews` is set in lines 16–21, and the `convertView` is returned on line 12.

That is the case of `convertView` being null. When the `getView()` method runs and `convertView` is not null, the code on line 14 is executed. No new `Views` are created. A call to the method to `getTag()` retrieves the embedded `ViewHolder` object that was associated with `convertView`. The `getTag()` method retrieves the `viewHolder` that was previously attached to the `View` with `setTag()`. Because a `ViewHolder` object has been provided that contains the already created `TextViews`, those views are populated as before on lines 16–21.

When using the view holder pattern, the goal is to avoid creating new `View` objects.

LISTING 8.4   Using the View Holder Pattern

```
1:  public View getView(int position, View convertView, ViewGroup parent) {
2:    ViewHolder viewHolder;
3:    if (convertView == null) {
4:        convertView = mInflater.inflate(R.layout.pie_view_item, null);
5:        viewHolder = new ViewHolder();
6:        viewHolder.textViewName = (TextView)
7:                    convertView.findViewById(R.id.textViewName);
8:        viewHolder.textViewDescription = (TextView)
9:                    convertView.findViewById(R.id.textViewDescription);
10:       viewHolder.textViewPrice = (TextView)
11:                   convertView.findViewById(R.id.textViewPrice);
12:       convertView.setTag(viewHolder);
13:    } else {
14:        viewHolder = (ViewHolder) convertView.getTag();
15:    }
16:    Pie currentPie = mPies.get(position);
17:    viewHolder.textViewName.setText(currentPie.mName);
18:    viewHolder.textViewDescription.setText(currentPie.mDescription);
19:    NumberFormat formatter = NumberFormat.getCurrencyInstance();
20:    String price = formatter.format(currentPie.mPrice);
21:    viewHolder.textViewPrice.setText(price);
22:    return convertView;
23:  }
```

For completeness, the complete listing for the `ViewHolderActivity` is shown. By examining the full listing, you can understand the structure of the code. The classes `PieAdapter` and `ViewHolder` are defined within the `Activity` class.

The method `makePies()` is used to populate an `ArrayList` of `Pie` objects:

```
package com.bffmedia.hour8application;
import android.app.Activity;
import android.content.Context;
import android.os.Bundle;
import android.view.LayoutInflater;
import android.view.View;
import android.view.ViewGroup;
import android.widget.AdapterView;
import android.widget.BaseAdapter;
import android.widget.ListView;
import android.widget.TextView;
import android.widget.Toast;

import java.text.NumberFormat;
import java.util.ArrayList;
```

```
public class ViewHolderActivity extends Activity {
    ListView pieListView;
    ArrayList<Pie> pies;

    @Override
    protected void onCreate(Bundle savedInstanceState) {
        super.onCreate(savedInstanceState);
        setContentView(R.layout.activity_main);
        pieListView = (ListView) findViewById(R.id.listView);
        pies = makePies();
        PieAdapter adapter = new PieAdapter(this, pies);
        pieListView.setAdapter(adapter);

        pieListView.setOnItemClickListener(new AdapterView.OnItemClickListener() {
            @Override
            public void onItemClick(AdapterView<?> parent, View view,
                                    int position, long id) {
                Toast.makeText(getApplicationContext(),
                        pies.get(position).mName, Toast.LENGTH_SHORT).show();
            }
        });
    }
    public class PieAdapter extends BaseAdapter {
        Context mContext;
        ArrayList<Pie>  mPies;
        LayoutInflater mInflater;
        public PieAdapter(Context c, ArrayList<Pie> pies) {
            mContext = c;
            mPies = pies;
            mInflater = (LayoutInflater) mContext.getSystemService(
                    Context.LAYOUT_INFLATER_SERVICE);

        }
        public int getCount() {
            return  mPies.size();
        }
        public Object getItem(int position) {
            return mPies.get(position);
        }
        public long getItemId(int position) {
            return position;
        }
        public View getView(int position, View convertView, ViewGroup parent) {
            ViewHolder viewHolder;
            if (convertView == null) {
                convertView = mInflater.inflate(R.layout.pie_view_item, null);
                viewHolder = new ViewHolder();
                viewHolder.textViewName = (TextView)
```

```java
                    convertView.findViewById(R.id.textViewName);
                viewHolder.textViewDescription = (TextView)
                        convertView.findViewById(R.id.textViewDescription);
                viewHolder.textViewPrice = (TextView)
                        convertView.findViewById(R.id.textViewPrice);
                convertView.setTag(viewHolder);
            } else {
                viewHolder = (ViewHolder) convertView.getTag();
            }
            Pie currentPie = mPies.get(position);
            viewHolder.textViewName.setText(currentPie.mName);
            viewHolder.textViewDescription.setText(currentPie.mDescription);
            NumberFormat formatter = NumberFormat.getCurrencyInstance();
            String price = formatter.format(currentPie.mPrice);
            viewHolder.textViewPrice.setText(price);
            return convertView;
        }
    }

    private static class ViewHolder {
        public TextView textViewName;
        public TextView textViewDescription;
        public TextView textViewPrice;
    }

    private ArrayList<Pie> makePies(){
        ArrayList<Pie> pies = new ArrayList<Pie>();
        pies.add(new Pie("Apple","An old-fashioned favorite. ", 1.5));
        pies.add(new Pie("Blueberry","Made with fresh Maine blueberries.", 1.5));
        pies.add(new Pie("Cherry","Delicious and fresh made daily.", 2.0));
        pies.add(new Pie("Coconut Cream","A customer favorite.", 2.5));
        return pies;
    }

    private class Pie {
        String mName;
        String mDescription;
        double mPrice;
        public Pie (String name, String description, double price){
            this.mName = name;
            this.mDescription = description;
            this.mPrice = price;
        }
    }
}
```

Summary

In this hour, you learned about `ListViews` and adapters. Adapters make the connection between a set of data and how that data is displayed in a view. An `ArrayAdapter` is used to display an array of data. A `BaseAdapter` can be extended to handle different types of data and to display that data as required. An `ArrayList` of `Pie` objects was used to show the implementation of a `BaseAdapter` called `PieAdapter`. The layout for a child view in the list included all three members of the `Pie` class. The view holder pattern is used to improve performance.

Q&A

Q. Will I always use a `BaseAdapter` with a `ListView`?

A. Android Lollipop introduced a `RecyclerView`, which is covered in the next chapter. There is also a `CursorAdapter` that is used for associating SQLite database data with views.

Q. What are alternatives to `ListViews`, and how do they work?

A. You can use a `GridView` and a number of other view container `Views`. All work with `Adapters`.

Workshop

Quiz

1. What does the view holder pattern eliminate to make displaying items in a list more efficient?

2. Which method in `BaseAdapter` returns a `View`?

3. What does the `setTag()` method on a `View` do?

Answers

1. Methods to create new `Views` are eliminated when using the view holder pattern. Those calls are resource intensive and slow down the list.

2. The `getView()` method returns a `View`. In `getView()`, the UI controls like `TextViews` are populated with data. The whole `View` is returned for display.

3. The `setTag()` method associates an object with a `View`. The view holder pattern relies on using `setTag()` and `getTag()` methods.

Exercises

1. How do you modify the `PieAdapter` to change the background color of every other pie listed? The first pie would have a white background and the second light gray. Alternating colors would continue:

   ▶ In `getView()`, check whether `position` is odd or even. You can use the modulo operator (%). If `position % 2 == 0`, `position` is an even number.

   ▶ Set the background color of the `RelativeLayout` view appropriately.

   ▶ The `RelativeLayout` view will be the `convertView` when you are using the view holder pattern. You can use these methods to set the color:

      ▶ `convertView.setBackgroundColor(Color.LTGRAY);`

      ▶ `convertView.setBackgroundColor(Color.WHITE);`

   ▶ Make sure that the background color is set in all cases.

2. Try using one layout within another; specifically, create a `LinearLayout` with vertical orientation. Add a `FrameLayout` and a `Button`. Then add an `ImageView` to the `FrameLayout`.

3. Create an XML layout that uses `RelativeLayout`. Place an `ImageView` and `TextView` in the layout. Now, use that layout as an `include` in another layout.

HOUR 9
Material Design

What You'll Learn in This Hour:

▶ Evolution of app design

▶ Introducing material design

▶ Implementing material design

Material design is Google's new design language. It is not just for Android. Material design applies to web apps, too. When you look at the Google Inbox app on a Chrome browser or on an Android device, the same design elements are present. In this hour, you consider design aspects of app creation and some of the key features of material design. You code material design into your apps and consider compatibility with older versions of Android.

The Evolution of App Design

Personal computers have existed for about a generation, and smartphones and apps were introduced less than 10 years ago. When personal computers (PCs) were introduced, an important usability idea was to make analogies to the real world. A desktop, file cabinet, and trashcan were all things found in a real-world office that were carried over as concepts into computer operating systems (OS).

Skeuomorphism

The concept of using real-world objects as an analogy in your design is called *skeuoumorphism.* Skeuomorphism did not begin with personal computing or app creation. A car with fake wood siding paneling is an example of skeuomorphism. Early digital devices incorporated dials in the user interface.

Early PCs used an analogy of the desktop. Apps on the iPhone also mirrored real-world objects. Notebooks, journals, and calendars looked like their real-world counterparts. The advantage to this type of design is an immediate familiarity for the user. A journal app looks like a journal.

Apple's iOS design was based on skeuomorphism until iOS 7.

Flat Design

In the past few years, skeuomorphism has taken a backseat to flat design. Flat design is based more on color and typography than on an analogy to a real-world object. As people used PCs and smartphones for a number of years, the need for a real-world analogy decreased. Apps were just apps. Clarity in purpose and action became more important than the analogy to a real-world object.

One goal of flat design is to remove stylistic choices from interface design. Things such as shadows surrounding buttons or icons are not part of flat design. There is no embellishment.

Microsoft's Windows Phone and iOS 7 use flat design. Flat design is also common on many websites.

Microsoft's home page is a good example of flat design. Note the bold colors, typography, and lack of embellishments in Figure 9.1.

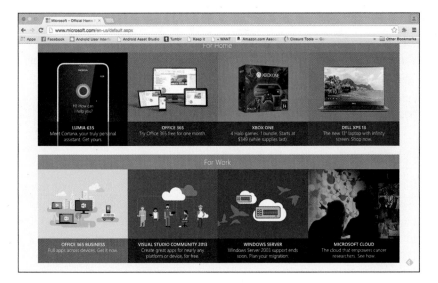

FIGURE 9.1
Flat design of Microsoft home page.

Introducing Material Design

Google introduced material design with the launch of the Lollipop version of Android. Material design is similar to flat design in some ways. Color and typography is important, but material design is not flat design at all. The concept behind material design is based on using paper for creating user interfaces. Think of pieces of construction paper of different colors and sizes. Those pieces of paper can be layered. One piece of paper can be on top of another. In that case, depth or elevation is important. One piece of paper could cast a shadow on another. Depending on the elevation between pieces of paper, the shadow could be large or small.

What material design does is to take design elements like elevation and shadows and to give them meaning in the user interface. They are no longer embellishments. They are meaningful.

3D Space and Shadows

The material environment is a 3D space. All objects have x, y, and z dimensions (that is, width, height, and depth). In material design in Android, you can set an object's elevation. Objects in the material environment follow rules of physical objects. Objects can be stacked and attached to each other, but they cannot pass through one another.

Objects will cast shadows, and those shadows add meaning to the user interface. Shadows are the result of the elevation being set.

The soft large shadow in Figure 9.2 indicates that the floating action button (FAB) is at a higher elevation than the app bar.

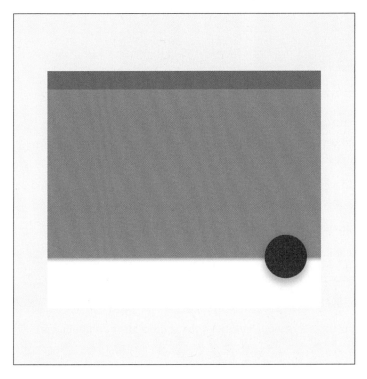

FIGURE 9.2
Shadows indicate elevation.

Graphics

The material design specification covers color, images, and icons in detail. Like flat design, colors in material design should be bold and colorful. Google has provided palettes of suggested colors to use in your designs. The primary colors should be used in your app, with additional colors being used as accents.

In Figure 9.3, the colors with number 500 are considered the primary colors, and the others the accents. The idea is that these colors will work well together.

Red		Pink		Purple	
500	#F44336	500	#E91E63	500	#9C27B0
50	#FFEBEE	50	#FCE4EC	50	#F3E5F5
100	#FFCDD2	100	#F8BBD0	100	#E1BEE7
200	#EF9A9A	200	#F48FB1	200	#CE93D8
300	#E57373	300	#F06292	300	#BA68C8
400	#EF5350	400	#EC407A	400	#AB47BC
500	#F44336	500	#E91E63	500	#9C27B0
600	#E53935	600	#D81B60	600	#8E24AA
700	#D32F2F	700	#C2185B	700	#7B1FA2
800	#C62828	800	#AD1457	800	#6A1B9A
900	#B71C1C	900	#880E4F	900	#4A148C

FIGURE 9.3
Palette suggestions.

The design section of the Android developer site includes swatches of colors that can be down-loaded for consideration in your design.

Images in material design should be prominent and help convey information. Images should be useful. They should enhance the user experience.

The material design guidelines provides five principles for using images:

▶ **Personal relevance:** Is the image relevant to the user?

▶ **Information:** Does the image convey meaningful information?

▶ **Delight:** Does the image make your product feel special to your user?

▶ **Appreciation of context:** Is the image appropriate for the context? Is it an intelligent choice for the context?

▶ **Be immersive:** Use color and content overlays to provide an in-depth immersive experience.

Typography

Typography is an important element of both flat design and material design. There are two specific fonts that are used on Android. Roboto is the standard typeface on Android. Noto is the standard typeface for all languages that do not support Roboto. Noto is also used on Chrome OS.

Roboto supports languages that use the Latin, Greek, and Cyrillic scripts. That includes English, French, Greek, and Russian.

Noto covers all major languages, including English, Greek, Russian, Arabic, Hebrew, Chinese, Japanese, Korean (CJK), Hindi, Bengali, and more.

Figure 9.4 shows examples of the Roboto font.

FIGURE 9.4
Roboto font.

Animation

Like other aspects of material design, the use of animation should both delight the user and convey information. Animation has a sense of movement, and movement can be used to convey information.

Animation can be used to show a responsive interaction. When the user touches the screen, something appropriate and logical happens. At that point, an animation can convey meaning to the user. The most basic response is an acknowledgment that the touch was received.

Small interactions, like a raise in elevation, can indicate that an element in the design is active.

Animation is particularly useful to indicate a meaningful transition. When a user selects a thumbnail of photos from a grid, you can just show a full screen image of the photo. Alternatively, you can add a meaningful transition by having the thumbnail expand to fill the screen.

Cards

A card contains unique related data. The Google Now app introduced the wide use of cards. Cards have a slight elevation and shadow. It is common in material design to show groups of cards and to show cards in a `ListView`. Figure 9.5 shows cards in the Google Now app.

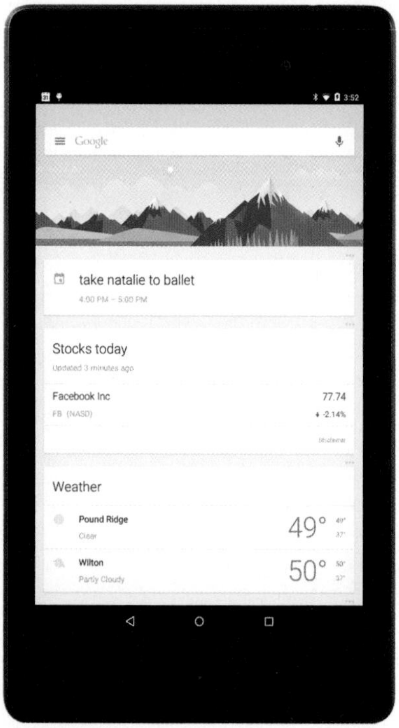

FIGURE 9.5
Cards in the Google Now app.

Implementing Material Design

Setting the theme for your app and setting the elevation on individual elements are two easy steps to implementing material design. Implementing a `CardView` and `RecyclerView` are coding tasks similar to adding a `ListView` with the view holder pattern. You'll create a simple animation and add a floating access button (FAB) to your app.

Setting Theme and Elevation

Setting the theme in Android Studio is easy. Figure 9.6 shows a button in Android Studio marked as App Theme. When you click that button, you can then set the app theme to Material Dark or Material Light. That is the first step in an application with material design.

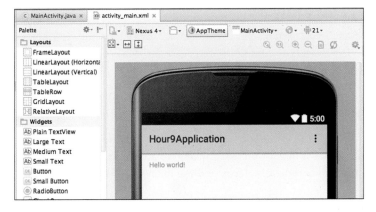

FIGURE 9.6
Setting your app theme.

Setting the elevation property for a widget is just as simple. Elevation is just another property for a widget. You can change elevation using the properties grid in Android Studio. You can also make edits directly in the XML layout file to add elevation. This snippet sets the elevation on a `TextView` to 12dp:

```
<TextView android:text="@string/hello_world"
        android:layout_width="wrap_content"
        android:layout_height="wrap_content"
        android:elevation="12dp" />
```

Setting the Material Theme for Your App and Adding Elevation
By adding a theme and using elevation, your app will take on the look used with material design:

1. Create a new Android project.

2. Change the app theme to `Material.light`.

3. Set the elevation for the generated `TextView` to 12dp.

4. Experiment with the light and dark theme and various elevations for the `TextView`.

CardView and RecyclerView

In Hour 8, "ListViews and Adapters," you used a `ListView`, `BaseAdapter`, and the view holder pattern to display a list of pies. The `CardView` and `RecyclerView` can work together to provide a similar list of pies that implement material design guidelines.

`CardView` and `RecyclerView` are part of the Android support library. The Android support library helps to bring new Android features to older versions of the platform. That means that these views can be used in apps that predate Lollipop and material design.

You need to add the appropriate libraries to your project. In Android Studio, in Project view, find the app folder and locate the build.gradle file. Then, add the following to the dependencies section:

```
compile 'com.android.support:cardview-v7:21.0.+'
compile 'com.android.support:recyclerview-v7:21.0.+'
```

Figure 9.7 shows the full dependencies section and build.gradle file in context.

Adding a CardView

After you add the support library, you can use a `CardView` in your design. `CardView` extends the `FrameLayout` class. It is easy to add a child view to a `CardView`. In the following snippet of an XML layout, a `CardView` contains a single `TextView`. Note that the `cardCornerRadius` value is 4dp. That is a property of `CardViews`:

```
<android.support.v7.widget.CardView
    xmlns:card_view="http://schemas.android.com/apk/res-auto"
    android:id="@+id/card_view"
    android:layout_width="200dp"
    android:layout_height="200dp"
    android:layout_centerInParent="true"
    android:layout_gravity="center"
    card_view:cardCornerRadius="4dp">
```

```
<TextView
    android:id="@+id/info_text"
    android:layout_width="wrap_content"
    android:layout_height="wrap_content"
    android:text="Information for this card" />
</android.support.v7.widget.CardView>
```

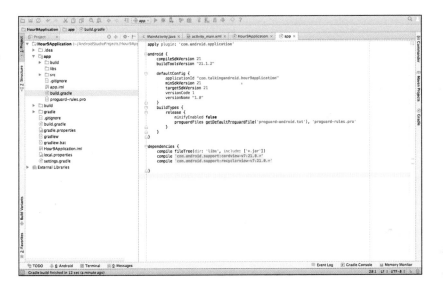

FIGURE 9.7
Adding required libraries.

Figure 9.8 shows this View in Android Studio design view.

You can have more control over the contents of a CardView by adding a layout like RelativeLayout as the first child element. That is, you will add a RelativeLayout to the CardView, and then you add child views to the RelativeLayout.

TRY IT YOURSELF ▼

Adding a CardView

A CardView is an important element in material design. These are the steps to add a CardView:

1. Add the support library to your project.

2. Add a CardView to the XML layout file.

3. Add a RelativeLayout to the CardView.

4. Add a TextView and an ImageView to the RelativeLayout.

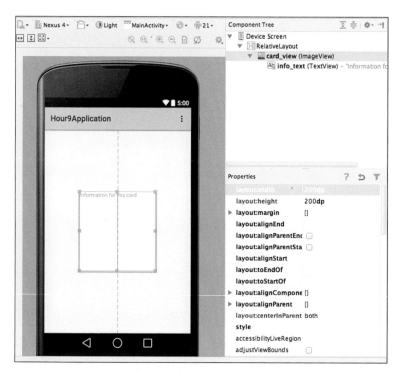

FIGURE 9.8
CardView in Android Studio.

Using a RecyclerView

In Hour 8, you used a `ListView` in a number of ways. The `RecyclerView` is a replacement for `ListView` that can be used when you have large data sets that you would like to scroll very quickly. The `RecyclerView` leverages the view holder pattern for efficiency.

The `RecyclerView` includes basic animations for displaying data and is easier to implement than the view holder pattern.

One of the examples in Hour 8 showed a `ListView` with a more complex visual display. It showed the list of pies with short descriptions. You will use a `RecyclerView` to create a similar experience.

Implementing the `RecyclerView` as a replacement for `ListView` requires:

▶ Creating an XML layout file that uses the `RecyclerView`

▶ Coding your `Activity` to refer to the `RecyclerView`

▶ Implementing a `RecyclerView.Adapter` instead of `BaseAdapter`

The XML layout file for replaces the `ListView` with a `RecyclerView`. As a reminder, you must first include a reference to the `RecyclerView` in your build.gradle file.

This XML layout file includes a `RecyclerView`. This layout file is the same as the one from Hour 8, but `RecyclerView` replaces `ListView`:

```
<RelativeLayout xmlns:android="http://schemas.android.com/apk/res/android"
    xmlns:tools="http://schemas.android.com/tools"
    android:layout_width="match_parent"
    android:layout_height="match_parent"
    android:paddingBottom="@dimen/activity_vertical_margin"
    android:paddingLeft="@dimen/activity_horizontal_margin"
    android:paddingRight="@dimen/activity_horizontal_margin"
    android:paddingTop="@dimen/activity_vertical_margin"
    tools:context=".MainActivity">

    <android.support.v7.widget.RecyclerView
        android:id="@+id/recyclerView"
        android:scrollbars="vertical"
        android:layout_width="match_parent"
        android:layout_height="match_parent"/>
</RelativeLayout>
```

The code for an activity that uses a `RecyclerView` is similar to the code for using a `ListView` and `BaseAdapter`. The `RecyclerView` is defined and tied to a `RecyclerView.Adapter`. The `RecyclerView.Adapter` has methods that must be implemented to create a view holder and to display the proper data for an item.

Listing 9.1 shows the complete implementation for an activity and adapter. This uses the pie data from Hour 8, and the same methods are called.

The `onCreate()` method on lines 19–30 for Listing 9.1 is similar to the work from Hour 8. A `RecyclerView` is used instead of a `ListView`, and the `PieAdapter` that is used is extended from `RecyclerView.Adapter` rather than from `BaseAdapter`.

Line 24 is new. The method `RecyclerView.setHasFixedSize(true)` means that each item displayed is the same size. If you know that to be the case, calling this method makes the list more efficient.

Implementing a `RecyclerView.Adapter` is different and simpler than using a `BaseAdapter`. The adapter is on lines 32–62 of Listing 9.1.

A constructor and three methods must be implemented for a `RecyclerView.Adapter`:

▶ **Constructor:** The constructor public `PieAdapter(ArrayList<Pie> pies)` is passed the data set to use. In this case, that is an `ArrayList` of `Pie` objects.

▶ **onCreateViewHolder():** A view holder is created in this method. It is in this method that you will inflate a view using an XML layout file that defines a single item.

▶ **onBindViewHolder():** Ties the data you are working with to a view. A single unit of data is displayed in a view. In this case, the information for a single `Pie` object is displayed.

▶ **getItemCount():** Provides the number of objects in the data set.

LISTING 9.1 An Activity with a RecyclerView

```
 1: package com.talkingandroid.hour9application;
 2: import android.app.Activity;
 3: import android.content.Context;
 4: import android.os.Bundle;
 5: import android.support.v7.widget.LinearLayoutManager;
 6: import android.support.v7.widget.RecyclerView;
 7: import android.view.LayoutInflater;
 8: import android.view.View;
 9: import android.view.ViewGroup;
10: import android.widget.TextView;
11: import java.text.NumberFormat;
12: import java.util.ArrayList;
13:
14: public class MainActivity extends Activity {
15:     RecyclerView pieRecyclerView;
16:     private RecyclerView.LayoutManager pieLayoutManager;
17:     ArrayList<Pie> pies;
18:
19:     @Override
20:     protected void onCreate(Bundle savedInstanceState) {
21:         super.onCreate(savedInstanceState);
22:         setContentView(R.layout.activity_main);
23:         pieRecyclerView = (RecyclerView) findViewById(R.id.recyclerView);
24:         pieRecyclerView.setHasFixedSize(true);
25:         pies = makePies();
26:         pieLayoutManager = new LinearLayoutManager(this);
27:         pieRecyclerView.setLayoutManager(pieLayoutManager);
28:         PieAdapter adapter = new PieAdapter(pies);
29:         pieRecyclerView.setAdapter(adapter);
30:     }
31:
```

```
32:     public class PieAdapter extends RecyclerView.Adapter<ViewHolder> {
33:         Context mContext;
34:         ArrayList<Pie> mPies;
35:         LayoutInflater mInflater;
36:
37:         public PieAdapter(ArrayList<Pie> pies) {
38:             mPies = pies;
39:         }
40:
41:       @Override
42:       public ViewHolder onCreateViewHolder(ViewGroup parent, int viewType) {
43:             View v = LayoutInflater.from(parent.getContext())
44:                     .inflate(R.layout.pie_view_item, parent, false);
45:             return new ViewHolder(v);
46:       }
47:
48:       @Override
49:       public void onBindViewHolder(ViewHolder holder, int position) {
50:             Pie currentPie = mPies.get(position);
51:             holder.textViewName.setText(currentPie.mName);
52:             holder.textViewDescription.setText(currentPie.mDescription);
53:             NumberFormat formatter = NumberFormat.getCurrencyInstance();
54:             String price = formatter.format(currentPie.mPrice);
55:             holder.textViewPrice.setText(price);
56:       }
57:
58:       @Override
59:       public int getItemCount() {
60:             return mPies.size();
61:       }
62:     }
63:
64:     private  class ViewHolder  extends RecyclerView.ViewHolder{
65:         public TextView textViewName;
66:         public TextView textViewDescription;
67:         public TextView textViewPrice;
68:         public ViewHolder(View v) {
69:             super(v);
70:             textViewName = (TextView) v.findViewById(R.id.textViewName);
71:             textViewDescription =
72:                         (TextView) v.findViewById(R.id.textViewDescription);
73:             textViewPrice = (TextView) v.findViewById(R.id.textViewPrice);
74:         }
75:     }
76:
77:     private ArrayList<Pie> makePies(){
78:       ArrayList<Pie> pies = new ArrayList<Pie>();
79:       pies.add(new Pie("Apple","An old-fashioned favorite. ", 1.5));
```

```
80:        pies.add(new Pie("Blueberry","Made with fresh Maine blueberries.", 1.5));
81:        pies.add(new Pie("Cherry","Delicious and fresh made daily.", 2.0));
82:        pies.add(new Pie("Coconut Cream","A customer favorite.", 2.5));
83:        return pies;
84:    }
85:
86:    private class Pie {
87:        String mName;
88:        String mDescription;
89:        double mPrice;
90:        public Pie (String name, String description, double price){
91:            this.mName = name;
92:            this.mDescription = description;
93:            this.mPrice = price;
94:        }
95:    }
96: }
```

Looking at the RecyclerView.Adapter in more detail, you can see that the PieAdapter defined on line 32 extends RecyclerView.Adapter.

The constructor is on lines 37–39 and is passed an ArrayList of Pie objects.

Lines 41–46 define the onCreateViewHolder(). In this method, the XML layout file R.layout.pie_view_item is inflated and returned as a View.

The onBindViewHolder() is implemented in lines 48–56. In this method, you get the current Pie object by using the position that is passed to the method. That is, you are using an ArrayList to hold the data. You can access a single item in the ArrayList if you know its position. This method passes the position, so you can retrieve the data to be displayed. This method also passes a ViewHolder. Once you have the data, you use it to populate the child views of that ViewHolder.

Lines 58–61 implement the getItemCount() method.

A ViewHolder is defined on lines 64–75. This is a very important class. Note that this class extends RecyclerView.ViewHolder. This class is passed a view that corresponds to the one you inflated in the onCreateViewHolder() method. You now use that view to assign individual items.

Lines 77–95 are the same as used in the code in Hour 8. A Pie object is defined, and a method to make an ArrayList of pie objects is implemented.

NOTE

RecyclerView: Where Is OnItemClickedListener()?

The `ListView` class includes support for `OnItemClickedListener`, but the `RecyclerView` does not. There are various strategies to handle this. They involve defining your own listener or adding click actions for items within the view.

One additional thing that you can do is place the listed items on cards by using the `CardView`. The following layout uses a `CardView` that holds a `RelativeLayout`. Figure 9.9 shows the result.

```xml
<?xml version="1.0" encoding="utf-8"?>
<RelativeLayout xmlns:android="http://schemas.android.com/apk/res/android"
    android:layout_width="match_parent" android:layout_height="match_parent"
    android:paddingBottom="2dp">

    <android.support.v7.widget.CardView
        xmlns:card_view="http://schemas.android.com/apk/res-auto"
        android:id="@+id/card_view"
        android:layout_width="match_parent"
        android:layout_height="wrap_content"
        card_view:cardCornerRadius="4dp"
        android:padding="12dp"
        android:layout_margin="4dp">

        <RelativeLayout
            android:layout_width="match_parent"
            android:layout_height="match_parent">

            <TextView
                android:layout_width="wrap_content"
                android:layout_height="wrap_content"
                android:textAppearance="?android:attr/textAppearanceLarge"
                android:text="Large Text"
                android:id="@+id/textViewName"
                android:layout_alignParentTop="true"
                android:layout_alignParentStart="true"
                android:paddingStart="10dp" />

            <TextView
                android:layout_width="wrap_content"
                android:layout_height="wrap_content"
                android:textAppearance="?android:attr/textAppearanceMedium"
                android:text="Medium Text"
                android:id="@+id/textViewDescription"
```

```
            android:layout_below="@+id/textViewName"
            android:layout_alignParentStart="true"
            android:paddingStart="10dp" />

        <TextView
            android:layout_width="wrap_content"
            android:layout_height="wrap_content"
            android:textAppearance="?android:attr/textAppearanceLarge"
            android:text="Large Text"
            android:id="@+id/textViewPrice"
            android:layout_alignParentTop="true"
            android:layout_alignParentEnd="true"
            android:paddingEnd="10dp" />
    </RelativeLayout>

    </android.support.v7.widget.CardView>
</RelativeLayout>
```

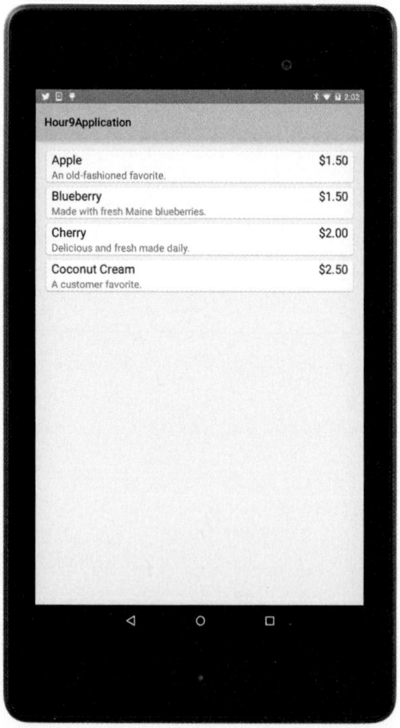

FIGURE 9.9
RecyclerView with items on cards.

Floating Action Button (FAB)

A floating action button (FAB) may be an important component of your application. It works very well in some designs. If your application shows a list of items and there is an option to add a new item, a FAB works very well. It will be the component you use to initiate adding new items.

For a real example, the Inbox mail app from Google uses a FAB to initiate writing a new email. It its regular state, the FAB shows a plus sign (+) icon. When selected, the icon expands to show the option to compose a new message or to select a contact to email. Figure 9.10 shows two states of the FAB.

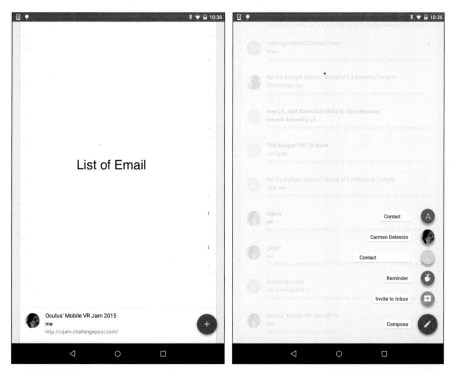

FIGURE 9.10
Two states of FAB.

A FAB is a circular button that is elevated above the layout. They are used to direct the user to a "promoted action." A FAB highlights an action that is something the user is likely to do and that is core to your app. The design definition of FAB says that a FAB is "made of paper that lifts and emits ink reactions on press." A FAB changes characteristics when it is pressed. The ink is sort of an animated shadow. FABs come in two specific sizes.

There is a sample project called Floating Action Button Basic that you can import into Android Studio to learn more about FAB. A FAB must be customized to your needs and your design. The sample app shows a FAB with a plus sign that changes to a check when selected. Figure 9.11 shows the two states of FAB for the sample app.

FIGURE 9.11
Two states of FAB.

Importing the Sample Project Floating Action Button Basic

Android Studio included sample projects, including this one, for a FAB. You will import the project and examine the code.

1. Choose File in Android Studio.

2. Choose Import Sample.

3. Find the Floating Action Button Basic Project under the UI section.

4. Import the project.

You can view the source code for the project on GitHub at https://github.com/googlesamples/android-FloatingActionButtonBasic/.

After you have imported the project, you can explore many aspects of the FAB implementation for this example.

Here are some things to check:

▶ `colors.xml`: Resource that defines the colors used in the project.

▶ `fab_icons.xml`: Resource that defines the two icons used in the project.

▶ `fab_background.xml`: Background that uses the ripple effect based on the checked state of the button.

▶ `fab_anim.xml`: Animation used to raise the z-level or elevation of the button when pressed.

▶ `fab_layout.xml`: Layout that includes two FABs.

▶ `FloatingActionButton.java`: Code for `FloatingActionButton`. A `FrameLayout` is extended, and the `Checkable` interface is implemented. The code to make the button into a circle occurs here.

Using a RippleDrawable in FAB

The fab_background.xml file defines a drawable in XML that has two states. One state is for a checked item, and the other state is for an unchecked item. Different colors are used for the two different states.

The items use a ripple effect that is tied to a `RippleDrawable`. A `RippleDrawable` is a new type of drawable introduced in Lollipop (API level 21). A ripple effect is shown in response to state changes.

This is what is in the fab_background.xml file:

```xml
<?xml version="1.0" encoding="UTF-8"?>
<selector xmlns:android="http://schemas.android.com/apk/res/android">

    <item android:state_checked="true">
        <ripple android:color="@color/fab_color_2_muted">
            <item>
                <shape>
                    <solid android:color="@color/fab_color_2" />
                </shape>
            </item>
        </ripple>
    </item>

    <item>
        <ripple android:color="@color/fab_color_1_muted">
            <item>
                <shape>
                    <solid android:color="@color/fab_color_1" />
                </shape>
            </item>
        </ripple>
    </item>
</selector>
```

The background is set for the FABs in the fab_layout.xml layout file:

```
android:background="@drawable/fab_background"
```

Adding Animation to FAB

In the sample, an animation is defined in the fab_anim.xml resource file in the res/animator folder. The animation elevates the object if it is pressed. It does that by setting the `TranslationZ` property to 9dp when the state is enabled or pressed.

The animator is set for the FABs in the fab_layout.xml layout file:

```
android:stateListAnimator="@animator/fab_anim"
```

This is what the fab_anim.xml file contains:

```xml
<?xml version="1.0" encoding="UTF-8"?>
<selector xmlns:android="http://schemas.android.com/apk/res/android">
```

```
<item
    android:state_enabled="true" android:state_pressed="true">
    <objectAnimator
        android:duration="@android:integer/config_shortAnimTime"
        android:propertyName="translationZ"
        android:valueTo="@dimen/fab_press_translation_z"
        android:valueType="floatType" />
</item>

<item>
    <objectAnimator
        android:duration="@android:integer/config_shortAnimTime"
        android:propertyName="translationZ"
        android:valueTo="0"
        android:valueType="floatType" />
</item>

</selector>
```

Summary

In this hour, you learned about design concepts and material design. Material design is Google's design language for Android and other platforms, like Chrome. You covered specific components of material design, such as graphics, typography, and cards. You learned how to use a RecyclerView and a CardView and learned about the use of animation and ripple effects in a FAB.

Q&A

Q. Should I always use a `RecyclerView` instead of a `ListView`?

A. No, for many cases, a ListView and a simple adapter like an ArrayAdapter will be sufficient. If you are implementing the view holder pattern using a ListView and a BaseAdapter, consider using a RecyclerView. By understanding view holder pattern in the ListView implementation, you can see the differences and potential advantages of using a RecyclerView.

Q. Can I used a `RecyclerView` to show a grid instead of a list?

A. Yes, in Listing 9.1, you set the RecyclerView.LayoutManager to use an LinearLayout this way: pieLayoutManager = new LinearLayoutManager(this);. By changing the LayoutManager, you can get a different view. To show a grid, you use pieLayoutManager = new GridLayoutManager(this, 2);.

Workshop

Quiz

1. What three methods must be implemented in a `RecyclerView.Adapter`?

2. Which fonts should be used in Android, and why are there two recommended fonts?

3. Explain what elevation is in material design?

Answers

1. The three methods that must be implemented are `onCreateViewHolder()`, `onBind-ViewHolder()`, and `getItemCount()`.

2. The two fonts are Roboto and Noto. They support different languages and alphabets.

3. The elevation is how far an object is elevated above the user interface in material design. In 3D space, elevation is the z-axis. When elevated, an object will cast a shadow.

Exercise

How would modify the `PieAdapter` to change the background color of every other pie listed? The first pie would have a white background and the second light gray. Alternating colors would continue. This is the same exercise as Hour 8, but now you must implement this change in the `RecyclerView.Adapter`.

More Views and Controls

What You'll Learn in This Hour:

- ▶ Controls for collecting information
- ▶ Indicating progress
- ▶ Displaying data
- ▶ Even more views

You have used basic controls like `Button`, `EditText`, and `TextView`. You have also dug into the details of using a `ListView` with an `Adapter`. In this hour, you explore additional controls. Some controls use adapters and are similar to `ListView` controls.

Controls for Collecting Information

An `EditText` collects data from the user. That data is a string of information that is entered by the user via a keyboard. The `getText()` method is used to retrieve data that is entered in an `EditText` control. Other controls for collecting data look different visually and may even include adapters for displaying selections for the user. A `Spinner` and an `AutoCompleteTextView` are examples of controls that collect data from the user.

Using a Spinner Control

The `Spinner` control is a version of a drop-down list. A single option is shown as the default selection. When the `Spinner` is clicked, additional choices are displayed and can be selected by the user. Figure 10.1 shows a `Spinner` with several options displayed for selection.

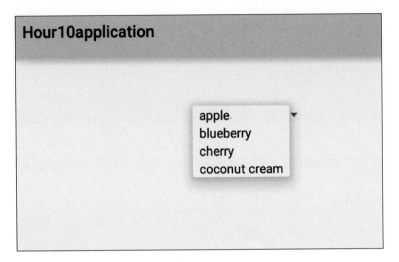

FIGURE 10.1
`Spinner` control showing data.

Adding Data for the Spinner

For a `Spinner` to function, you must provide a list of data to be displayed. In Hour 8, "ListViews and Adapters," you used an adapter to associate data with a `ListView`. You will do the same to populate the data for a `Spinner`. To show data in the control, you can use an `ArrayAdapter` as you did previously.

Similar to Hour 8, in the Strings.xml file in the res/values/ folder, create an array called pie_array, as follows:

```
<string-array name="pie_array">
    <item>apple</item>
    <item>blueberry</item>
    <item>cherry</item>
    <item>coconut cream</item>
</string-array>
```

To use this data, you create the `Spinner` in the `onCreate()` method of an `Activity`, retrieve the data from the array that you defined in the resource file, and tie the `Spinner` to that data using an `ArrayAdapter`. Listing 10.1 shows the full code for an activity that populates a `Spinner`.

LISTING 10.1 Using a Spinner with an ArrayAdapter

```
1: package com.bffmedia.hour10application;
2: import android.app.Activity;
3: import android.content.res.Resources;
```

```
 4: import android.os.Bundle;
 5: import android.view.View;
 6: import android.widget.AdapterView;
 7: import android.widget.ArrayAdapter;
 8: import android.widget.Spinner;
 9: import android.widget.Toast;
10:
11: public class MainActivity extends Activity {
12:     Spinner spinner;
13:     String[] pies;
14:     @Override
15:     protected void onCreate(Bundle savedInstanceState) {
16:         super.onCreate(savedInstanceState);
17:         setContentView(R.layout.activity_data_collection);
18:         spinner = (Spinner)findViewById(R.id.spinner);
19:         Resources resources = getResources();
20:         pies = resources.getStringArray(R.array.pie_array);
21:         spinner.setAdapter(new ArrayAdapter<String>(this,
22:                 android.R.layout.simple_spinner_item, pies));
23:         spinner.setOnItemSelectedListener(new
24:                             AdapterView.OnItemSelectedListener() {
25:             @Override
26:             public void onItemSelected(AdapterView<?> parent, View,
27:                                 int position, long id) {
28:                 Toast.makeText(getApplicationContext(),
29:                     pies[position], Toast.LENGTH_SHORT).show();
30:             }
31:
32:             @Override
33:             public void onNothingSelected(AdapterView<?> parent) {
34:
35:             }
36:         });
37:     }
38: }
```

On line 18, a Spinner is defined using the findViewById() method. Lines 19–20 create a String array named pies that holds the data to display in the Spinner. On lines 21 and 22, an ArrayAdapter is defined and used to associate the data in the pies array with the Spinner. Having provided the data, a view, and an adapter, you are now able to display the data in the Spinner in your activity.

Getting Data from a Spinner

To retrieve data from a Spinner, you should use the setOnItemSelectedListener() method, as shown in lines 23–24 of Listing 10.1. When you use an OnItemSelected Listener, you must implement the onItemSelected() and onNothingSelected()

methods. All the action occurs in the `onItemSelected()` method. In this case, a `Toast` is displayed with the value of the selected item based on the position in the `pies` array.

Using an AutoCompleteTextView

An `AutoCompleteTextView` is an input field that provides a list of suggestions based on user input. The user may select one of the suggestions or make a new entry. Figure 10.2 shows several states of an `AutoCompleteTextView` based on the text entered. The list of possible values is the same that was used for the `Spinner`. The top image shows the `hint` property.

When "ap" is entered, the choice "apple" is shown.

FIGURE 10.2
`AutoCompleteTextView` based on entered data.

Setting up an `AutoCompleteTextView` is similar to setting up a `Spinner`. An adapter is defined and bound to the view:

```
autoCompleteTextView = (AutoCompleteTextView) findViewById(
                    R.id.autoCompleteTextView);
autoCompleteTextView.setAdapter(new ArrayAdapter<String>(this,
                    android.R.layout.simple_spinner_dropdown_item, pies));
```

To retrieve data from an `AutoCompleteTextView`, the method `getText()` is used. An `AutoCompleteTextView` is similar to an `EditText` but with the additional capability of having a list of preset values.

CheckBoxes and RadioButtons

A `CheckBox` is either checked or unchecked and provided a value of true or false when read. When the `CheckBox` has a checkmark, the value is true. You would use a `CheckBox` when showing one or more true/false choices to the user. Each `CheckBox` is independent of any others.

A RadioButton works in the same way, but there is a significant difference. A RadioButton can be part of a RadioGroup. When a RadioButton is part of a RadioGroup, only one CheckBox within that group can be selected. You can provide a multiple-choice style question in which only one answer can be selected.

Figure 10.3 shows an example showing a single CheckBox and a RadioGroup that contains two RadioButtons.

FIGURE 10.3
Single CheckBox with RadioGroup.

When you create layout files that include CheckBoxes or RadioButtons, you can set the checked property to true. This layout file for the RadioGroup shown in Figure 10.3 indicates that the RadioButton with id radioButtonPositive is checked. The value android:checked is set to "true":

```
<RadioGroup
    android:layout_width="wrap_content"
    android:layout_height="wrap_content"
    android:layout_below="@+id/textView"
    android:id="@+id/radioGroup">

    <RadioButton
        android:layout_width="wrap_content"
        android:layout_height="wrap_content"
        android:text="@string/postive"
        android:id="@+id/radioButtonPositive"
        android:layout_gravity="center_horizontal"
        android:checked="true" />

    <RadioButton
        android:layout_width="wrap_content"
        android:layout_height="wrap_content"
        android:text="@string/negative"
        android:id="@+id/radioButtonNegative"
        android:layout_gravity="center_horizontal" />

</RadioGroup>
```

Use the `isChecked()` method on an individual `RadioButton` or `CheckBox` to determine whether it is selected. A Boolean value will be returned.

For a `Checkbox` named `checkbox`, you use the following:

```
checkbox.isChecked()
```

For two `RadioButtons` called `radioButtonNegative` and `radioButtonPositive`, you use the following:

```
Boolean yesChecked = radioButtonPositive.isChecked();
Boolean noChecked = radioButtonNegative.isChecked();
```

There is no need to check each individual `RadioButton` when using a `RadioGroup`. You can use the `getCheckedRadioButtonId()` method of the `RadioGroup` to determined which `RadioButton` was selected. The returned value is the `id` of the `RadioButton`.

▼ TRY IT YOURSELF

Retrieving a Selected RadioButton from a RadioGroup

You will create a single `Activity` that has a `RadioGroup` that contains at least two radio buttons. Use the `getCheckedRadioButtonId()` method of the `RadioGroup` to determine what was selected:

1. Create a new project with an `Activity`.

2. Change the XML layout file to include a `RadioGroup` with at least two `RadioButtons`.

3. Add a `Button` to the design.

4. Add an `OnClickListener` to the `Button`.

5. When the `Button` is clicked, use `getCheckedRadioButtonId()` to get the `id` of the selected `RadioButton`. (Hint: If the selected `RadioButton` was defined with an id of `radioButtonPositive`, the value `R.id. radioButtonPositive` is returned in your code.)

6. Show a `Toast` message that indicates which `RadioButton` was selected.

Indicating Progress

`ProgressBars` and `SeekBars` help tell the status of an event that is occurring. For example, you may want to show a `ProgressBar` to indicate to the user that data is being retrieved or a long-running process in occurring.

A `ProgressBar` that is circular and indicates that something is occurring is known as an *indeterminate* `ProgressBar`. A horizontal `ProgressBar` can represent what percentage of a task is complete. A `SeekBar` is similar to a horizontal `ProgressBar`, but the user can set the `SeekBar` to a specific location. A `SeekBar` can be used to set the location within a `VideoView`, for example.

Figure 10.4 shows a `ProgressBar`, `HorizontalProgressBar`, and a `SeekBar` in an `Activity`.

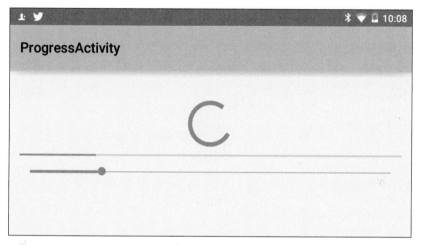

FIGURE 10.4
Showing progress.

In Hour 5, "Responsive Apps: Running in the Background," you used the `AsyncTask` class and learned about running tasks in the background without affecting what was occurring on the UI thread. To show how `ProgressBars` and `SeekBars` work, you will use an `AsyncTask` to do some work in the background and to indicate the progress of that background processing.

The `AsyncTask` class has two methods that help with indicating and showing progress: `publishProgress()` and `onProgressUpdate()`. These two methods work together. The `publishProgress()` method runs in the background and is called from the `doInBackground()` method. The `onProgressUpdate()` method runs on the UI thread whenever `publishProgress()` is called:

▶ **`publishProgress()`:** This method, called from the `doInBackground()` method, periodically informs the UI thread about the background process progress. This method sends information to the UI process. Use this opportunity to send updated progress for a `ProgressBar` that the user can see.

▶ **onProgressUpdate()**: This method runs on the UI thread whenever the `doInBackground()` method calls `publishProgress()`. This method receives information from the background process. Use this opportunity to update a `ProgressBar` control that the user can see.

Listing 10.2 shows the complete code for an activity called `ProgressActivity` that displays an indeterminate `ProgressBar`, a horizontal `ProgressBar`, and a `SeekBar`. The horizontal `ProgressBar` and `SeekBar` are updated using the `onProgressUpdate()` method of an `AsyncTask` named `ProgressTask`.

LISTING 10.2　Activity Showing ProgressBar and SeekBar

```
 1: package com.bffmedia.hour10application;
 2: import android.app.Activity;
 3: import android.os.AsyncTask;
 4: import android.os.Bundle;
 5: import android.os.SystemClock;
 6: import android.view.View;
 7: import android.widget.ProgressBar;
 8: import android.widget.SeekBar;
 9: import android.widget.TextView;
10:
11: public class ProgressActivity extends Activity {
12:     ProgressBar progressBar;
13:     ProgressBar progressBarHorizontal;
14:     SeekBar seekBar;
15:     TextView textView;
16:
17:     @Override
18:     protected void onCreate(Bundle savedInstanceState) {
19:         super.onCreate(savedInstanceState);
20:         setContentView(R.layout.activity_progress);
21:         progressBar= (ProgressBar) findViewById(R.id.progressBar);
22:         progressBarHorizontal= (ProgressBar)
findViewById(R.id.progressBarHorizontal);
23:         seekBar= (SeekBar) findViewById(R.id.seekBar);
24:         textView = (TextView) findViewById(R.id.textView);
25:         new ProgressTask().execute();
26:     }
27:
28:     class ProgressTask extends AsyncTask<Integer, Integer, Integer> {
29:
30:         @Override
31:         protected void onPostExecute(Integer result) {
32:             progressBar.setVisibility(View.GONE);
33:             progressBarHorizontal.setVisibility(View.GONE);
```

```
34:                seekBar.setVisibility(View.GONE);
35:                textView.setVisibility(View.VISIBLE);
36:            }
37:
38:            @Override
39:            protected Integer doInBackground(Integer... params) {
40:                for (int i=0; i < 5; i++){
41:                    SystemClock.sleep(1000);
42:                    publishProgress(i+1);
43:                }
44:                return 0;
45:            }
46:
47:            @Override
48:            protected void onProgressUpdate(Integer... progress){
49:                progressBarHorizontal.setProgress(progress[0]);
50:                seekBar.setProgress(progress[0]);
51:            }
52:    }
53: }
```

The big idea of Listing 10.2 is simple. You display two `ProgressBars` and a `SeekBar` until a background task finishes. When the task finishes, the `ProgressBars` and `SeekBar` disappear, and a `TextView` with the text "Finished" appears. The `HorizontalProgressBar` and the `SeekBar` will show incremental progress.

Any `View` can have one of three states of visibility. A `View` can be visible, invisible, or gone. An invisible `View` still takes up space. A gone `View` does not.

Changing visibility is easy. You use the `setVisibility()` method, as follows:

```
seekBar.setVisibility(View.GONE);
textView.setVisibility(View.VISIBLE);
```

When user interface for `ProgressActivity` is shown, the `ProgressBar` and `SeekBar` are visible. The `TextView` saying "Finished" has visibility set to gone. When the background task finishes, the `ProgressBars` and `SeekBar` are hidden, and the `TextView` is set to visible.

TIP

Setting Maximum Values for Horizontal ProgressBars and SeekBars

A property for horizontal `ProgressBars` and `SeekBars` is the maximum value. It is indicated in the layout file as `android:max="5"`. To indicate progress, you need to know the maximum value. You can then indicate your progress relative to the maximum. To set the max value in code, use `seekBar.setMax(5);`.

The work of Listing 10.2 occurs in the `AsyncTask` class `ProgressTask`. There is a `for` loop in the `doInBackround()` method that sleeps for 1 second and then makes a call to `publishProgess()`. That occurs in lines 38–45. The `for` loop increments from 0 to 4. On the first increment of 0, a 1-second delay occurs, followed by a call to `publishProgess()` with a value of 1. The progress indicates the time delay that has been completed. On the last iteration, the `publishProgess()` passes a 5. The horizontal `ProgressBar` and the `SeekBar` are set to have a maximum value of 5. The result is that they indicate that the progress is at 100%.

The `onProgressUpdate()` method accepts that value passed by `publishProgess()` and updates the horizontal `ProgressBar` and `SeekBar` appropriately.

Displaying Data

There are many ways to display data or images or views in Android. In Hour 8, you used a `ListView` and a number of different adapters to display a list of pie flavors. The simplest implementation used an `ArrayAdapter`.

You created a `ListView` in the XML layout file and populated it using an `ArrayAdapter`. The array was populated from the Strings.xml resource file. This code snippet will populate the `ListView` and show a `Toast` message when an item in the list is selected:

```
public class ArrayAdapterActivity extends Activity {
    ListView pieListView;
    String[] pies;

    @Override
    protected void onCreate(Bundle savedInstanceState) {
        super.onCreate(savedInstanceState);
        setContentView(R.layout.activity_main);
        Resources resources = getResources();
        pies = resources.getStringArray(R.array.pie_array);
        pieListView = (ListView) findViewById(R.id.listView);
        pieListView.setAdapter(new ArrayAdapter<String>(this,
                R.layout.text_view_item, pies));
        pieListView.setOnItemClickListener(new AdapterView.OnItemClickListener() {
            @Override
            public void onItemClick(AdapterView<?> parent, View,
                                    int position, long id) {
                Toast.makeText(getApplicationContext(),
                        pies[position], Toast.LENGTH_SHORT).show();
            }
        });
    }
}
```

Using a GridView

A `GridView`(`android.widget.GridView`) displays data in a grid containing columns and rows. A `GridView` functions precisely the same was as a `ListView`. You decide which data to display in the view and then create an appropriate adapter.

In a `GridView`, you can specify the number of columns.

A basic `GridView` can be defined in a layout file with the following properties:

```
<GridView
    android:layout_width="match_parent"
    android:layout_height="wrap_content"
    android:id="@+id/gridView"
    android:layout_alignParentTop="true"
    android:layout_alignParentStart="true"
    android:numColumns="2" />
```

In this case, the number of columns is set to 2.

TRY IT YOURSELF ▼

Displaying Data in a GridView

You will create a single activity with a `GridView`. The goal is to display data from the pie array in the `GridView`. The code can be modeled on the `ArrayAdapter` code that was used to display data in a `ListView`. The result should look like Figure 10.5:

1. Create a new project with an activity.

2. Change the XML layout file to include a `GridView` with two columns.

3. Add the `pie` array definition to the Strings.xml resource file.

4. In the `onCreate()` method for the `Activity`, use `findViewById()` to get the `GridView`.

5. Get the `String` array of pies from the Strings.xml resource file.

6. Use an `ArrayAdapter` to display the array of pie data in the `GridView`. If the data is an array called `pies` and the `GridView` is in a variable called `gridView`, you can use the following:

   ```
   gridView.setAdapter(new ArrayAdapter<String>(this, android.R.layout.simple_
   list_item_1, pies));
   ```

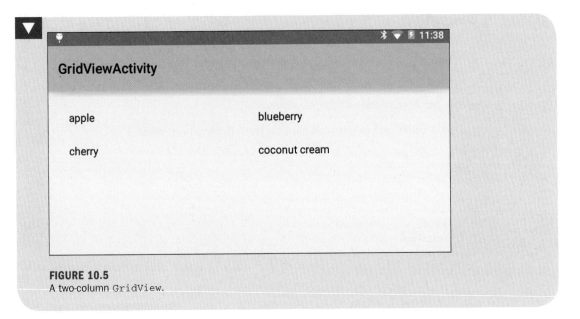

FIGURE 10.5
A two-column `GridView`.

Using an AdapterViewFlipper

An `AdapterViewFlipper` displays one view at a time and provides the ability to flip between views. You can use an `AdapterViewFlipper` in the same way that you used a `ListView` or `GridView`. The `AdapterViewFlipper` has an option to flip between views automatically. Think of that as the ability to create a slideshow of `Views`.

You can use the same `pie` array to flip through the display of pie flavors. The view being displayed in the `AdapterViewFlipper` will be the `TextView` specified in the `ArrayAdapter`. This is a simple example to show how an `AdapterViewFlipper` works and to show the similarity between containers that use an `Adapter`.

Listing 10.3 shows the code for an `Activity` that uses an `AdapterViewFlipper`.

LISTING 10.3   Activity with an AdapterViewFlipper

```
1:   import android.app.Activity;
2:   import android.content.res.Resources;
3:   import android.os.Bundle;
4:   import android.view.View;
5:   import android.widget.AdapterView;
6:   import android.widget.AdapterViewFlipper;
7:   import android.widget.ArrayAdapter;
8:   import android.widget.Toast;
9:
```

```
10:   public class AdapterViewFlipperActivity extends Activity {
11:       AdapterViewFlipper adapterViewFlipper;
12:       String[] pies;
13:
14:       @Override
15:       protected void onCreate(Bundle savedInstanceState) {
16:           super.onCreate(savedInstanceState);
17:           setContentView(R.layout.activity_adapter_view_flipper);
18:           adapterViewFlipper = (AdapterViewFlipper)
19:                           findViewById(R.id.adapterViewFlipper);
20:           Resources resources = getResources();
21:           pies = resources.getStringArray(R.array.pie_array);
22:           adapterViewFlipper.setAdapter(new ArrayAdapter<String>(this,
23:                   android.R.layout.simple_list_item_1, pies));
24:           adapterViewFlipper.setAutoStart(true);
25:           adapterViewFlipper.setFlipInterval(2000);
26:       }
27:   }
```

Listing 10.3 defines the `AdapterViewFlipper`. On line 22, the `setAdapter()` method is used to associate the data in the `pies` `String[]` array with the view. Line 24 indicates that the view should start flipping automatically, and line 25 indicates that the interval to show each view is 2 seconds. The view being shown in the `AdapterViewFlipper` is the `TextView` defined by `android.R.layout.simple_list_item_1`. It is specified in the `setAdapter` call on line 23.

Other useful methods available for the `AdapterViewFlipper` include `showNext()`, `showPrevious()`, `stopFlipping()`, and `startFlipping()`.

Page Flipping and Horizontal Scrolling

In addition to the `AdapterViewFlipper`, you have options for displaying content with horizontal scrolling or page flipping. With the `AdapterViewFlipper`, you were able to take advantage of using a control that works with an adapter. The `AdapterViewFlipper` and other containers that work with an adapter extend the `AdapterView` class.

You can find more information about the `AdapterView` in the Android documentation:

http://developer.android.com/reference/android/widget/AdapterView.html

Other options include the `HorizontalScrollView`, `ViewFlipper`, and `ViewPager`.

Table 10.1 shows the available views with a description and API level listed.

TABLE 10.1   Options for Horizontal Scrolling or Paging

View	Description	API Level/Availability
Gallery	Horizontal scrolling for views. Extends `AdapterView`.	Since API level 1, deprecated API level 16
AdapterViewFlipper	Flip between `Views`. Extends `AdapterView`.	Since API level 11
ViewFlipper	Flip between `Views`.	Since API level 1
ViewPager	Flip between `Views`. Use a `PagerAdapter` to generate the pages to show.	Support library
HorizontalScrollView	A layout container for horizontal scrolling.	Since API level 3

More Views

You may choose to use additional views in your Android applications. Some views are used on forms and are appropriate for collecting data. Others are useful to display data or indicate a status to this user. As you use the design palette in Android Studio, you will see many additional widgets and containers. Many are similar or have similar properties to what you have already reviewed in this hour. Others are unique. You'll consider two additional views now: a `WebView` and a `ScrollView`. The `ImageView` is covered in detail in the next hour.

GO TO ▶ CHAPTER 11, "IMAGEVIEWS AND BITMAPS," to see more on `ImageViews`.

WebView

A `WebView` is used to display web pages. The content for those pages can be defined by a URL for a website or can be local data that is loaded into the `WebView`.

To load a web page, you will use the `loadUrl()` method and pass a URL:

```
webView.loadUrl("http://developer.android.com/index.html");
```

To load HTML from a source within your app (for instance, a `String` containing HTML), you use the `loadData()` method. The parameters are the HTML data, MIME type, and encoding to use:

```
webView.loadUrl(htmlString, "text/html", null);
```

To detect events occurring within a `WebView`, you can set a `WebViewClient`. You can override certain methods within the `WebViewClient` to detect events and to decide whether to override the action associated with a particular URL. When you override the `shouldOverrideUrlLoading()` method, you decide whether to let the `WebView` display the URL provided or to take another action. If you return true, it means that your code is taking responsibility for what will occur. If you return false, the `WebView` displays the passed URL.

Listing 10.4 shows a `WebView` that specifies a `WebViewClient` called `CustomWebViewClient`. The `WebView` initially displays the Google search page. Any search or URL that contains the word "android" caused the `WebView` to display the Android Developer site.

LISTING 10.4   WebView Using a WebViewClient

```
 1:   package com.bffmedia.hour10application;
 2:   import android.app.Activity;
 3:   import android.os.Bundle;
 4:   import android.webkit.WebView;
 5:   import android.webkit.WebViewClient;
 6:
 7:   public class WebViewActivity extends Activity {
 8:       WebView webView;
 9:
10:       @Override
11:       protected void onCreate(Bundle savedInstanceState) {
12:           super.onCreate(savedInstanceState);
13:           setContentView(R.layout.activity_web_view);
14:           webView = (WebView)findViewById(R.id.webView);
15:           webView.setWebViewClient(new CustomWebViewClient());
16:           webView.loadUrl("https://www.google.com");
17:       }
18:
19:       private class CustomWebViewClient extends WebViewClient {
20:           @Override
21:           public boolean  shouldOverrideUrlLoading (WebView  view, String  url){
22:               if (url.contains("android")){
23:                   view.loadUrl
24:                           ("http://developer.android.com/develop/index.html");
25:                   return true;
26:               }
27:               return false;
28:           }
29:       }
20:   }
```

In Listing 10.4, a `WebView` is defined. On line 16, the URL for the Google website is loaded. On line 15, the `WebViewClient` is set to `CustomWebViewClient`. `CustomWebViewClient` is defined on lines 19–29.

The `CustomWebViewClient` overrides the `shouldOverrideUrlLoading()` method. On line 22, a check is made to determine whether the passed URL contains the string `"android"`. If the URL contains "android," the passed view is loaded with the URL specified on line 24. That view is the `WebView`. True is returned on line 25 to indicate that the app has handled loading this URL. If the passed URL does not contain "android," the method returns false, and the passed URL is loaded.

In your own apps, you will likely never need to override any URL containing the word "android," but overriding URLs for different purposes is a common occurrence.

Figure 10.6 shows a `WebView` filling the screen for an activity. Note that a `WebView` does not include common web controls, such as next/back or an address bar.

FIGURE 10.6
Displaying a `WebView`.

CAUTION

Internet Permission Is Required

When you use a `WebView` to load a URL, you must set the Internet permission in your Android manifest file. Make sure to add the following:

```
<uses-permission android:name="android.permission.INTERNET" />
```

When to Use a ScrollView

A `ScrollView` may contain one view. Typically, you would add a `Layout` to a `ScrollView`. If you know that your display will be bigger than the page, a `ScrollView` comes in handy.

Summary

Different views and containers were considered in this hour. You learned about using views to collect data in a form, `ProgressBars` to display status, and multiple ways to display data. Those included a `GridView` and an `AdapterViewFlipper`. You saw that populating data for a `GridView` and an `AdapterViewFlipper` was very similar to loading data in a `ListView`. The adapters you used in Hour 8 can be used. In this hour, you used an `ArrayAdapter` to tie an array of string data to the display. A `WebView` was covered, as was when to use a `ScrollView`.

Q&A

Q. Will I always use a `BaseAdapter` with a `ListView`?

A. Android Lollipop introduced a `RecyclerView`, which is covered in the next hour. Also, a `CursorAdapter` is used to associate SQLite database data with views.

Workshop

Quiz

1. What does a hint do in an `AutoCompleteTextView`?

2. What is the difference between an indeterminate `ProgressBar` and a horizontal `ProgressBar`?

3. What does `publishProgess` mean when discussing an `AsyncTask`?

Answers

1. The hint is displayed in the `EditText` view as a prompt for the user. It is overwritten by user input.

2. An indeterminate `ProgressBar` is shown as a spinning circle and does not show the actual status of the current task. A horizontal `ProgressBar` reflects the status of the background process. If the background task is 50% complete, the horizontal `ProgressBar` will be at the halfway mark.

3. The `publishProgress()` is called from the `doInBackground()` method. When `publishProgress()` is called, the method `onProgressUpdate` runs, and the user interface can be updated. So, `publishProgress` can be used to indicate that the user interface associated with a background task can be updated. You used this method to update a horizontal `ProgressBar`.

Exercise

Create an activity that uses a `Spinner` to display a list of three countries: England, France, and the United States. If United States is selected, display another `Spinner` that shows a list of 50 states. Include a `Button` that reads the selected values and displays the result in a `Toast` message.

ImageViews and Bitmaps

What You'll Learn in This Hour:

▶ Examining `ImageView` Bitmaps

▶ Using `Bitmaps` and `Canvas`

▶ Introducing Picasso

Images and media can play an important role in creating an exceptional Android app. In this chapter, you look at the details of handling images and bitmaps, including creating bitmaps, using drawing commands, and handling very large images.

Examining ImageView

You learned about different types of views in Hour 10, "More Views and Controls." An `ImageView` is a view that displays an image, but you will find that there are unique aspects to working with images. An `ImageView` can display any drawable image. The source of the image can be a resource, a drawable, or a bitmap.

Displaying an Image

There are four methods available for setting an image in an `ImageView`. They differ by how the image to display is defined. The image can be a `bitmap`, `drawable`, `Uri`, or resource `id`. The methods are as follows:

▶ **`setImageDrawable()`:** Set a drawable as the content of the `ImageView`.

▶ **`setImageBitmap()`:** Set a `Bitmap` as the content of the `ImageView`.

▶ **`setImageResource()`:** Use a resource `id` to set the content of the `ImageView`.

▶ **`setImageUri()`:** Use a URI to set the content of the `ImageView`.

To set an `ImageView` to an image resource defined by `R.drawable.mainImage`, you use the following:

```
ImageView mainImage = (ImageView) findViewById(R.id.imageView1);
mainImage.setImageResource(R.drawable.mainImage)
```

To populate a `Drawable` object from a resource, use the `getResources.getDrawable()` method:

```
Drawable myDrawable = getResources().getDrawable(R.drawable.ic_launcher);
```

In this hour, you populate an `ImageView` using a resource `id` as the source and then explore several properties of how an `ImageView` can display an image.

Using ScaleTypes in ImageView

`ImageViews` include a `ScaleType` property. The `ScaleType` defines how the image will be displayed within the `ImageView`. Using `ScaleType`, you can have an image fill the entire `ImageView`, be centered in the `ImageView`, or be cropped and centered in the `ImageView`.

The options for `ScaleType` are defined in `ImageView.ScaleType`. For example, `ImageView.ScaleType.CENTER` refers to a scale type in which the image is centered in the `ImageView`. The complete set of `ScaleTypes` are as follows:

▶ **ImageView.ScaleType.CENTER:** Center the image with no scaling. The image dimensions are unchanged.

▶ **ImageView.ScaleType.CENTER_CROP:** Scales the image and keeps the aspect ratio until either the width of height of the image is the same as the width or height of the `ImageView`. For a small image, this has the effect of enlarging the entire image. For a large image, this has the effect of showing the center of the image.

▶ **ImageView.ScaleType.CENTER_INSIDE:** The image is scaled, and the aspect ratio is maintained. The width and height of the image fit within the `ImageView`.

▶ **ImageView.ScaleType.FIT_CENTER:** Maintain aspect ratio and fit the image in the center of the `ImageView`.

▶ **ImageView.ScaleType.FIT_START:** Maintain aspect ratio and fit the image in the left and top edge of the `ImageView`.

▶ **ImageView.ScaleType.FIT_END:** Maintain aspect ratio and fit the image in the right and bottom edge of the `ImageView`.

▶ **ImageView.ScaleType.FIT_END:** Maintain aspect ratio and fit the image in the right and bottom edge of the `ImageView`.

▶ **ImageView.ScaleType.MATRIX:** Scale using a matrix.

You can change scaleType dynamically in your code. Listing 11.1 show the code for an app that displays an ImageView and includes a RadioGroup and set of RadioButtons for changing the scale type. When a radio button is selected, the scaleType for the ImageView is updated.

LISTING 11.1 Changing ScaleType Programatically

```
 1:  package com.talkingandroid.hour11application;
 2:  import android.app.Activity;
 3:  import android.os.Bundle;
 4:  import android.widget.ImageView;
 5:  import android.widget.RadioGroup;
 6:
 7:  public class ScaleActivity extends Activity {
 8:      RadioGroup radioGroup;
 9:      ImageView imageView;
10:
11:      @Override
12:      protected void onCreate(Bundle savedInstanceState) {
13:          super.onCreate(savedInstanceState);
14:          setContentView(R.layout.activity_scale);
15:          radioGroup = (RadioGroup) findViewById(R.id.radioGroup);
16:          imageView = (ImageView) findViewById(R.id.imageView);
17:          radioGroup.setOnCheckedChangeListener(new
18:                      RadioGroup.OnCheckedChangeListener() {
19:              @Override
20:              public void onCheckedChanged(RadioGroup group, int checkedId) {
21:                  switch (checkedId){
22:                      case R.id.radioCenter:
23:                          imageView.setScaleType(ImageView.ScaleType.CENTER);
24:                          break;
25:                      case R.id.radioCenterCrop:
26:                          imageView.setScaleType(ImageView.ScaleType.CENTER_CROP);
27:                          break;
28:                      case R.id.radioCenterInside:
29:                          imageView.setScaleType(ImageView.ScaleType.CENTER_INSIDE);
30:                          break;
31:                      case R.id.radioFitCenter:
32:                          imageView.setScaleType(ImageView.ScaleType.FIT_CENTER);
33:                          break;
34:                      case R.id.radioFitStart:
35:                          imageView.setScaleType(ImageView.ScaleType.FIT_START);
36:                          break;
37:                      case R.id.radioFitEnd:
38:                          imageView.setScaleType(ImageView.ScaleType.FIT_END);
39:                          break;
40:                      case R.id.radioFitXY:
```

```
41:                          imageView.setScaleType(ImageView.ScaleType.FIT_XY);
42:                          break;
43:                      }
44:                  }
45:          });
46:      }
47:}
```

On line 17 of Listing 11.1, an `OnCheckChangeListener()` is set for the `RadioGroup`. When the change is detected, the select `RadioButton id` is checked, and the appropriate `scaleType` is set on the image.

The image used in the code for Listing 11.1 is shown in Figure 11.1. The image is 900 pixels wide and 200 pixels high. It is used in several other examples in this chapter.

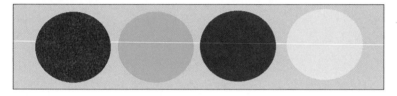

FIGURE 11.1
Base image for showing `ScaleType` (scaletest.png).

By using this simple image with four circles of different colors, it is easy to see the effect of the changing `ScaleType`.

The `ImageView` is set to match the parent width and height. When the image `scaleType` is set to `CENTER_INSIDE`, the image is shown taking the full width of the `ImageView` and is centered with a height that is proportional to the width.

Figure 11.2 shows the base image using the `scaleTypes` set to `CENTER`, `CENTER_CROP`, and `CENTER_INSIDE`. Using `CENTER` shows the image in actual size. Because the size of the image is larger than the `ImageView`, the green and blue circles in the center are shown. `CENTER_CROP` shows half of the green and blue circle. The height of the image fills the `ImageView`. `CENTER_INSIDE` shows the entire image centered in the `ImageView`.

Figure 11.3 shows the base image using the `ScaleTypes` `FIT_CENTER`, `FIT_START`, `FIT_END`, and `FIT_XY`. The aspect ratio is maintained in the first three, but when using `FIT_XY`, the image fills the `ImageView` and "stretches" the image to fit.

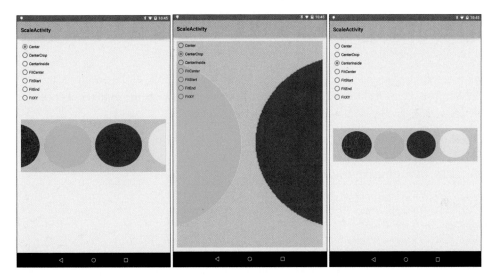

FIGURE 11.2
ScaleTypes `CENTER`, `CENTER_CROP`, and `CENTER_INSIDE`.

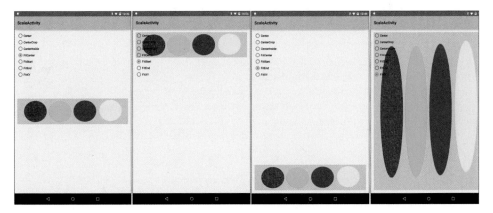

FIGURE 11.3
ScaleTypes `FIT_CENTER`, `FIT_START`, `FIT_END`, and `FIT_XY`.

Rotating an Image

An `ImageView` contains several methods for rotating an image. When you rotate an image, you must set the point in the image to rotate around. That is the *pivot point*. The method `setPivotX()` and `setPivotY()` are used to set the pivot point.

Once the pivot point is set, you can call the `setRotation()` method to make the image actually rotate.

The idea in Listing 11.2 is to set the pivot point to the center of the `ImageView` and to rotate the image 30 degrees each time the button is clicked. The `ImageView` is defined to have height and width set to `match_parent`. The `ImageView` occupies the entire screen.

To get the center of the `ImageView`, the width and height are divided by 2. To continuously rotate, the number of clicks count is kept. The angle to rotate is 30 times the number of clicks. So, if the button is clicked twice, the image is rotated 60 degrees.

Figure 11.4 shows the rotated image.

LISTING 11.2   Rotating an Image

```
 1: package com.talkingandroid.hour11application;
 2: import android.app.Activity;
 3: import android.os.Bundle;
 4: import android.view.View;
 5: import android.widget.Button;
 6: import android.widget.ImageView;
 7:
 8: public class RotateActivity extends Activity {
 9:     Button rotateButton;
10:     ImageView imageView;
11:     int numClicks = 1;
12:
13:     @Override
14:     protected void onCreate(Bundle savedInstanceState) {
15:         super.onCreate(savedInstanceState);
16:         setContentView(R.layout.activity_rotate);
17:         imageView = (ImageView)findViewById(R.id.imageView);
18:         rotateButton = (Button) findViewById(R.id.button);
19:         rotateButton.setOnClickListener(new View.OnClickListener() {
20:             @Override
21:             public void onClick(View v) {
22:                 imageView.setPivotX(imageView.getWidth()/2);
23:                 imageView.setPivotY(imageView.getHeight() / 2);
24:                 imageView.setRotation(30*numClicks);
25:                 numClicks++;
26:             }
27:         });
28:     }
29: }
```

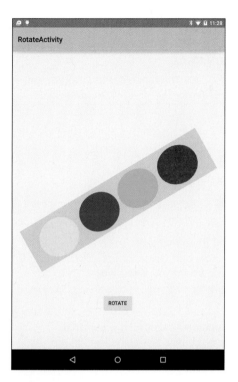

FIGURE 11.4
Rotated image.

Considering a Matrix

As an alternative to using the built-in rotation method, you can use a matrix with an `ImageView`. In graphics programming, a matrix is used to transform an image. Simple transformations include scaling, translating, or rotating an image. Android includes a `Matrix` class (`android.graphics.Matrix`) to support these graphic transformations.

Setting Alpha

Alpha level indicates the opacity of an image. An image can be completely transparent, completely opaque, or somewhere in the middle. The alpha level can be set on an `ImageView` using the `setAlpha()` method or, since API level 11, the `setImageAlpha()` method. These methods take an integer parameter. A parameter of 0 indicates complete transparency and 255 for complete opacity.

▼ TRY IT YOURSELF

Using a SeekBar to Dynamically Change Alpha Values

You'll create an `Activity` with a `SeekBar` and an `ImageView`. The range of the `SeekBar` will be from 0 to 255. As the `SeekBar` moves, set the alpha value for the `ImageView` and watch the change:

1. Create a new project with an `Activity`.

2. Change the XML layout file to include a `SeekBar` and an `ImageView`.

3. The `ImageView` should have the `src` value set to an existing image.

4. Use `setOnSeekBarChangeListener()` to set an `OnSeekBarChangeListener` for the `SeekBar`.

5. In the `OnSeekBarChangeListener`, you implement three methods: `onProgressChanged()`, `onStartTrackingTouch()`, and `onEndTrackingTouch()`. If you are using Android Studio, these methods are created for you if you type `"new OnSeekBarChangeListener()"` as a parameter to the `setOnSeekBarChange Listener()` method.

6. The `onProgressChanged()` method includes a parameter called `progress` that indicates the value on the `SeekBar`. Use that value to change the alpha level of the `ImageView`. You will use `imageView.setImageAlpha(progress);`.

Using Bitmaps and Canvas

The `Bitmap(android.graphics.Bitmap)` class represents a bitmap image. Bitmaps are created via the `BitmapFactory(android.graphics.BitmapFactory)` class.

Three typical ways use `BitmapFactory` to create `Bitmaps` are to create a bitmap from a resource, file, or `InputStream`. To create a `Bitmap` from a resource, use the `BitmapFactory` method `decodeResource()`:

```
Bitmap = BitmapFactory.decodeResource(getResources(), R.drawable.someImage);
```

The other two methods are similar to `decodeResource()`: `decodeFile()` and `decodeStream()`.

Handling Large Images

There are techniques for avoiding the dreaded out-of-memory (OOM) exception. Large images can have a significant impact on memory use in your app. To demonstrate this, you'll create an unrealistically large image to display in an `ImageView`. If the unmodified image is loaded into an `ImageView`, the app fails with an OOM error. A `java.lang.OutOfMemory` exception occurs. You'll fix the memory error for this case by checking the image size and display side.

The idea is to display the image at an appropriate size for the device. There is no point in showing a 10-foot mural in a 6-inch frame. Similarly, there is no point in showing a 20-inch image on a 3-inch device screen. You will scale down the image size and save memory.

The details of your app will influence your memory usage and the techniques that will work best in your case. This example shows how to handle a single large image.

To demonstrate this, you'll start with an image and increase it to an *unrealistic* size. You will use a photo that is 72 inches x 54 inches and that has a 28MB file size.

The image is in the `drawable` resource folder and has the id `R.drawable.largeimage`.

You can cause the app to fail with an OOM error by trying to set an `ImageView` to this resource. You have an `ImageView` named `imageView`. This line of code that causes the app to fail is this:

```
imageView.setImageResource(R.drawable.largeimage);
```

Some work is required, but it is possible to handle an image this large. In all cases, it would be better to work with appropriately sized images, but that does not always happen.

The approach is to get the dimensions of the underlying `Bitmap` without actually rendering it. Getting those dimensions is not a memory-intensive activity. Once you have the `Bitmap`, you can determine an appropriate size for the `Bitmap` that will fit in our display. If you have a 20-inch image and a 4-inch display, you'll request that the `Bitmap` that is created in memory fill the 4-inch display.

Using BitmapFactory.Options

The `BitmapFactory.Options` class is used with the `BitmapFactory` class. It is essential for handling large bitmaps.

You'll use the following options from the `BitmapFactoryOptions` class:

- **`inJustDecodeBounds`:** If set to true, this option indicates that the `Bitmap` dimensions should be determined by the `BitmapFactory` but that the `Bitmap` itself should not be created. This is the key to getting the `Bitmap` dimensions without the memory overhead of creating the `Bitmap`.

- **`outWidth`:** The width of the image set when `inJustDecodeBounds` is used.

- **`outHeight`:** The height of the image set when `inJustDecodeBounds` is used.

- **`inSampleSize`:** This integer indicates how much the dimensions of the `Bitmap` should be reduced. Given an image of 1000x400, an `inSampleSize` of 4 will result in a `Bitmap` of 250x100. The dimensions are reduced by a factor of 4.

Listing 11.3 shows the code to address this.

LISTING 11.3   Displaying a Large Image

```
 1: package com.talkingandroid.hour11application;
 2: import android.app.Activity;
 3: import android.graphics.Bitmap;
 4: import android.graphics.BitmapFactory;
 5: import android.os.Bundle;
 6: import android.view.Display;
 7: import android.widget.ImageView;
 8:
 9: public class LargeImageActivity extends Activity {
10:
11:     @Override
12:     protected void onCreate(Bundle savedInstanceState) {
13:         super.onCreate(savedInstanceState);
14:         setContentView(R.layout.activity_large_image);
15:         ImageView imageView = (ImageView) findViewById(R.id.imageView);
16:         Display display = getWindowManager().getDefaultDisplay();
17:         int displayWidth = display.getWidth();
18:         BitmapFactory.Options options = new BitmapFactory.Options();
19:         options.inJustDecodeBounds = true;
20:         BitmapFactory.decodeResource(getResources(), R.drawable.largeimage,
21:             options);
22:         int width = options.outWidth;
23:         if (width > displayWidth) {
24:             int widthRatio = Math.round((float) width / (float) displayWidth);
25:             options.inSampleSize = widthRatio;
26:         }
27:         options.inJustDecodeBounds = false;
28:         Bitmap scaledBitmap =  BitmapFactory.decodeResource(getResources(),
29:                             R.drawable.largeimage, options);
30:         imageView.setImageBitmap(scaledBitmap);
31:     }
32: }
```

On lines 16 and 17, you get the size of the device display. You'll use this as the target size for reducing the image size.

On lines 18–22, you determine the size of the current `Bitmap`. You do that by creating a `BitmapFactory.Options` class and setting the `inJustDecodeBounds` value to `true`. On line 20, the `Bitmap` is decoded to get the dimensions. Using this method, you get the dimensions without the memory overhead of creating the `Bitmap`. The result is available in `options.outWidth`. On line 22, you assign `options.outWidth` to the `int` variable `width`.

In this example, you use a simple test for the size of the image. On line 23, you check whether the width of the `Bitmap` is greater than the size of the display. If that is the case, you must determine the `inSampleSize` to use. That is done on lines 24 and 25. If the width of the `Bitmap` is 1000 pixels and the size of the display is 250 pixels, you get an `inSampleSize` of 4 by dividing the width of the `Bitmap` by the width of the display. For simplicity, you are not checking the height.

With the `imSampleSize` set to an appropriate value, you can render the image.

On line 27, the `inJustDecodeBounds` value is set to false. That means the image will be decoded and a `Bitmap` object will be created.

Lines 28 and 29 use the `BitmapFactory.decodeResource()` method to actually decode the image and create the `Bitmap`. The bitmap is assigned to the variable `scaledBitmap`. It is important to note that in this call, the `BitmapFactory.Options` variable `options` is passed as a parameter. That is how you indicate to the `BitmapFactory` what `inSampleSize` to use. The value for `options.inSampleSize` was set on line 25.

It is certainly not recommended to display a 72-inch image on a device, but Figure 11.5 shows that it can be done!

FIGURE 11.5
Very large photo displayed on device.

Drawing Directly on a Canvas

There is one more thing that you can do with an `ImageView` and `Bitmap`. You'll create a
`Bitmap` and draw directly on the `Canvas` that is associated with the `Bitmap`. A `Canvas` is an
object that you can draw on by calling drawing commands.

You will use an `ImageView` to display the `Bitmap`. You will also use an `ImageView` to determine the dimensions when creating the `Bitmap` and for drawing. In Listing 11.4, you draw the
word "Hello" in the center of the screen.

LISTING 11.4   Drawing on a Canvas

```
 1: package com.talkingandroid.hour11application;
 2: import android.app.Activity;
 3: import android.graphics.Bitmap;
 4: import android.graphics.Canvas;
 5: import android.graphics.Color;
 6: import android.graphics.Paint;
 7: import android.os.Bundle;
 8: import android.view.View;
 9: import android.widget.Button;
10: import android.widget.ImageView;
11:
12: public class DrawActivity extends Activity {
13:     ImageView imageView;
14:     Button drawButton;
15:
16:     @Override
17:     protected void onCreate(Bundle savedInstanceState) {
18:         super.onCreate(savedInstanceState);
19:         setContentView(R.layout.activity_draw);
20:         imageView = (ImageView) findViewById(R.id.imageView);
21:         drawButton = (Button)findViewById(R.id.button);
22:         drawButton.setOnClickListener(new View.OnClickListener() {
23:             @Override
24:             public void onClick(View v) {
25:                 Bitmap imageBitmap = Bitmap.createBitmap(imageView.getWidth(),
26:                     imageView.getHeight(), Bitmap.Config.ARGB_8888);
27:                 Canvas canvas = new Canvas(imageBitmap);
28:                 float scale = getResources().getDisplayMetrics().density;
29:                 Paint p = new Paint();
30:                 p.setColor(Color.BLUE);
31:                 p.setTextSize(48*scale);
32:                 canvas.drawText("Hello", imageView. getWidth()/2,
33:                                 imageView.getHeight()/2, p);
34:                 imageView.setImageBitmap(imageBitmap);
35:             }
36:         });
37:     }
38: }
```

A new `Bitmap` is created on lines 25 and 26 by using the method `Bitmap.create Bitmap()`. Note that the width and height of the bitmap are set using the width and height of the `ImageView`. The `Bitmap.Config (android.graphics.Bitmap.Config)` is set to `Bitmap.Config.ARGB_8888`.

When looking at the documentation for the `Bitmap` class, there are a number of `createBitmap()` methods that take different parameters. These methods may return a *mutable* or an *immutable* `Bitmap`. That is important; only a mutable `Bitmap` can be used for drawing.

On line 27, a `Canvas` is instantiated based on the `Bitmap` that you created.

Simple drawing commands are applied to the canvas in lines 28–33. You create a `Paint` object and set the `Color` to blue and set the text size. Line 28 gets the density of the display. That is used to set the text size properly. Recall that you previously learned about converting density independent pixels to pixels. On line 32, you draw the word "Hello" in the center of the `Canvas`.

On line 34, you update the `ImageView` to show your generated `Bitmap`.

Figure 11.6 shows the result.

FIGURE 11.6
Drawing on a `Canvas`.

Introducing Picasso

Picasso is an open source Android library from the team at Square. Picasso is an image downloading and caching library. When you use Picasso to download and display an image, the library keeps track of whether it has a copy of the image in memory or stored locally on the disk. The response time for retrieving and showing images in Picasso is very fast.

Picasso uses a context that is often your current `Activity`. In this example, the context is indicated by `this`, which refers to the `Activity`. Basic usage for displaying an image from a resource file into an `ImageView` is as follows:

```
Picasso.with(this).load(R.drawable.ic_launcher).into(imageView);
```

There are many other methods for Picasso; you can learn more at http://square.github.io/picasso/.

▼ TRY IT YOURSELF

Installing and Using Picasso

Picasso enhances your app when you work with images and bitmaps. These are the steps to download and use Picasso:

1. Go to http://square.github.io/picasso/ to learn more about Picasso.

2. In Android Studio, in Project view, find the app folder and locate the build.gradle file.

3. Add the line **compile 'com.squareup.picasso:picasso:2.5.0'** to the dependencies. That adds the Picasso library to the project.

4. Create an `Activity` with an `ImageView`.

5. Display an image from the drawable resources folder into the `ImageView` using Picasso.

Summary

In this hour, you looked at `ImageViews` and `Bitmaps`. You learned how `ScaleType` is used to change how images display in `ImageViews` and saw how rotation can be used in `ImageViews`. You learned about the `Matrix` class. You handled the display of an unrealistically large image by reading the dimensions of the bitmap before displaying it. You drew the word "Hello" on `Canvas` and displayed it in an `ImageView` to learn about the relationship between an `ImageView`, `Canvas`, and `Bitmap`. Picasso, an open source image library, was introduced.

Q&A

Q. If I am developing an app that displays images in a `ListView`, should I use `BitmapFactory.Options` to check the size of each image?

A. If you do not have control of the size of the images coming from the server, it is important to check size. If you do have control over the images, the ideal scenario is to have appropriately sized images. You can also use Picasso for handling images in code.

Workshop

Quiz

1. What is the purpose of `inJustDecodeBounds`?

2. What does mutable mean?

3. What is a pivot point?

Answers

1. In `BitmapFactory.Options`, `inJustDecodeBounds` is used to decode a `Bitmap` to get the dimensions but not actually create a `Bitmap` in memory.

2. Mutable means changeable, and that is important when you create `Bitmaps`. Some methods return mutable `Bitmaps` and others return immutable `Bitmaps`.

3. When you rotate an image, there must be a point to rotate around. That is the pivot point.

Exercise

For this exercise, use your own images or images that you find on the web. Create an `Activity` that includes two `ImageViews`. The first `ImageView` will take up the whole screen, with width and height set to `match_parent`. The second `ImageView` will have a fixed size. It will be smaller than the first `ImageView` and will appear over the first `ImageView` aligned on the bottom of the first `ImageView`. The goal is to use `scaleTypes` to display one image full size in the large view and to create a good thumbnail image in the smaller view. This exercise is an opportunity to experiment with displaying modified images. Try making the smaller image a set square size and use `CENTER_CROP` for the `scaleType`.

Using VideoViews and Media

What You'll Learn in This Hour:

▶ Playing a video

▶ Using `VideoView` events

▶ Playing audio

Videos can supplement your app or be an integral part of what you are trying to accomplish. You can easily add a video tutorial or demo to your app. This hour covers the basics of playing a video and how a `VideoView` functions. That includes overriding `VideoView` events and how a `VideoView` interacts with a media controller and media player. In addition to video, a basic example of playing audio using the media player is covered.

Playing Video

The most direct way to play a video is to use an intent and let the video player on the device take control. That usually ensures a good experience and an experience that the user has seen before when playing videos. The default player has basic controls and the ability to pause and restart a video.

Using an Intent

This code snippet creates a URI using the string `http://bffmedia.com/bigbunny.mp4`. An `Intent` is created with the action set to `ACTION_VIEW` and the MIME type `video/mp4`. When `startActivity()` is called with this intent, the specified video begins to play.

That video display includes a pause button, fast-forward, rewind, and a `SeekBar` that indicates your progress through the video (see Figure 12.1):

```
    String videoToPlay = "http://bffmedia.com/bigbunny.mp4";
  Uri videoUri = Uri.parse(videoToPlay);
  Intent= new Intent();
```

```
intent.setAction(Intent.ACTION_VIEW);
intent.setDataAndType(videoUri, "video/mp4");
startActivity(intent);
```

FIGURE 12.1
Using an Intent to display a video.

NOTE

Remember Your Permissions

To show a video where the source is on the Internet, you must specify the uses Internet permission in your Android manifest:

```
<uses-permission android:name="android.permission.INTERNET" />
```

Using a VideoView

Playing a video using a VideoView is similar to using an intent. You specify the video to play and start the video. The difference is that you first create a layout file that includes a VideoView widget. When you define a widget with the ID set to VideoView, the following snippet plays a video in the VideoView:

```
VideoView videoView = (VideoView) findViewById(R.id.videoView);
String videoToPlay = "http://bffmedia.com/bigbunny.mp4";
Uri video = Uri.parse(videoToPlay);
videoView.setVideoURI(video);
videoView.start();
```

When you use the basic `VideoView` widget, no controls, like play or pause, are shown.

TRY IT YOURSELF ▼

Playing a Video in a VideoView

Here are the steps to create an `Activity` that shows a video in a `VideoView`:

1. Create a new project with an `Activity`.

2. Change the XML layout file to include a single `VideoView` with width set to `match_parent` and height set to `wrap_content`. The `VideoView` should be centered in the parent.

3. Assign the `VideoView` in your activity's `onCreate()` method.

4. Using the code snippet as a model, create a URI from a video.

5. Set the URI in the `VideoView` and start the video.

Adding a MediaController to a VideoView

One way to easily introduce these controls is by adding a `MediaController`.

Listing 12.1 shows an activity that defines a `VideoView` and adds a `MediaController`.

Line 15 defines the `MediaController`, and line 16 sets the `MediaController` to be the anchorView of the `VideoView` using the `MediaController`'s `setAnchorView()` method. That means that the `MediaController` will be positioned at the bottom of the `VideoView`.

On line 19, the `VideoView` sets its `MediaController` to the `MediaController` defined on line 15. The `VideoView` and `MediaController` refer to each other.

The rest of the code in Listing 12.1 is used to display a video in the `VideoView`. Lines 18 and 19 define the URI of the video to play. Lines 20 and 21 assign the video URI and start the video. Figure 12.2 shows the result.

LISTING 12.1 VideoView with MediaController

```
1: package com.talkingandroid.hour12applicaton;
2:
3: import android.app.Activity;
4: import android.net.Uri;
5: import android.os.Bundle;
6: import android.widget.MediaController;
7: import android.widget.VideoView;
8:
```

```
 9: public class VideoViewMediaControllerActivity extends Activity {
10:     @Override
11:     protected void onCreate(Bundle savedInstanceState) {
12:         super.onCreate(savedInstanceState);
13:         setContentView(R.layout.activity_video_view);
14:         VideoView videoView = (VideoView) findViewById(R.id.videoView);
15:         MediaController mediaController = new MediaController(this);
16:         mediaController.setAnchorView(videoView);
17:         String videoToPlay = "http://bffmedia.com/bigbunny.mp4";
18:         Uri video = Uri.parse(videoToPlay);
19:         videoView.setMediaController(mediaController);
20:         videoView.setVideoURI(video);
21:         videoView.start();
22:     }
23: }
```

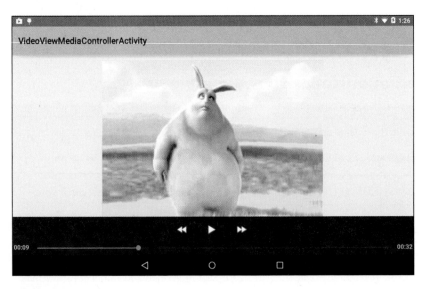

FIGURE 12.2
Using a VideoView with a MediaController.

Starting, Pausing, and Positioning a Video

For controlling a video, the VideoView includes methods called start(), pause(), and seekTo(). The start() and pause() methods start and stop the video. The seekTo() method positions the video at a specific location and is based on milliseconds. If you call seekTo() with 10,000, you will position the video at the tenth second. You can get the current position and duration of the video with the methods `getCurrentPosition()` and `getDuration()`. To skip ahead 10 seconds in the video, use the following:

```
videoView.seekTo(mVideo.getCurrentPosition + 10000);
```

Adding a Custom Play/Pause Button

You can customize how your app interacts with a `VideoView`. Follow these steps to create an app that does that:

1. Create a new project with an `Activity`.

2. Change the XML layout file to include a single `VideoView` with width set to `match_parent` and height set to `wrap_content`. The `VideoView` should be centered in the parent.

3. Add a pause `Button` to the layout.

4. When the pause `Button` is clicked, pause the video and change the text on the `Button` to say "Play."

5. If the `Button` shows "Play," begin playing the video and change the text on the `Button` to say "Pause."

Handling VideoView Events

Several states are tied to playing a video in a `VideoView`. Videos do not start playing immediately. First, they are downloaded and buffered. You have the opportunity to provide your own user interface before the video begins during that time. You can also take an action when a video completes playing.

Listening for the States of a VideoView

Two listeners are unique to a `VideoView`: the `OnPreparedListener` and the `OnCompletionListener`. When a video is ready to play, the `OnPreparedListener()` code is run. You have the opportunity to provide your own user interface before the video begins, and when the video is prepared, you can do something else. One option is to show a `ProgressBar` before the video starts and then hide it in the `onPreparedListener`.

The `OnCompletionListener` is triggered when the video is done playing. It is an opportunity to repeat the video, start a new video, or change the user interface to prompt the user about what to do next.

Listing 12.2 shows a video and adds an `OnPreparedListener()` and `OnCompletionListener` to the `VideoView`. In the `OnPreparedListener`, the `ProgressBar` is hidden, and a custom pause `Button` displays. In the `OnCompletionListener`, the video is repositioned to the beginning, and a play button is shown.

LISTING 12.2   Listening for VideoView Events

```
 1: package com.talkingandroid.hour12applicaton;
 2: import android.app.Activity;
 3: import android.media.MediaPlayer;
 4: import android.net.Uri;
 5: import android.os.Bundle;
 6: import android.view.View;
 7: import android.widget.Button;
 8: import android.widget.ProgressBar;
 9: import android.widget.TextView;
10: import android.widget.VideoView;
11:
12: public class VideoViewPlayPause extends Activity {
13:     Boolean isPaused = false;
14:
15:     @Override
16:     protected void onCreate(Bundle savedInstanceState) {
17:         super.onCreate(savedInstanceState);
18:         setContentView(R.layout.activity_video_view_play_pause);
19:         final ProgressBar progressBar = (ProgressBar)
20:                 findViewById(R.id.progressBar);
21:         final TextView textView= (TextView) findViewById(R.id.textView);
22:         final VideoView videoView = (VideoView) findViewById(R.id.videoView);
23:         final Button pauseButton= (Button) findViewById(R.id.pauseButton);
24:         pauseButton.setOnClickListener(new View.OnClickListener() {
25:             public void onClick(View v) {
26:                 if (isPaused){
27:                     videoView.start();
28:                     pauseButton.setText("Pause");
29:                     isPaused=false;
30:                 }else{
31:                     videoView.pause();
32:                     pauseButton.setText("Play");
33:                     isPaused=true;
34:                 }
35:             }
36:         });
37:         String videoToPlay = "http://bffmedia.com/bigbunny.mp4";
38:         Uri video = Uri.parse(videoToPlay);
39:         videoView.setVideoURI(video);
40:
```

```
41:         videoView.setOnPreparedListener(new MediaPlayer.OnPreparedListener(){
42:             public void onPrepared(MediaPlayer mp) {
43:                 int height = mp.getVideoHeight();
44:                 int width = mp.getVideoWidth();
45:                 int duration = mp.getDuration();
46:                 textView.setText("Video: " + width +" " +height+
47:                         " " + duration +" milliseconds");
48:                 progressBar.setVisibility(View.GONE);
49:                 pauseButton.setVisibility(View.VISIBLE);
50:                 videoView.requestFocus();
51:                 videoView.start();
52:             }
53:         });
54:
55:         videoView.setOnCompletionListener(new
56:                     MediaPlayer.OnCompletionListener() {
57:             @Override
58:             public void onCompletion(MediaPlayer mp) {
59:                 mp.seekTo(0);
60:                 isPaused = true;
61:                 pauseButton.setText("Play");
62:             }
63:         });
64:   }
65:}
```

You can consider the code in Listing 12.2 in sections. All the work occurs in the onCreate() method, where a video is set to play in a VideoView. There is a ProgressBar displayed until the video is prepared, and there is a custom play/pause button:

▶ **Lines 37–39**: Set up video to play

▶ **Lines 23–36**: OnClickListener for play/pause button

▶ **Lines 41–53**: The VideoView OnPreparedListener

▶ **Lines 55–63**: The VideoView OnCompletionListener

The OnClickListener for the play/pause button uses the VideoView start() and pause() methods to control the video play.

When the activity begins, an indeterminate ProgressBar displays. On line 48 in the OnPreparedListener code, the ProgressBar's visibility is set to View.GONE.

On line 42, a MediaPlayer object is passed to the onPrepared() method. The MediaPlayer class is used to control media playback for both audio and video. A MediaPlayer is tied to the VideoView class. Using the MediaPlayer, you can get information about the contents of the media. In the `OnPreparedListener` on lines 43–47, the width, height, and duration of the video are retrieved and displayed.

Figure 12.3 shows a paused video with the width, height, and duration showing.

FIGURE 12.3
`VideoView` showing dimensions retrieved from `MediaPlayer`.

Like the `OnPreparedListener`, the `OnCompletionListener` in Listing 12.2 is passed a `MediaPlayer` object. In the `OnPreparedListener()` on line 59, the `seekTo()` method of the `MediaPlayer` is called with a parameter of 0. That resets the video to being played at the beginning. In the remainder of the `OnCompletionListener`, the custom play/pause button is set to play. Doing this leaves the video in paused state ready to play from the beginning. This is an example of what can be done when a video finishes. It is possible to replay the video to offer additional navigation choices. You may have a hidden layout with controls that appear only after the video has completed.

Playing Audio with MediaPlayer

You used a `MediaPlayer` in the `OnPreparedListener` and `OnCompletionListener` for the `VideoView`. You can use a `MediaPlayer` object directly to work with video and audio.

A simple case is to play an audio file that is stored in the assets folder of your project.

Although this is a simple case of using a `MediaPlayer`, you are responsible for the state of the `MediaPlayer`. The `MediaPlayer` must be prepared, started, and ultimately released. You'll prepare and start the `MediaPlayer` in your `Activity`'s `onResume()` method.

Then you'll release the `MediaPlayer` in the `onPause()` method. This is an example of taking advantage of the `Activity` lifecycle.

Listing 12.3 shows the code for an activity that pays an MP3 audio file. The audio file is in the assets folder for the project.

LISTING 12.3   Playing an MP3 Audio File

```
 1: package com.talkingandroid.hour12applicaton;
 2: import android.app.Activity;
 3: import android.content.res.AssetFileDescriptor;
 4: import android.media.MediaPlayer;
 5: import android.os.Bundle;
 6: import java.io.IOException;
 7:
 8: public class AudioActivity extends Activity {
 9:     MediaPlayer mediaPlayer = new MediaPlayer();
10:     AssetFileDescriptor audioFileDescriptor;
11:
12:     @Override
13:     protected void onCreate(Bundle savedInstanceState) {
14:         super.onCreate(savedInstanceState);
15:         setContentView(R.layout.activity_audio);
16:     }
17:     @Override
18:     protected void onResume() {
19:         super.onResume();
20:         try {
21:             audioFileDescriptor = getAssets().openFd("helloworld.mp3");
22:             mediaPlayer.setDataSource(audioFileDescriptor.getFileDescriptor());
23:             mediaPlayer.prepare();
24:             mediaPlayer.start();
25:         } catch (IOException e) {
26:             e.printStackTrace();
27:         }
28:     }
29:     @Override
30:     protected void onPause() {
31:         super.onPause();
32:         mediaPlayer.release();
33:     }
34: }
```

In Listing 12.3, you read a file called helloworld.mp3 from the assets directory. That is done in the `onResume()` method. The `MediaPlayer` is released in the `onPause()` method.

On line 21, the method `getAssets().openFd()` is called with helloworld.mp3 passed as the parameter. That MP3 file is in the assets folder for the project. Recall that assets are raw files that can be accessed directly. In the project folder structure, the hierarchy is /src/main/assets.

The call to `getAssets()` returns an `AssetManager`. An `AssetManager` is used to provide access to the raw files in the assets folder.

Calling `openFd()` gives you an `AssetFileDescriptor` called `audioFileDescriptor`. On line 22, the `audioFileDescriptor` is used to set the data source for the `MediaPlayer`. The method `audioFileDescriptor.getFileDescriptor()` returns a `FileDescriptor` that is passed to the `MediaPlayer setDataSource()` method.

With the data source set on line 22, the `MediaPlayer` is prepared on line 23 and started on line 24.

Because it is possible that the asset file will not exist, a `try/catch` clause that checks for an `IOException` must be included on lines 25–27. If you add the files to your assets folder in the project, that should not occur.

The `MediaPlayer` is released on line 32 in the `onPause()` method of the activity.

More Media

In this hour, you've considered `VideoViews` and were introduced to the `MediaPlayer`. If you are creating complex media apps, you want to dig deeper. There are other media-related topics for you to explore.

Using media in Android includes these classes:

▶ **AudioManager:** android.media.AudioManager

▶ **AudioFocus:** android.media.AudioManager.OnAudioFocusChangeListener

▶ **SoundPool:** android.media.SoundPool

▶ **AudioTrack:** android.media.AudioTrack

▶ **MediaPlayer:** android.media.MediaPlayer

▶ **Presentation:** android.app.Presentation

Summary

In this hour, you took a closer look at `VideoViews` and `MediaPlayers`. You learned about showing videos and listening for video-related events. You played an audio file from the assets folder in your app and learned about preparing, starting, and releasing a `MediaPlayer`. You also learned how to interact with a `VideoView` using a `MediaController` and how to use your own custom layout.

Q&A

Q. Is `VideoView` the only way to play a video on Android?

A. No, `VideoView` is one of the easier ways to play a video. As you learned, you can also play a video via an `ActionView` intent. You can also use a `MediaPlayer` directly.

Q. What are the advantages and disadvantages of using an `Intent` versus a `VideoView` to play video?

A. Using an `Intent` to play a video will show the default video player for the device. That will typically include controls like play, pause, and rewind. When you use a `VideoView`, you can create a custom user interface. Perhaps a news article includes a video to accompany the main story. Using a `VideoView` can provide the option for custom functionality. You could change the video to play in Spanish rather than English in an app that demonstrates new functionality.

Q. What happens if a `VideoView` is in an `Activity` that is rotated?

A. When an `Activity` is rotated, it restarts, and the video in the `VideoView` also restarts (see Hour 4, "Activities and Fragments"), and the methods to handle configuration change when using a `VideoView`. Another option is to prevent rotation in an activity that uses a `VideoView` by specifying portrait or landscape mode only.

Workshop

Quiz

1. How is `onPreparedListener()` used?

2. What object provides information on the width and height of a video to play?

3. How do you set the position of a video in a `VideoView` to be 32 seconds from the start of the video?

Answers

1. In a `VideoView`, `onPreparedListener` listens for when a video is prepared to play. In one example in this hour, you showed a `ProgressBar` until the video was prepared and then displayed the video.

2. A `MediaPlayer` object has width, height, and duration information about a video that is ready to play. A `MediaPlayer` is passed to both the `OnPreparedListener` and `OnCompletionListener`.

3. To set the position of a video within a `VideoView`, you use the `seekTo()` method. To set a `VideoView` called `videoView` to be positioned at the 32-second mark, use `videoView.seekTo(32000);`.

Exercise

Using Listing 12.2 as a starting point, develop an app with an `Activity` that includes a `VideoView`. Add a `SeekBar` to the layout. When the `SeekBar` is moved, set the video to the location in the video.

You need to know the duration of the video to set the max value for the `SeekBar`. You will use the `seekTo()` method to position the video.

HOUR 13
Adding Navigation

What You'll Learn in This Hour:

▶ Using the `ActionBar`

▶ Introducing the `Toolbar`

▶ Implementing sliding drawer navigation

In this hour, you use an `ActionBar`, `Toolbar`, and sliding drawer menu. All provide solutions for navigation and persistent presence of navigation controls in the app. You can use these features to always give your users a sense of where they are in your app and how they can navigate to other areas. Getting around a complex app requires consistent and thoughtful navigation. These tools are provided so that you can do that.

Using the ActionBar

Until version 3.0, all Android phones and devices included a hardware-based menu button. That ensured that the option to click Menu was persistent in apps. To add functionality to that hardware Menu button, you would use the options menu functionality.

Since Android 3.0, the options menu functionality has been incorporated into the `ActionBar(android.app.ActionBar)`.

The options menu provides a robust and simple mechanism for providing navigation and functionality that many applications require.

Displaying the Options Menu

You may have noticed that when you create a new `Activity` a corresponding resource file is created under the menu resource folder. For example, if you create an activity called `MainActivity`, a resource file named menu_main.xml is generated. In addition, the code to use that menu resource file is added to the MainActivity.java code.

The menu resource file menu_main.xml contains the following:

```
<menu xmlns:android="http://schemas.android.com/apk/res/android"
    xmlns:tools="http://schemas.android.com/tools" tools:context=".MainActivity">
    <item
        android:id="@+id/action_settings"
        android:title="@string/action_settings"
        android:orderInCategory="100"
        android:showAsAction="never" />
</menu>
```

This single item includes the following attributes:

- **id:** The id of this menu item.

- **orderInCategory:** The order that this item appears.

- **showAsAction:** Show this item as an action on the ActionBar.

- **title:** The title for the menu item.

In the source for MainActivity.java, the following code is generated:

```
@Override
    public boolean onCreateOptionsMenu(Menu menu) {
        // Inflate the menu; this adds items to the action bar if it is present.
        getMenuInflater().inflate(R.menu.menu_options_menu, menu);
        return true;
    }

    @Override
    public boolean onOptionsItemSelected(MenuItem item) {
        // Handle action bar item clicks here. The action bar will
        // automatically handle clicks on the Home/Up button, so long
        // as you specify a parent activity in AndroidManifest.xml.
        int id = item.getItemId();

        //noinspection SimplifiableIfStatement
        if (id == R.id.action_settings) {
            return true;
        }

        return super.onOptionsItemSelected(item);

    }
```

The onCreateOptionsMenu() method will inflate the menu items defined in the menu resource file menu_main.xml.

When you run the app, you will see an `ActionBar`, as shown in Figure 13.1. The icon with three vertical dots is known as the *overflow menu*.

FIGURE 13.1
`ActionBar` with overflow menu.

When menu items do not fit in the `ActionBar`, they are shown in the overflow menu. You can also specify items that should always be shown or never be shown in the `ActionBar`. That is the case with "Settings." It was defined to have `showAsAction` set to never:

```
android:showAsAction="never"
```

When selected, the overflow menu expands to show the `ActionBar` with the Settings item displayed (see Figure 13.2). The user can now select that option.

FIGURE 13.2
`ActionBar` with overflow menu open.

Understanding the showAsAction Attribute

You can specify how items are displayed in an `ActionBar` by using the `showAsAction` attribute. Table 13.1 shows the possible values.

TABLE 13.1   Values for the showAsAction Attribute

Value	Definition
always	Always show in `ActionBar`.
never	Never show in `ActionBar`.
ifRoom	Show in the `ActionBar` if there is room.
withText	Show with text from `android:Title`. Can be used with other values (`ifRoom|withText`).
collapseActionView	The `actionView` is collapsible. API level 14.

It is easy to expand the sample menu that is generated with a new `Activity`. This menu resource file includes three items for the overflow menu and four items set to be shown if there is room. The two states of this `ActionBar` are shown in Figures 13.3 and 13.4.

```
<menu xmlns:android="http://schemas.android.com/apk/res/android"
    xmlns:tools="http://schemas.android.com/tools"
    tools:context="com.talkingandroid.hour13application.ActionBarActivity">
    <item
        android:id="@+id/action_help"
        android:title="@string/action_help"
        android:orderInCategory="100"
        android:showAsAction="never" />
    <item
        android:id="@+id/action_settings"
        android:title="@string/action_settings"
        android:orderInCategory="110"
        android:showAsAction="never" />
    <item
        android:id="@+id/action_about"
        android:title="@string/action_about"
        android:orderInCategory="120"
        android:showAsAction="never" />

    <item
        android:id="@+id/action_item_1"
        android:orderInCategory="10"
        android:showAsAction="ifRoom"
        android:title="Action 1"/>
    <item
        android:id="@+id/action_item_2"
        android:orderInCategory="20"
        android:showAsAction="ifRoom"
        android:title="Action 2"/>
    <item
        android:id="@+id/action_item_3"
        android:orderInCategory="30"
        android:showAsAction="ifRoom"
        android:title="Action 3"/>
    <item
        android:id="@+id/action_item_4"
        android:orderInCategory="40"
        android:showAsAction="ifRoom"
        android:title="Action 4"/>
</menu>
```

FIGURE 13.3
`ActionBar` displaying items and overflow menu.

FIGURE 13.4
`ActionBar` displaying items and expanded overflow menu.

Adding Icons to Menu Items

An icon can be added to an item in the menu resource file with a single line:

```
android:icon="@+drawable/action_item"
```

In this case, a drawable named `action_item` must exist in the drawable resource folder.

Responding to the Options Menu

So far, you have displayed items on `ActionBar`. Responding to a click on an item is straight-forward. You created the menu with the `onCreateMenuOptions()` method. To respond when a menu item is clicked, you use the `onOptionsItemSelected()` method, as shown in Listing 13.1.

LISTING 13.1   Using onOptionsItemSelected()

```
1: package com.talkingandroid.hour13application;
2: import android.app.Activity;
3: import android.os.Bundle;
4: import android.view.Menu;
5: import android.view.MenuItem;
6:
7: public class ActionBarActivity extends Activity {
8:
```

```
 9:        @Override
10:        protected void onCreate(Bundle savedInstanceState) {
11:            super.onCreate(savedInstanceState);
12:            setContentView(R.layout.activity_action_bar);
13:        }
14:
15:        @Override
16:        public boolean onCreateOptionsMenu(Menu menu) {
17:            // Inflate the menu; this adds items to the action bar if it is present.
18:             getMenuInflater().inflate(R.menu.menu_action_bar, menu);
19:             return true;
20:        }
21:
22:        @Override
23:        public boolean onOptionsItemSelected(MenuItem item) {
24:            int id = item.getItemId();
25:            switch (id){
26:                case R.id.action_about:
27:                    return true;
28:                case R.id.action_help:
29:                    return true;
30:                case R.id.action_settings:
31:                    return true;
32:                case R.id.action_item_1:
33:                    return true;
34:                case R.id.action_item_2:
35:                    return true;
36:                case R.id.action_item_3:
37:                    return true;
38:                case R.id.action_item_4:
39:                    return true;
40:            }
41:            return super.onOptionsItemSelected(item);
42:        }
43: }
```

The onCreate() method for this Activity is on lines 9–13 of Listing 13.1. The setContent-
View() method is called on line 12.

Lines 15–20 show the onCreateOptionsMenu(), and that is where the menu is inflated.

The onOptionsItemSelected() method is on lines 22–42 of Listing 13.1. The parameter
menuItem is passed to this method. The menuItem contains the information defined for the
selected menuItem. You can access the id and the title, for example.

On line 24, the ID of the selected item is determined using the method getItemId(). On lines
25–40, a switch statement is used to determine what action to take based on the selected item.

In Listing 13.1, you just return true for each case. That true means that the menuItem response has been handled.

In your code, you determine what to do based on each item click. You might switch to a new fragment, navigate to an activity, and open a dialog window.

Adding Up Navigation

There is a design pattern in Android known as *up navigation*. The idea is that there is a parent activity that launches child activities. The child activities navigate back to the parent activity. Figure 13.5 shows a red circle around the icon used in a child activity to indicate the user can navigate back up to the parent activity.

Implementing up navigation for a child activity is very easy. In the Android manifest for the child activity, you include a reference to the parent activity.

This snippet defines an Activity called ActionBarBasicActivity that includes a title and a reference to the parent activity using android:parentActivityName:

```
<activity
        android:name=".ActionBarBasicActivity"
        android:label="@string/title_activity_action_bar"
        android:parentActivityName=".MainActivity" >
    </activity>
```

FIGURE 13.5
Highlighting up navigation.

TRY IT YOURSELF ▼

Adding an ActionBar with Up Navigation

These are the steps to add up navigation to the ActionBar. This is a common navigation pattern:

1. Create a new project with an activity called MainActivity.

2. Add an activity called ChildActivity.

3. Set ChildActivity to have MainActivity as a parent.

4. Add a button to navigate from MainActivity to ChildActivity.

Introducing the Toolbar

The `ActionBar` can be used for many applications for overall navigation and persistent presence. The `Toolbar` is a widget that was introduced in Lollipop that can be a replacement for the `ActionBar` or can be an additional toolbar that you add anywhere in your app.

A `Toolbar` is easy to customize. Because the `Toolbar` extends the `ViewGroup` class, you can add child views to the `Toolbar`.

NOTE

Maintaining Compatibility with Toolbars

There is both an `android.widget.Toolbar` class and an `android.support.v7.widget.Toolbar`. The `android.widget.Toolbar` was introduced in Lollipop (API level 21). The `android.support.v7.widget.Toolbar` can be used to support older versions of Android.

A Basic Toolbar

A basic `Toolbar` can replace an `ActionBar`. A `Toolbar` can include a title, subtitle, menu items, and up navigation. Because a `Toolbar` is a widget, you can add it to the layout file for your `Activity`.

This shows a layout file that includes a `Toolbar`:

```
<RelativeLayout  xmlns:android="http://schemas.android.com/apk/res/android"
    xmlns:tools="http://schemas.android.com/tools"
    android:layout_width="match_parent"
    android:layout_height="match_parent"
    tools:context="com.talkingandroid.hour13application.ToolbarActivity">

    <Toolbar android:layout_width="match_parent"
        android:layout_height="wrap_content"
        android:minHeight="?android:attr/actionBarSize"
        android:background="#FFC107"
        android:id="@+id/toolbar"
        />
```

This defines a simple `Toolbar` with the background color set.

You need to add code to your `Activity` class to make the `Toolbar` useful. Listing 13.2 shows the `Activity` code for this layout and `Toolbar`.

LISTING 13.2   Using a Toolbar

```
 1: package com.talkingandroid.hour13application;
 2: import android.app.Activity;
 3: import android.os.Bundle;
 4: import android.view.Menu;
 5: import android.view.MenuItem;
 6: import android.widget.Toolbar;
 7:
 8: public class ToolbarActivity extends Activity {
 9:   @Override
10: protected void onCreate(Bundle savedInstanceState) {
11:     super.onCreate(savedInstanceState);
12:       setContentView(R.layout.activity_toolbar);
13:       Toolbar toolbar = (Toolbar) findViewById(R.id.toolbar);
14:       toolbar.setTitle("TITLE");
15:       toolbar.setSubtitle("Sub-title");
16:       toolbar.setLogo(R.mipmap.ic_launcher);
17:       setActionBar(toolbar);
18:       getActionBar().setDisplayHomeAsUpEnabled(true);
19:     }
20:
21:     @Override
22:     public boolean onCreateOptionsMenu(Menu menu) {
23:         getMenuInflater().inflate(R.menu.menu_action_bar, menu);
24:         return true;
25:     }
26:
27:     @Override
28:     public boolean onOptionsItemSelected(MenuItem item) {
29:       int id = item.getItemId();
30:         if (id == R.id.action_settings) {
31:             return true;
32:         }
33:         return super.onOptionsItemSelected(item);
34:     }
35: }
```

On line 13 of Listing 13.2, the `Toolbar` is defined using the `findViewById()` method. The `Toolbar` is just another widget like a `Button` or `TextView`, so you access it like any other widget.

Lines 14 and 15 add a title and subtitle to the `Toolbar`. Line 16 adds a logo.

Line 17 is important. It tells the `Activity` to consider this `Toolbar` to be the `ActionBar`:

```
setActionBar(toolbar);
```

Line 18 is a programmatic way to implement up navigation:

```
getActionBar().setDisplayHomeAsUpEnabled(true);
```

CAUTION

Defining the Right Style for Your Activity

You cannot use a `Toolbar` as your `ActionBar` if your `Activity` is not properly defined in the AndroidManifest.xml file. There is an assumption that an `ActionBar` will be present. On line 18 of Listing 13.2, you replace the `ActionBar` with the `Toolbar`. To do that, you must define the `Activity` to have a style with no `ActionBar`.

This `Activity` definition in the AndroidManifest.xml refers to the style AppThemeNoActionBar:

```
<activity
    android:name=".ToolbarActivity"
    android:label="@string/title_activity_tool_bar"
    android:parentActivityName=".MainActivity"
    android:theme="@style/AppThemeNoActionBar" >
</activity>
```

The `AppThemeNoActionBar` style is defined in the styles.xml resource file as follows:

```
<style name="AppThemeNoActionBar" parent="android:Theme.Material.Light">
    <item name="android:windowNoTitle">true</item>
    <item name="android:windowActionBar">false</item>
</style>
```

Note that the `windowActionBar` attribute is set to `false`.

Putting together the layout file, the code, and the style will result in displaying a toolbar in your activity, as shown in Figure 13.6.

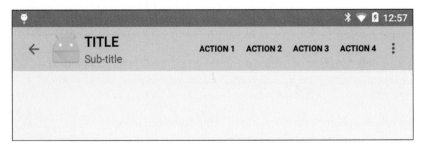

FIGURE 13.6
Adding a `Toolbar`.

In Figure 13.6, the overflow menu is present, and the items that were defined as part of the menu resource file are shown. Remember, you replaced the action bar with this toolbar, so the menu items are attached to the `Toolbar`. Check lines 21–25 of Listing 13.2 to see that the menu resource is inflated in the `onCreateOptionsMenu()` method.

Customizing a Toolbar

Follow these steps to customize a `Toolbar` to be appropriate for your app:

1. Start with the basic `Toolbar` from this hour.

2. Set the title and subtitle to something meaningful.

3. Update the menu resource file to include items to display in the `ActionBar` and the overflow menu.

Adding a Child View to a Toolbar

Because the `Toolbar` is a `ViewGroup`, you can add child views. That allows for a great amount of customization and functionality in the `Toolbar`.

In this case, you add a spinner to the `Toolbar`. The work will be similar to the basic toolbar. You start with a `Toolbar` in the layout. In this case, you add a `Spinner` as a child view to the `Toolbar`. This is the XML layout file for the `Activity`:

```
<RelativeLayout  xmlns:android="http://schemas.android.com/apk/res/android"
    xmlns:tools="http://schemas.android.com/tools"
    android:layout_width="match_parent"
    android:layout_height="match_parent"
    tools:context="com.talkingandroid.hour13application.ToolbarCustomViewActivity">
    <Toolbar android:layout_width="match_parent"
        android:layout_height="wrap_content"
        android:minHeight="?android:attr/actionBarSize"
        android:background="#FFC107"
        android:id="@+id/toolbar">
    <Spinner
        android:layout_width="wrap_content"
        android:layout_height="wrap_content"
        android:id="@+id/spinner" />
    </Toolbar>
</RelativeLayout >
```

The `Spinner` has ID set to `spinner` and is defined within the `Toolbar`.

The `ToolbarCustomViewActivity` code in Listing 13.3 is similar to the code for the basic toolbar. A `Spinner` is defined, and an `ArrayAdapter` is used to populate the contents of the spinner.

LISTING 13.3   Adding a Child View to a Toolbar

```
 1: package com.talkingandroid.hour13application;
 2: import android.app.Activity;
 3: import android.os.Bundle;
 4: import android.widget.ArrayAdapter;
 5: import android.widget.Spinner;
 6: import android.widget.Toolbar;
 7:
 8: public class ToolbarCustomViewActivity extends Activity {
 9:     Toolbar toolbar;
10:     Spinner spinner;
11:     String[] values = {"View 1", "View 2", "View 3", "View 4" };
12:     ArrayAdapter<String> spinnerAdapter;
13:
14:     @Override
15:      protected void onCreate(Bundle savedInstanceState) {
16:         super.onCreate(savedInstanceState);
17:         setContentView(R.layout.activity_action_bar_custom_view);
18:         toolbar = (Toolbar) findViewById(R.id.toolbar);
19:         toolbar.setTitle("TITLE");
20:         toolbar.setLogo(R.mipmap.ic_launcher);
21:         setActionBar(toolbar);
22:         getActionBar().setDisplayHomeAsUpEnabled(true);
23:         spinner = (Spinner) findViewById(R.id.spinner);
24:         ArrayAdapter<String> spinnerAdapter = new ArrayAdapter<String>
25:                 (this,android.R.layout.simple_spinner_dropdown_item,values);
26:         spinner.setAdapter(spinnerAdapter);
27:     }
28: }
```

Lines 18–22 of Listing 13.3 define the toolbar and handle the toolbar set up such as setting the title, setting the icon, and setting the toolbar as the action bar.

Lines 23–26 define the spinner and the associated adapter. In this case, the data to be displayed is defined in the code on line 11. The `Spinner` will show the strings `View 1`, `View 2`, `View 3`, and `View 4`.

Figure 13.7 shows the resulting `Toolbar`, and Figure 13.8 shows the `Toolbar` with the `Spinner` open.

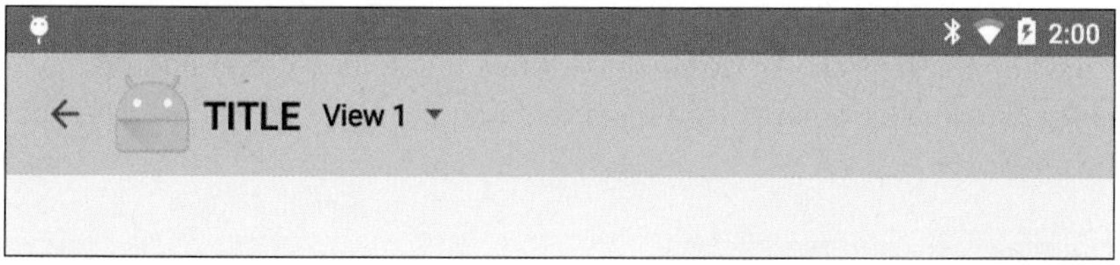

FIGURE 13.7
A `Toolbar` with a `View`.

If your app included different views of similar content, one way to navigate to the content is to use a `Spinner` in the `ActionBar`. You would need to add code to react to the `Spinner` item selected and update the `View` or switch out a `Fragment`.

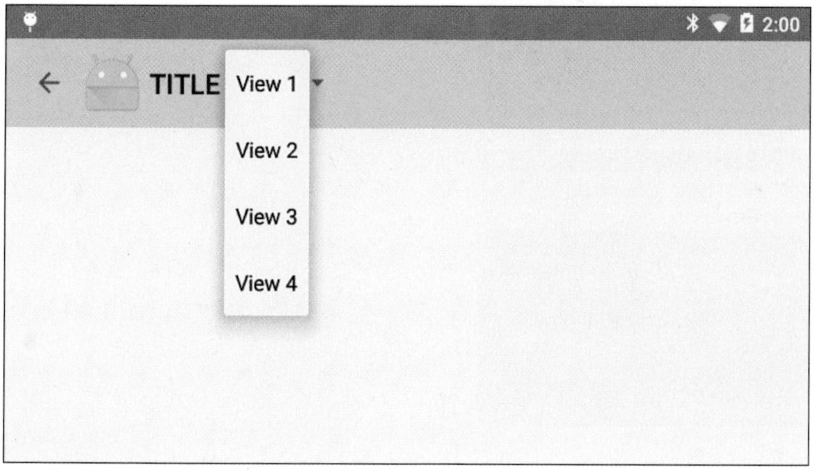

FIGURE 13.8
`Toolbar` with `Spinner` showing.

Sliding Drawer Navigation

You have probably seen apps that use the design pattern that Android calls sliding drawer navigation. There is an icon in the action bar that some call the "hamburger icon." When you select it, a menu list of options appears to slide out from the left side of your app. (It might also come from the right.) When you select an item from the list, the drawer slides back and the content you selected is displayed.

The sliding drawer is persistent and there is usually no up navigation or the idea that the user is going back to a previous screen. The action occurs in the sliding drawer.

In Figure 13.9, you can take a closer look at the three states of the icon for the sliding drawer. In the initial state, it is the hamburger icon. An arrow shows when the sliding drawer options are fully visible. Between the time the hamburger icon is selected and the arrow shows, the icon animates and the drawer slides out.

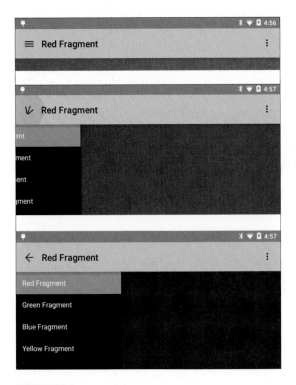

FIGURE 13.9
Sliding drawer animation.

Figure 13.9 shows the demo app that will be used in this hour. A single activity contains a sliding drawer with four options. There is a corresponding fragment to display for each option. The fragments in this example are simple. They just have different background colors and a different text message, but in your own apps, the sliding drawer can be used for showing fragments that look completely different and that contain very different functionality.

The Importance of Layouts

The layout for the main activity is important when implementing a sliding drawer. You need an action bar, a location for the contents of the sliding drawer, and a location for the contents to be displayed.

When the sliding drawer is not showing, you want the application contents to show on the entire screen. When the sliding drawer is showing, it displays over the current contents.

The view hierarchy used to accomplish this is shown in Figure 13.10, which is a screenshot of the component view in Android Studio.

FIGURE 13.10
Layout for sliding drawer.

An `android.support.v4.widget.DrawerLayout` is the top-level component. The `content_frame` is a `FrameLayout` that is the size of the whole screen. When a new fragment is displayed, it will occupy this content frame.

The `left_drawer_layout` is a `RelativeLayout`. This is the view that is displayed as the sliding drawer. The `left_drawer_layout` is 240dp wide. The `left_drawer_layout` contains a `ListView` called `left_drawer` that displays the list of choices to select.

The `FrameLayout` and the `RelativeLayout` are on the same level in the hierarchy. The `RelativeLayout` appears over the `FrameLayout`.

The `ListView` is a child view of the `RelativeLayout`. A sliding drawer does not just need to contain a `ListView`. It can be as simple or complex as necessary for your application.

This is the full XML layout file contents:

```
<android.support.v4.widget.DrawerLayout
    xmlns:android="http://schemas.android.com/apk/res/android"
    android:id="@+id/drawer_layout"
    android:layout_width="match_parent"
    android:layout_height="match_parent">

    <FrameLayout
        android:id="@+id/content_frame"
        android:layout_width="match_parent"
        android:layout_height="match_parent" />

    <RelativeLayout
        android:id="@+id/left_drawer_layout"
        android:layout_width="240dp"
        android:layout_height="match_parent"
        android:layout_gravity="start">
```

```
    <ListView
        android:id="@+id/left_drawer"
        android:layout_width="240dp"
        android:layout_height="match_parent"
        android:choiceMode="singleChoice"
        android:divider="@android:color/transparent"
        android:dividerHeight="0dp"
        android:background="#111"/>

  </RelativeLayout >
</android.support.v4.widget.DrawerLayout>
```

In the app, the choices for the sliding drawer will be displayed in the `ListView`. When an item in the `ListView` is selected, a fragment will be displayed in the `FrameLayout`.

The work to implement the app is to

▶ Wire the infrastructure for the sliding drawer.

▶ Populate the contents of the `ListView`.

▶ Show the `Fragment` that corresponds to the selected item in the `ListView`.

Setting Up the Sliding Drawer

In this section, you use the components defined in the layout file to implement the sliding drawer. You rely on properly setting up an `ActionBarDrawerToggle` to use the sliding drawer.

CAUTION

Using the ActionBarActivity

Your sliding drawer activity must extend an `ActionBarActivity(android.support.v7.app.ActionBarActivity)`. The `ActionBarActivity` is part of the app compatibility libraries in Android. Your activity will be defined using something like this: `public class NavigationDrawerActivity extends ActionBarActivity`.

Listing 13.4 shows the activity definition and a portion of the `onCreate()` method that is used to create the sliding drawer. The code continues in Listing 13.5.

LISTING 13.4   Implementing the Sliding Drawer

```
1: public class NavigationDrawerActivity extends ActionBarActivity {
2:     private DrawerLayout mDrawerLayout;
3:     private ListView mDrawerListView;
4:     private RelativeLayout  mDrawerRelativeLayout ;
5:     private ActionBarDrawerToggle mDrawerToggle;
```

```
 6:      String[] mDrawerOptionLabels;
 7:
 8:      @Override
 9:      protected void onCreate(Bundle savedInstanceState) {
10:          super.onCreate(savedInstanceState);
11:          setContentView(R.layout.activity_navigation_drawer);
12:          mDrawerLayout = (DrawerLayout) findViewById(R.id.drawer_layout);
13:          mDrawerListView = (ListView) findViewById(R.id.left_drawer);
14:          mDrawerRelativeLayout  = (RelativeLayout )
15:                              findViewById(R.id.left_drawer_layout);
16:          mDrawerLayout.setDrawerShadow(R.drawable.drawer_shadow,
17:               ·                    GravityCompat.START);
18:          getSupportActionBar().setDisplayHomeAsUpEnabled(true);
19:          getSupportActionBar().setHomeButtonEnabled(true);
20:          mDrawerToggle = new ActionBarDrawerToggle(
21:                  this,                       /* host Activity */
22:                  mDrawerLayout,              /* DrawerLayout object */
23:                  R.string.drawer_open,   /* "open drawer" for accessibility */
24:                  R.string.drawer_close   /* "close drawer" for accessibility */
25:          );
26:
27:          mDrawerLayout.setDrawerListener(mDrawerToggle);
28:          mDrawerToggle.syncState();
```

Lines 13–15 of Listing 13.4 define the components previously mentioned. There is a DrawerLayout, a RelativeLayout, and a ListView.

Lines 16–17 set the drawable that is used as a shadow over the contents when the sliding drawer is displayed using the setDrawerShadow() method.

Lines 18–19 set the action bar to use up navigation. In this case, you are not really using the up navigation to go to a parent activity. Instead, this is setting up the icon for the sliding drawer.

Lines 20–25 define the ActionBarDrawerToggle. This is the key to setting up the sliding drawer. The first parameter is the current activity. The second parameter is the DrawerLayout object. In Listing 13.4, the DrawerLayout object to use was defined on line 2 and populated using the findViewById() on line 12.

Line 27 sets the DrawerListener to the ActionBarToggle that was just created.

The ActionBarToggle in this case takes four parameters. If you are going to use a sliding drawer with a Toolbar instead of an ActionBar, there are five parameters that the Toolbar is passed:

```
mDrawerToggle = new ActionBarDrawerToggle(
    this,                   /* host Activity */
    mDrawerLayout,          /* DrawerLayout object */
    mToolbar,               /* Toolbar object */
```

```
     R.string.drawer_open,   /* "open drawer" for accessibility */
     R.string.drawer_close   /* "close drawer" for accessibility */
);
```

Populating ListView and Handling Selection

The sliding drawer contains a RelativeLayout, and that RelativeLayout contains a ListView. You can handle this ListView like any other. Listing 13.5 shows the code to populate the ListView and to handle a selection made on the sliding drawer.

LISTING 13.5   Handling the ListView in the Sliding Drawer

```
 1: Resources resources = getResources();
 2: mDrawerOptionLabels = resources.getStringArray(R.array.sliding_drawer_array);
 3: ArrayAdapter<String> drawerAdapter = new ArrayAdapter<String>(this,
 4:             R.layout.drawer_list_item, mDrawerOptionLabels);
 5: mDrawerListView.setAdapter(drawerAdapter);
 6: mDrawerListView.setOnItemClickListener(new AdapterView.OnItemClickListener()  {
 7:
 8:        @Override
 9:        public void onItemClick(AdapterView<?> parent, View,
10:                            int position, long id) {
11:            FragmentManager fragmentManager = getFragmentManager();
12:            Fragment = new RedFragment();
13:            switch (position){
14:                case 0:  //RED
15:                    fragment = new RedFragment();
16:                    break;
17:                case 1: //GREEN
18:                    fragment = new GreenFragment();
19:                    break;
20:                case 2: //BLUE
21:                    fragment = new BlueFragment();
22:                    break;
23:                case 3:  // YELLOW
24:                    fragment = new YellowFragment();
25:                    break;
26:            }
27:            fragmentManager.beginTransaction().
28:                    replace(R.id.content_frame, fragment).commit();
29:            setTitle(mDrawerOptionLabels[position]);
30:            mDrawerListView.setItemChecked(position, true);
31:            mDrawerLayout.closeDrawer(mDrawerRelativeLayout );
32:        }
33:        });
```

Lines 1 and 2 in Listing 13.5 read an array of strings from resources. The array contains the list of labels that correspond to the fragments to display.

Lines 3–5 set up an adapter for the `ListView` as you have done previously.

Lines 6–33 show the `onClickListener` for the `ListView`, and this is where the determination is made about which fragment to show. This code is responsible for showing the fragment and for closing the sliding drawer.

The position of the selected item in the list is passed as a parameter to the `onItemClick()` method of the `onClickListener`. See lines 9 and 10. You know that the position in the list corresponds to the fragment to display. The order is red, green, blue, yellow. So, if the first item is selected, the red fragment should be displayed.

Lines 11 and 12 define a `FragmentManager` and initialize a `Fragment` to use in this section.

A `switch` statement handles determining which `Fragment` is in use based on the item position. See lines 13–26.

When the `switch` statement is complete, a `Fragment` has been specified to be displayed. You can now display it and close the sliding drawer.

Lines 27 and 28 display the `Fragment`.

Line 31 closes the sliding drawer. Note that the parameter to the `closeDrawer()` method is the view that is displayed in the drawer layout. In this case, that is `mDrawerRelativeLayout`:

```
mDrawerLayout.closeDrawer(mDrawerRelativeLayout );
```

Line 29 sets the title in the `ActionBar` to have the same label as the item selected from the sliding drawer:

```
setTitle(mDrawerOptionLabels[position]);
```

Line 30 sets the selected item to checked in the sliding drawer:

```
mDrawerListView.setItemChecked(position, true);
```

The position of the selected item drives much of what occurs. You can make your sliding drawers dynamic and more complicated. In this case, the position directly corresponds to the data for the selected item.

Odds and Ends for the Sliding Drawer

The hamburger icon used in the sliding drawer design and the arrow used to close the sliding drawer must be handled as part of the options menu. In the `onOptionsItemSelected()` method, this is the code to have the `ActionBarDrawerToggle` handle when these are selected in the `ActionBar`. See lines 94–97 of Listing 13.6.

```
if (mDrawerToggle.onOptionsItemSelected(item)) {
        return true;
    }
```

When you implement a sliding drawer, you should handle configuration changes.

Listing 13.6 shows the complete code for the sliding drawer activity. Configuration changes are handled in the `PostCreate()` and `onConfigurationChanged()` methods. See lines 75–85 of Listing 13.6.

To handle the case of displaying an initial fragment when the app starts and nothing has been selected from the sliding drawer menu, check for the state where `savedInstance` is null. That occurs on lines 65–72. In that case, the red fragment is displayed directly.

LISTING 13.6 Full Code for Sliding Drawer Activity

```
 1: public class NavigationDrawerActivity extends ActionBarActivity {
 2:     private DrawerLayout mDrawerLayout;
 3:     private ListView mDrawerListView;
 4:     private RelativeLayout  mDrawerRelativeLayout ;
 5:     private ActionBarDrawerToggle mDrawerToggle;
 6:     String[] mDrawerOptionLabels;
 7:
 8:     @Override
 9:     protected void onCreate(Bundle savedInstanceState) {
10:         super.onCreate(savedInstanceState);
11:         setContentView(R.layout.activity_navigation_drawer);
12:         mDrawerLayout = (DrawerLayout) findViewById(R.id.drawer_layout);
13:         mDrawerListView = (ListView) findViewById(R.id.left_drawer);
14:         mDrawerRelativeLayout  = (RelativeLayout )
15:                         findViewById(R.id.left_drawer_layout);
16:         mDrawerLayout.setDrawerShadow(R.drawable.drawer_shadow,
17:                         GravityCompat.START);
18:         getSupportActionBar().setDisplayHomeAsUpEnabled(true);
19:         getSupportActionBar().setHomeButtonEnabled(true);
20:         mDrawerToggle = new ActionBarDrawerToggle(
21:                 this,                 /* host Activity */
22:                 mDrawerLayout,        /* DrawerLayout object */
23:                 R.string.drawer_open,  /* "open drawer" for accessibility */
24:                 R.string.drawer_close  /* "close drawer" for accessibility */
25:         );
26:
27:         mDrawerLayout.setDrawerListener(mDrawerToggle);
28:         mDrawerToggle.syncState();
29:       Resources resources = getResources();
30:         mDrawerOptionLabels =
31:                     resources.getStringArray(R.array.sliding_drawer_array);
32:         ArrayAdapter<String> drawerAdapter = new ArrayAdapter<String>(this,
```

```
33:                          R.layout.drawer_list_item, mDrawerOptionLabels);
34:
35:          mDrawerListView.setAdapter(drawerAdapter);
36:          mDrawerListView.setOnItemClickListener(new
37:              AdapterView.OnItemClickListener() {
38:              @Override
39:              public void onItemClick(AdapterView<?> parent, View,
40:                          int position, long id) {
41:                  FragmentManager fragmentManager = getFragmentManager();
42:                  Fragment = new RedFragment();
43:                  switch (position){
44:                      case 0:  //RED
45:                          fragment = new RedFragment();
46:                          break;
47:                      case 1: //GREEN
48:                          fragment = new GreenFragment();
49:                          break;
50:                      case 2: //BLUE
51:                          fragment = new BlueFragment();
52:                          break;
53:                      case 3:  // YELLOW
54:                          fragment = new YellowFragment();
55:                          break;
56:                  }
57:                  fragmentManager.beginTransaction().
58:                              replace(R.id.content_frame, fragment).commit();
59:                  setTitle(mDrawerOptionLabels[position]);
60:                  mDrawerListView.setItemChecked(position, true);
61:                  mDrawerLayout.closeDrawer(mDrawerRelativeLayout );
62:              }
63:          });
64:
65:      if (savedInstanceState == null) {
66:          FragmentManager fragmentManager = getFragmentManager();
67:          Fragment = new RedFragment();
68:          fragment = new RedFragment();
69:          fragmentManager.beginTransaction().
70:              replace(R.id.content_frame, fragment).commit();
71:          setTitle(mDrawerOptionLabels[0]);
72:      }
73:  }
74:
75:  @Override
76:  protected void onPostCreate(Bundle savedInstanceState) {
77:      super.onPostCreate(savedInstanceState);
78:      mDrawerToggle.syncState();
79:  }
80:
```

```
81:    @Override
82:    public void onConfigurationChanged(Configuration newConfig) {
83:        super.onConfigurationChanged(newConfig);
84:        mDrawerToggle.onConfigurationChanged(newConfig);
85:    }
86:
87:    @Override
88:    public boolean onCreateOptionsMenu(Menu menu) {
89:        getMenuInflater().inflate(R.menu.menu_navigation_drawer, menu);
90:        return true;
91:    }
92:
93:    @Override
94:    public boolean onOptionsItemSelected(MenuItem item) {
95:        if (mDrawerToggle.onOptionsItemSelected(item)) {
96:            return true;
97:        }
98:
99:        int id = item.getItemId();
100:        if (id == R.id.action_settings) {
101:            return true;
102:        }
103:        return super.onOptionsItemSelected(item);
104:    }
105:}
```

Summary

In this hour, you learned about the `ActionBar` and the `Toolbar`. You learned that by configuring a menu resource file, you have great control over what appears in an action bar. You saw that a toolbar is a widget-based version of an action bar that can be customized and that can hold child views. The relationship between styles and how an activity is defined in the Android manifest is important when working with toolbars. You also learned about the up navigation pattern and how to implement a sliding drawer menu.

Q&A

Q. When should I use a sliding drawer instead of a `Toolbar`?

A. A short answer is that you should use a sliding drawer if you have a lot of different navigable content in your app. There are some guidelines in the online Android documentation that say to use a sliding drawer for navigation if you have more than three top-level views or if you have deep navigation branches and want to provide a way to more easily navigate to content at lower levels.

Q. In the sliding drawer example, one activity was used, and `Fragments` were displayed as different content. Is that a good model for using the `ActionBar` and `Toolbar`?

A. Yes, you can use `Fragments` to display content in a consistent manner regardless of the navigation. You can also use activities and dialogs depending on your app. It may make sense to have a help option in the overflow menu that displays a dialog or an item in the action bar that navigates to a different activity. It will largely depend on your design, but fragments can be very useful.

Workshop

Quiz

1. What is a difference between an `ActionBar` and a `Toolbar`?

2. How would you indicate that a menu item should always be displayed in the overflow menu?

3. What would you do to implement the up navigation pattern if you had an `Activity` called `ChildActivity` that will navigate to `MainActivity` when the up navigation icon is selected?

Answers

1. A `Toolbar` is a widget that can be added to an XML layout file. An `ActionBar` is not a widget.

2. In the menu resource file, you set the item to never show as an action by using `android:showAsAction="never"`.

3. To use up navigation with `ChildActivity` and `MainActivity`, you modify the AndroidManifest.xml file entry for `ChildActivity` to indicate that `MainActivity` was its parent:

```
android:parentActivityName=".MainActivity"
```

Exercise

Use a `Toolbar` instead of `ActionBar` to implement a sliding drawer. You can use the code in the hour as a starting point. You need to add a toolbar to the layout. You need to use the proper constructor for the `ActionBarToggle`.

PART III

Working with Data

Using the File System

What You'll Learn in This Hour:

▶ File system overview

▶ Saving data privately in your app

▶ Saving data in public folders

In this hour, you learn about creating files and saving data for your apps. Data can be used exclusively by your app, or it can be public for other apps to access. Android provides file storage for different scenarios that include different rules for storage. For example, a file stored as part of the "cache" folder may be deleted if the system requires more file space. The specific differences are included in this hour.

File System Overview

There are multiple methods for storing data in Android. The proper method depends on how you will use the data, whether it is public or private, and whether you are using internal or external storage.

To store data, you can use the following:

▶ **Internal storage:** To store data privately using device memory.

▶ **External storage:** To store data on the shared external storage. Large files should use external storage.

▶ **Shared preferences:** To store data in key/value pairs

▶ **SQLite databases:** To store structured data in a private database.

In addition to considering public and private data, you may decide that some data is cached. That means that it is available for use in your app, but is not critical and may be deleted by the system at some point.

GO TO ▶ **CHAPTER 15, "USING SHAREDPREFERENCES,"** to learn more about shared preferences.

GO TO ▶ **CHAPTER 16, "SAVING DATA IN A SQLITE DATABASE,"** to learn more about SQLite.

Understanding Internal and External Storage

In the past, Android devices typically included a built-in storage area and an external storage area like a micro-SD card. The built-in storage was known as internal storage, and the removable micro-SD card was known as external storage. Now some devices divide permanent storage into internal and external storage areas.

The Android application programming interfaces (APIs) support the concept of internal and external storage regardless of the physical storage on the device.

Internal Storage

Internal storage has these characteristics:

▶ Typically, files saved in internal storage are accessible only by your application.

▶ Because internal storage cannot be removed (like a micro-SD card), it is always available.

▶ If a user uninstalls your app, all files on internal storage are deleted.

▶ No additional permissions are required for the use of internal storage.

Internal storage can ensure that the data you store is only accessed by your app.

External Storage

External storage has these characteristics:

▶ Files saved in external storage can be read by anyone.

▶ Because external storage might be removable, it may not be available.

▶ Typically, if the user uninstalls your app, these files will not be deleted. The exception is if they were saved with the `getExternalFilesDir()` method.

▶ Additional permissions are required for the use of external storage.

External storage might be used to make public files like pictures available to other apps or to store nonsensitive data that does not require access restrictions.

The permission required in your manifest file to write to external storage is `WRITE_EXTERNAL_STORAGE`. It will appear in the manifest as follows:

```
<uses-permission android:name="android.permission.WRITE_EXTERNAL_STORAGE"/>
```

There is also a READ_EXTERNAL_STORAGE permission. All apps that use the WRITE_EXTERNAL_STORAGE are granted READ_EXTERNAL_STORAGE permission.

Starting in API level 19, Android 4.4 (KitKat), you do not need to declare these permissions if you are using the methods getExternalFilesDir(String) and getExternalCacheDir(). Those methods provide directories for external storage that are exclusive to your app. If the user deletes your app, these files are deleted.

Understanding Public and Private Storage

Generally, when you use internal storage in your app, the data is private. You can use the method getFilesDir() to get a directory to write files using internal storage for your app.

You may need to use external storage for large files that you consider private to your app. Any file that should be deleted if your app is deleted should be considered private. This is data that belongs to your app.

Certain apps create content that clearly belongs to the user. If you had a photo app or a PDF document creator, you would not expect your photos or PDFs to be deleted if your app was deleted.

Android provides mechanisms for handling private app data and for public user content.

The methods getExternalFilesDir(String) and getExternalCacheDir() are used for external storage that should be exclusive to your app.

The method Environment.getExternalStoragePublicDirectory() is used for public external storage.

Understanding Cached Storage

You sometimes need to temporarily store noncritical data for your app to run efficiently. You cache this data or content temporarily. If is not available, your app will likely retrieve it again. That is the concept of caching data.

Because the data is noncritical, the Android system might reclaim storage if necessary. That means your cached files might be deleted. Typically, you check to see whether the data you need is available in cache. It if is, you rely on the data in that file. If the file is not there, you will have an alternate method of retrieving the data (for example, downloading it). At the point that you retrieve new data, you cache it in the file system for future use.

To get a directory that can be used for cached data, you use a getExternalCacheDir().

The following methods are used to create a directory for storing data in your app:

▶ **Context.getFilesDir()**: Returns a directory to use for the private internal storage for your app. This is used for internal storage. These files are deleted if your app is deleted.

► `Context.getCacheDir()`: Returns a directory for internal storage that is exclusive to your app. These files are deleted if your app is deleted and may be deleted if space is needed by the system.

► `Context.getExternalFilesDir()`: Returns a directory for external storage that is exclusive to your app. These files are deleted if your app is deleted.

► `Environment.getExternalStoragePublicDirectory()`: This is public external data. This content is not deleted if your app is deleted.

Saving Data Privately in Your App

As you can see, there are many methods for saving data privately for use in your app. You can use internal storage for app data. You can decide to use cache storage.

Figure 14.1 shows the user interface for an activity that will read data from the user and write that data to a file. There is an option to read the data and display the file contents, and there is an option to delete the file.

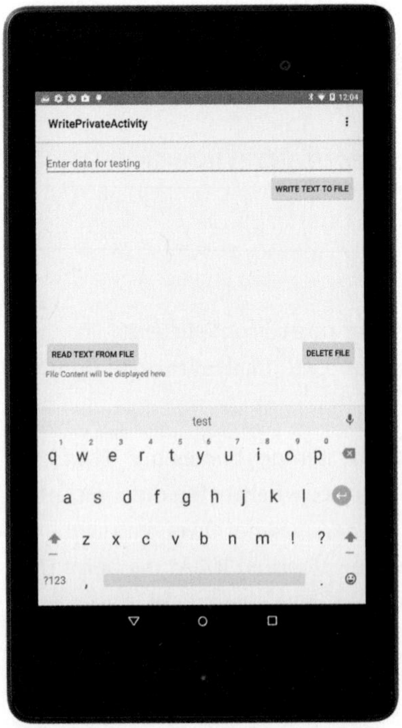

FIGURE 14.1
User interface to test file reading and writing.

The layout of the activity shown in Figure 14.1 has an `EditText` for input, a `TextView` to display the content, and three buttons to read, write, and delete a file.

The code for the activity shown in Figure 14.1 is shown in Listing 14.1.

LISTING 14.1   Reading and Writing App Data

```
 1: package com.talkingandroid.hour14application;
 2: import android.app.Activity;
 3: import android.os.Bundle;
 4: import android.view.View;
 5: import android.widget.Button;
 6: import android.widget.EditText;
 7: import android.widget.TextView;
 8: import java.io.BufferedReader;
 9: import java.io.BufferedWriter;
10: import java.io.File;
11: import java.io.FileNotFoundException;
12: import java.io.FileReader;
13: import java.io.FileWriter;
14: import java.io.IOException;
15:
16: public class WritePrivateActivity extends Activity {
17:     EditText editText;
18:     TextView textView;
19:     Button readButton;
20:     Button writeButton;
21:     Button deleteButton;
22:     private static String demoFile = "demo_file.txt";
23:     File file;
24:
25:     @Override
26:     protected void onCreate(Bundle savedInstanceState) {
27:         super.onCreate(savedInstanceState);
28:         setContentView(R.layout.activity_read_write);
29:         editText = (EditText) findViewById(R.id.editText);
30:         textView = (TextView) findViewById(R.id.textView);
31:         file  = new File(this.getFilesDir(), demoFile);
32:         writeButton = (Button) findViewById(R.id.writeButton);
33:         writeButton.setOnClickListener(new View.OnClickListener() {
34:             @Override
35:             public void onClick(View v) {
36:                 try {
37:                     FileWriter fileWriter = new FileWriter(file, true);
38:                     BufferedWriter bufferedWriter = new
39:                                     BufferedWriter(fileWriter);
40:                     String data = editText.getText().toString();
41:                     bufferedWriter.write(data);
```

```
42:                    bufferedWriter.close();
43:                    fileWriter.close();
44:                } catch (FileNotFoundException e) {
45:                    e.printStackTrace();
46:                } catch (IOException e) {
47:                    e.printStackTrace();
48:                }
49:            }
50:        });
51:
52:        readButton = (Button) findViewById(R.id.readButton);
53:        readButton.setOnClickListener(new View.OnClickListener() {
54:            StringBuffer stringBuffer = new StringBuffer();
55:            @Override
56:            public void onClick(View v) {
57:                try {
58:                    FileReader fileReader = new FileReader(file);
59:                    BufferedReader bufferedReader = new
60:                                        BufferedReader(fileReader);
61:                    int readData;
62:                    while ((readData = bufferedReader.read()) != -1) {
63:                        char data = (char) readData;
64:                        stringBuffer.append(data);
65:                    }
66:                    bufferedReader.close();
67:                    fileReader.close();
68:                    textView.setText("");
69:                    textView.setText(stringBuffer.toString());
70:                } catch (FileNotFoundException e1) {
71:                    e1.printStackTrace();
72:                } catch (IOException e1) {
73:                    e1.printStackTrace();
74:                }
75:            }
76:        });
77:
78:        deleteButton = (Button) findViewById(R.id.deleteButton);
79:        deleteButton.setOnClickListener(new View.OnClickListener() {
80:            @Override
81:            public void onClick(View v) {
82:                boolean result = file.delete();
83:                if (result){
84:                    textView.setText("File deleted");
85:                }else{
86:                    textView.setText("File NOT deleted");
87:                }
88:            }
89:        });
90:    }
```

The key to Listing 14.1 is how the file that you are writing data to was defined. On line 31, the `getFilesDir()` method is used:

```
file  = new File(this.getFilesDir(), demoFile);
```

The `getFilesDir()` method returns a directory that uses internal storage and is completely private to your app. That directory is the first parameter to the `File` constructor. The second parameter is the `String` for the filename. The field `demoFile` has the value `"demo_file.txt"` and is defined on line 22.

Lines 33–50 are the code for the button that writes the entered data to a file. A `FileWriter` and `BufferFileWriter` are used. The `FileWriter` is defined on line 37. The second parameter to the `FileWriter` constructor indicates that data should be appended to this file:

```
FileWriter fileWriter = new FileWriter(file, true);
```

Similarly, to see how this file is read, see lines 52–76 of Listing 14.1. A `FileReader` and `BufferedReader` are used.

The code to delete the file occurs on lines 78–89.

TRY IT YOURSELF ▼

Saving Your App Data to a File in the Cache Directory

Using the cache directory can be useful for saving large, but temporary, files. Saving a bitmap for immediate use is an example:

1. Use Listing 14.1 as a starting point.

2. Change the code to save your app data in a cache directory.

NOTE

Alternative Techniques

An alternative to using `Context.getFilesDir()` is to use the `openFileOutput()` method. If you define a `FileOutputStream` called `outputStream`, you can open a file to write using `openFileOutput`. You use

```
outputStream = openFileOutput(filename, Context.MODE_PRIVATE)
```

where *filename* is the name of the file to use. The parameter `Context.MODE_PRIVATE` indicates that the contents are private to your app.

Saving Data in Public Folders

Files stored on external storage can be viewed by other apps. Looking at files on external storage is like looking at files on your hard drive. You can use the `getExternalFilesDir()` method to return a directory for external files that are exclusive to your app. These files will be deleted if your app is deleted.

You use `getExternalFilesStoragePublicDirectory()` to store data in a file in a public directory that will be read by other apps. If you store a picture, in the pictures directory, it will be available in the Gallery and other apps. These files are not deleted if your app is deleted.

When you use external storage, you must check to see that it is available. If an SD card is pulled from the phone, you will not be able to access the storage. That is one example that shows the need to check for storage.

To check for the availability of external storage, you check the external storage state to see whether the media is mounted. If the media is mounted, it is available for writing:

```
String state = Environment.getExternalStorageState();
if (Environment.MEDIA_MOUNTED.equals(state)) {
    // you can write to external storage
}
```

When you use an external directory, you should specify the type of content that the directory holds. That is true whether you are using the `getExternalFilesDir()` method or the `getExternalFilesStoragePublicDirectory()` method.

The possible values to use for standard directories are as follows:

▶ `Environment.DIRECTORY_ALARMS`: Any audio files that the user can select as an alarm

▶ `Environment.DIRECTORY_DCIM`: Used for pictures and videos from a camera

▶ `Environment.DIRECTORY_DOCUMENTS`: Documents that have been created by the user

▶ `Environment.DIRECTORY_DOWNLOADS`: Any downloads

▶ `Environment.DIRECTORY_MOVIES`: Movies

▶ `Environment.DIRECTORY_MUSIC`: Music

▶ `Environment.DIRECTORY_NOTIFICATIONS`: Any audio files that the user can select as a notification

▶ `Environment.DIRECTORY_PICTURES`: Pictures

▶ `Environment.DIRECTORY_PODCASTS`: Podcasts

▶ `Environment.DIRECTORY_RINGTONES`: Any audio files that can be used as ringtones

You could change Listing 14.1 to use external storage by changing line 31 from:

```
file  = new File(this.getFilesDir(), demoFile);
```

to:

```
file = new File(this.getExternalFilesDir(Environment.DIRECTORY_DOCUMENTS),
demoFile);
```

You can call `getExternalFilesDir()` with a null value to save files for your apps that may not fit into the categories of the standard directories.

When you use external storage, you really should check to see whether the media is available by checking the external storage state.

CAUTION

Remember Your Permissions

Beginning in KitKat (Android 4.4), you do not need to set permission to write to external storage if you are writing to your own app directory. So, if you use `getExternalFilesDir()` on KitKat and later, no permission is required. You need permission for earlier versions and to write to public directories using `getExternalFilesStoragePublicDirectory()`.

The method `getExternalFilesStoragePublicDirectory()` works somewhat differently than the other methods you have been using. When you use `getExternalFilesDir()`, a directory is created if it does not exist.

With `getExternalFilesStoragePublicDirectory()`, you request the public directory and make your file using that directory. You cannot assume the directory exists, so you must call the method `mkdirs()` to make the directory and create your file.

When you use `getExternalFilesDir()`, you can say the following:

```
file  = new File(this.getFilesDir(), demoFile);
```

With `getExternalFilesStoragePublicDirectory()`, use this:

```
path = Environment.getExternalStoragePublicDirectory(
        Environment.DIRECTORY_DOCUMENTS);
file = new File(path, demoFile);
path.mkdirs();
```

where `path` and `file` are both of type `File`.

▼ TRY IT YOURSELF

Saving Your App Data to a File in the External Public Directory

When you save a file in an external public directory, you are ensuring that the user has access even if your app is uninstalled. For apps that create pictures or documents, that is critical.

1. Use Listing 14.1 as a starting point.

2. Set the proper permission.

3. Check for external storage state.

4. Write to the public documents directory.

5. If you have a device, use a file-viewing app to check for the file.

Summary

In this hour, you learned about storing data on the file system. You focused on internal/external storage and on public/private storage. You can keep data that is exclusive to your app and private or save user items like documents and pictures that will persist if your app is deleted.

Q&A

Q. Is this how files are accessed on all versions of Android?

A. The methods in this chapter were introduced in API level 8. That is Froyo (Android 2.2). All devices actually in use can use these methods. Froyo has less than 1% Android distribution, and earlier versions of Android have even less.

Workshop

Quiz

1. When and why do you need to check the external storage state?

2. If your app is deleted, which files are not deleted?

3. True or false: It is impossible for you to read a list of podcasts on a device.

Answers

1. When you use external storage, you must check the external storage state. It is possible that external storage may not be available.

2. Files in public external directories, like `Environment.DIRECTORY_PICTURES`, will not be deleted.

3. False. If they exist, you can read a list of podcasts from the `DIRECTORY_PODCASTS` standard directory.

Exercise

If you have a file that represents a directory, you can get a list of available filenames by using the `list()` method. So, given a directory named path, you populate `fileList` with an array of filenames using this code:

```
String[] fileList = path.list();
```

Using SharedPreferences

What You'll Learn in This Hour:

▶ Using `SharedPreferences` to store data

▶ Setting user preferences

▶ Creating a `PreferencesFragment`

▶ Generating a `PreferencesActivity`

`SharedPreferences` is a class that provides the ability to store data in key/value pairs. This data can be set and retrieved in any `Activity`. Android provides a robust Preferences application programming interface (API) for user settings that use `SharedPreferences` as the underlying data store. In this hour, you learn how to use `SharedPreferences` for your app settings. You also develop a user interface for the user settings in your app.

Using SharedPreferences to Store Data

`SharedPreferences` provides a mechanism for storing and retrieving data as key/value pairs. You will create a single `Activity` app to demonstrate how preferences can be used just for storing data. In this app, your goal is to show a different message to a first time user than for a returning user.

Setting Preferences

The idea of a key/value pair is that a key can be used to look up information. The key is associated with a value. The key is a string. The value can be an integer, Boolean, `String`, or other simple type.

To determine first time use, you can use a Boolean that is set to true the first time the user runs the app. After that, the first time value is false. The key will be the `String` `"com.talking android.hour15application.firstUse"`. The package name for your app should be the

first part of the key. If the package name is com.example.app, you use com.example.app.
firstUse as the key. You can define this key in a resource file or in your app. Declaring a static
field is common:

```
public static final String FIRST_USE_SETTING = "com.talkingandroid.
hour15application.firstUse";
```

The key/value pair will be retained across uses of the app. You will access the stored data by
retrieving the SharedPreferences for the app with a call to the getSharedPreferences()
method. The method takes two parameters: name and mode. Name is the filename where the
key/value pairs are stored. It is a String and should be start with the package name. The mode
parameters represent the type of file storage that should be used. Use Context.MODE_PRIVATE,
indicating that the settings are private.

To write to shared preferences, you use a shared preferences editor. You must define the Editor,
write the values, and then call commit() on the Editor.

With key shared preferences and a key defined as follows

```
public static final String SETTINGS = "com.talkingandroid.hour15application.
settings";
public static final String FIRST_USE_SETTING = "com.talkingandroid.
hour15application.firstUse";
```

you would define shared preferences and write a new value to the key using an editor like this:

```
SharedPreferences = getSharedPreferences(SETTINGS, MODE_PRIVATE);
Editor editor = preferences.edit();
editor.putBoolean(FIRST_USE_SETTING, false);
editor.commit();
edit.commit();
```

Reading from SharedPreferences

You will want to read the values from shared preferences in your app! In a typical case, you will
have occasions to write or update data and other times when you will read the data.

Listing 15.1 is the entire code for an activity where writing a reading shared preferences occurs in
the onCreate() method. This is the case of showing a different message to a first time user and
a returning user.

The string values for shared preferences storage and the first use key are defined on lines 9–12 of
Listing 15.1.

LISTING 15.1   Reading and Setting Preferences

```
 1: package com.talkingandroid.hour15application;
 2: import android.app.Activity;
 3: import android.content.SharedPreferences;
 4: import android.content.SharedPreferences.Editor;
 5: import android.os.Bundle;
 6: import android.widget.TextView;
 7:
 8: public class ReadWritePreferences extends Activity {
 9:     public static final String SETTINGS =
10:             "com.talkingandroid.hour15application.settings";
11:     public static final String FIRST_USE_SETTING =
12:             "com.talkingandroid.hour15application.firstUse";
13:     TextView textView;
14:
15:     @Override
16:     protected void onCreate(Bundle savedInstanceState) {
17:         super.onCreate(savedInstanceState);
18:         setContentView(R.layout.activity_read_write_preferences);
19:         textView = (TextView) findViewById(R.id.textView);
20:       // Get Preferences
21:       SharedPreferences = getSharedPreferences(SETTINGS, MODE_PRIVATE);
22:       // Read the FIRST_USE_SETTING
23:       boolean firstUse = preferences.getBoolean(FIRST_USE_SETTING, true);
24:        if (firstUse){
25:             textView.setText(R.string.first_time_message);
26:             // Create Preferences Editor and update settings
27:             Editor editor = preferences.edit();
28:             editor.putBoolean(FIRST_USE_SETTING, false);
29:             editor.commit();
30:        } else{
31:             textView.setText(R.string.return_user_message);
32:        }
33:     }
34: }
```

On line 21, a SharedPreferences object called preferences is populated with a call to getSharedPreferences(). Once preferences is available, you can read data from it. On line 23, the Boolean firstUse is read from preferences. To read preferences, you must use the appropriate method. In this case, that is getBoolean(). The first parameter is the key to read and the second parameter is a default value. The key is FIRST_USE_SETTING, and the default value is true.

After the first time in the app, you need to set the FIRST_USE_SETTING to false. That occurs on lines 27–29 of Listing 15.1, where an editor is created and the data is updated.

▼ TRY IT YOURSELF

Reading and Writing to Shared Preferences

Write data to shared preferences in one activity and display the stored value:

1. Create a new Android project with a `MainActivity`.

2. Include an `EditText`, a save `Button`, and a display `Button` for `MainActivity`.

3. When the save `Button` is pressed, save the contents of `EditText` to a shared preference.

4. Create a new activity called `DisplayActivity` that includes a `TextView`.

5. When the display `Button` is pressed, start `DisplayActivity` and display the value that was stored.

In the case of a first time user, you are using `SharedPreferences` as a storage mechanism for key/value pairs. Nothing is directly entered by the user. In a similar way, `SharedPreferences` can be used for timestamps and other mechanisms for simple tracking.

You can count the number of times a user takes a certain action in your app and store the value in `SharedPreferences`. At a certain threshold, you might prompt the user to rate your app or take some other action.

In another example, you can use the system time to set time stamps and then check for elapsed time.

Data Types and Methods in SharedPreferences

Common types are stored and retrieved from `SharedPreferences`. There are methods for `getBoolean()`, `getFloat()`, `getInt()`, `getLong()`, `getString()`, and `getStringSet()`.

In addition, there is a `getAll()` method and a `contains()` method. The `getAll()` method will get all key/value pairs as a `Map` where the key is a string and the value is whatever was put into `SharedPreferences`. The `contains()` method take a `String` as a parameter. The `String` is the key to check. The `contains()` method returns true if the key is contained in `SharedPreferences`.

NOTE

Listening for Changes in SharedPreferences

`SharedPreferences` also includes a `registerOnSharedPreferenceChangeListener()` method. This allows your app to listen for changes to preferences and react if necessary. There is a corresponding `unregisterOnSharedPreferenceChangeListener()` method.

Setting User Preferences

`SharedPreferences` implements a data store for key/value pairs. Android uses the `SharedPreferences` data store together with a set of Preferences APIs to provide a robust way to implement user settings.

Either a `PreferenceActivity` or a `PreferenceFragment` can be used as the user interface for settings. The user changes the settings and the `SharedPreferences` data store is updated.

The `Preference` class is extended to provide subclasses to handle specific types of settings. Each subclass of `Preference` includes properties for the setting and a user interface for displaying the preference. For example, a `CheckBoxPreference` presents a check box and a message to the user. The user may check or uncheck the check box. The value associated with a `CheckBoxPreference` is a Boolean, with true indicating that the check box is checked.

Creating a PreferencesFragment

When creating a `PreferenceFragment` or `PreferenceActivity`, an XML file is used to define the preferences. This is not a res/layout XML file. Layout files define views. In this case, the XML file defines preferences. The preference XML file is put in a res/xml folder. You will use the filename preferences.xml to create a `PreferenceFragment`.

Listing 15.2 shows the entire `SettingsFragment` class. `SettingsFragment` extends `PreferenceFragment` and implements onSharedPreferenceChangeListener. On line 12, within the `onCreate()` method, a call is made to `addPreferencesFromResource()`. That will read the data in the `R.xml.preferences` file and show the appropriate user settings.

LISTING 15.2   Extending PreferencesFragment

```
 1: package com.talkingandroid.hour15application;;
 2: import android.content.SharedPreferences;
 3: import android.content.SharedPreferences.OnSharedPreferenceChangeListener;
 4: import android.os.Bundle;
 5: import android.preference.PreferenceFragment;
 6: import android.util.Log;
 7: public class SettingsFragment extends PreferenceFragment
 8: implements OnSharedPreferenceChangeListener {
 9:     @Override
10:     public void onCreate(Bundle savedInstanceState) {
11:         super.onCreate(savedInstanceState);
12:         addPreferencesFromResource(R.xml.preferences);
13:     }
14:     @Override
15:     public void onResume() {
16:         super.onResume();
17:         getPreferenceScreen().getSharedPreferences().
```

```
18:                              registerOnSharedPreferenceChangeListener(this);
19:       }
20:       @Override
21:       public void onPause() {
22:            super.onPause();
23:          getPreferenceScreen().getSharedPreferences().
24:                              unregisterOnSharedPreferenceChangeListener(this);
25:       }
26:       @Override
27:       public void onSharedPreferenceChanged(SharedPreferences
28:                                 sharedPreferences, String key) {
29:          Log.d("Settings", key);
30:       }
31:   }
```

The onSharedPreferenceChangeListener is implemented. The registerOnShared
PreferenceChangeListener() method is called on lines 17–18 in the fragment's onRe-
sume() method. It is unregistered in the onPause() method on lines 23–24. When a change
is detected in the onSharedPreferenceChanged() method, we just log the passed key. This
allows us to see when a change occurs using LogCat.

How the SettingsFragment looks when displayed to the user is determined by the contents of
the preferences.xml file. There are a set of preference elements and attributes that are interpreted
and then properly displayed

CheckBoxPreference

A check box is displayed using a CheckBoxPreference. Listing 15.3 shows a sample prefer-
ences.xml file. A PreferenceScreen contains a CheckBoxPreference. Lines 4–7 include the
attributes for the preference. The key is used to store the associated data. The title and summary
are used for display. The default value indicates the initial setting for the preference. With a
default value of false, the check box is not enabled.

Figure 15.1 shows the SettingsFragment when the preference.xml file defined in Listing 15.3
is used.

LISTING 15.3   **CheckBoxPreference Definition**

```
1:   <?xml version="1.0" encoding="utf-8"?>
2:   <PreferenceScreen xmlns:android="http://schemas.android.com/apk/res/android">
3:       <CheckBoxPreference
4:           android:key="hires"
5:           android:title="Hi-Res Images"
6:           android:summary="Show high quality images. These take longer to load"
7:           android:defaultValue="False" />
8:   </PreferenceScreen>
```

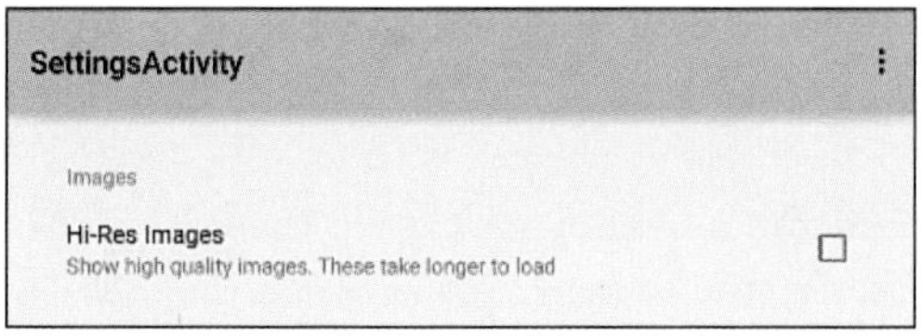

FIGURE 15.1
SettingsFragment with one CheckBoxPreference.

Note that in the app, the SettingsFragment is used in a SettingsActivity. The SettingsActivity just uses setContentView() to display a layout that contains the SettingsFragment. The activity_settings.xml layout file is shown here:

```
<RelativeLayout xmlns:android="http://schemas.android.com/apk/res/android"
    xmlns:tools="http://schemas.android.com/tools" android:layout_width="match_
parent"
    android:layout_height="match_parent"
    android:paddingLeft="@dimen/activity_horizontal_margin"
    android:paddingRight="@dimen/activity_horizontal_margin"
    android:paddingTop="@dimen/activity_vertical_margin"
    android:paddingBottom="@dimen/activity_vertical_margin"
    tools:context="com.talkingandroid.hour15application.SettingsActivity">

    <fragment
        android:layout_width="fill_parent"
        android:layout_height="fill_parent"
        android:name="com.talkingandroid.hour15application.SettingsFragment"
        android:id="@+id/fragment"
        android:layout_alignParentTop="true"
        android:layout_alignParentStart="true" />
</RelativeLayout>
```

Table 15.1 lists the reference types, including CheckBoxPreference.

TABLE 15.1   Preference Types

Preference Type	Stored Value	API Level	Description
CheckBoxPreference	Boolean	1	Show a check box
EditTextPreference	String	1	Enter data in an EditText
ListPreference	String	1	Select from a list
MultiSelectListPreference	Set of Strings	11	Show a dialog with multiple values
SwitchPreference	Boolean	14	An on/off toggle for Boolean values

In addition to these simple preference types, there are options for titles and subscreens.

SwitchPreference and ListPreference

Listing 15.4 shows an additional SwitchPreference and a ListPreference. The SwitchPreference indicates whether the user likes pie. The ListPreference lets the user indicate which type of pie he or she likes.

In the ListPreference definition on lines 7–15, note several things. Line 8 indicates a dependency on "pie," which is the SwitchPreference defined on lines 1–5. That means that the ListPreference will not be available if the SwitchPreference with the key "pie" is not selected. Figure 15.2 shows the two states for this.

LISTING 15.4   **ListPreference and Dependency**

```
1: < SwitchPreference
2:         android:key="pie"
3:         android:title="Pie"
4:         android:summary="Like Pie"
5:         android:defaultValue="true" />
6:
7: <ListPreference
8:         android:dependency="pie"
9:         android:key="pie_type"
10:        android:title="Pie Type"
11:        android:summary="Preferred pie type for eating"
12:        android:dialogTitle="Type of Pie"
13:        android:entries="@array/pie_array"
14:        android:entryValues="@array/pie_array"
15:        android:defaultValue="apple" />
```

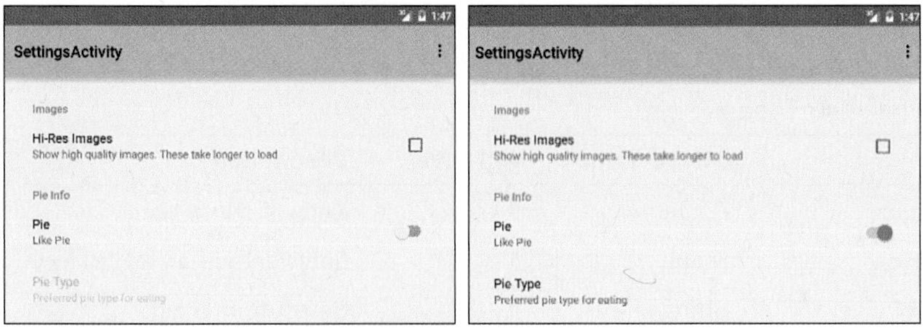

FIGURE 15.2
ListPreference depends on SwitchPreference.

The `ListPreference` refers to the `@array/pie_array` that is defined in the res/values/Strings. xml file. Entries are what is displayed to the user. `EntryValues` are the corresponding values. In this case, the name of the pies is both the `entries` and the `entryValues`. In other cases, the display name might differ from the `entryValue`. For example, a country code might be stored while a country name is displayed. A `defaultValue` is specified. Figure 15.3 shows the `ListPreference` display.

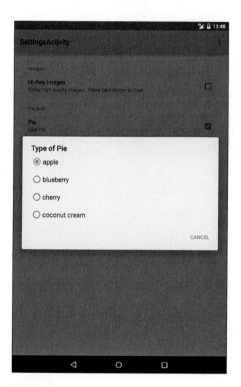

FIGURE 15.3
`ListPreference` displaying options.

EditTextPreference

Another type of preference is the `EditTextPreference`, which gives a user free-form entry. The following XML snippet defines an `EditTextPreference`. The resulting display is shown in Figure 15.4. (The `SettingsActivity` screen and the dialog to accept additional data are shown.)

```
<EditTextPreference
 android:key="more_info"
 android:title="More Info"
 android:summary="More about pies"
 android:defaultValue="" />
```

FIGURE 15.4
`EditPreference` example.

Adding Titles and Subscreens

Adding titles to organize content for settings is easy. Each set of related content that appear under a title should be wrapped in the XML in a `PreferenceCategory` with a title. A sample `PreferenceCategory` is shown. This is how the Pie Info title is displayed:

```
<PreferenceCategory android:title="Pie Info">

  ...add preferences here

</PreferenceCategory>
```

In addition to titles, a subscreen can be used to organize content on the setting page. Subscreens are defined in a nested `PreferenceScreen` element. Listing 15.5 shows the entire preferences. xml file, including titles and subscreens.

Figure 15.5 shows the resulting settings page. The title is shown on the main settings page. When that title is selected, the subscreen is shown.

LISTING 15.5   Showing a Subscreen

```
1:   <?xml version="1.0" encoding="utf-8"?>
2:   <PreferenceScreen xmlns:android="http://schemas.android.com/apk/res/android">
3:       <PreferenceCategory
4:           android:title="Images">
5:           <CheckBoxPreference
```

```
 6:                    android:key="hires"
 7:                    android:title="Hi-Res Images"
 8:                    android:summary="Show high quality images. These take longer to
load"
 9:                    android:defaultValue="False" />
10:          </PreferenceCategory>
11:          <PreferenceCategory
12:                  android:title="Pie Info">
13:                  <SwitchPreference
14:                      android:key="pie"
15:                      android:title="Pie"
16:                      android:summary="Like Pie"
17:                      android:defaultValue="true" />
18:
19:                  <ListPreference
20:                      android:dependency="pie"
21:                      android:key="pie_type"
22:                      android:title="Pie Type"
23:                      android:summary="Preferred pie type for eating"
24:                      android:dialogTitle="Type of Pie"
25:                      android:entries="@array/pie_array"
26:                      android:entryValues="@array/pie_array"
27:                      android:defaultValue="apple" />
28:
29:                  <EditTextPreference
30:                      android:key="more_info"
31:                      android:title="More Info"
32:                      android:summary="More about pies"
33:                      android:defaultValue="" />
34:          </PreferenceCategory>
35:          <PreferenceScreen
36:                  android:key="second_preferencescreen"
37:                  android:title="Second Screen of Settings">
38:                  <EditTextPreference
39:                      android:key="extraA"
40:                      android:title="More Data"
41:                      android:summary="Another EditTextPreference"
42:                      android:defaultValue="" />
43:                  <EditTextPreference
44:                      android:key="ExtraB"
45:                      android:title="Even More Info"
56:                      android:summary="What more can we say"
47:                      android:defaultValue="" />
48:          </PreferenceScreen>
49:  </PreferenceScreen> >
```

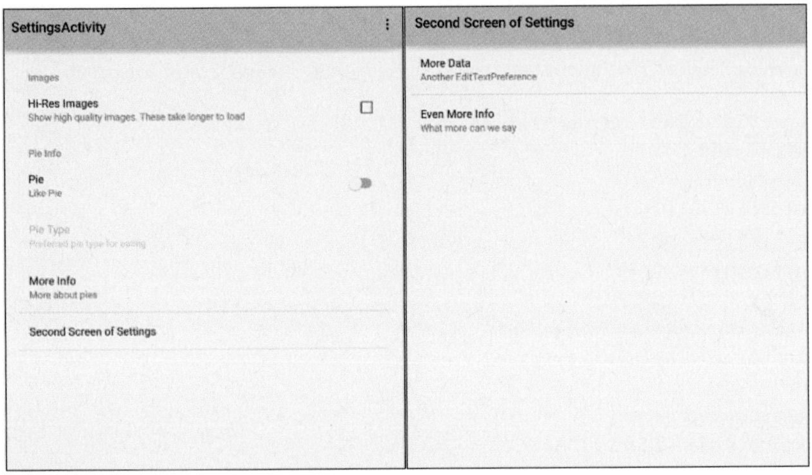

FIGURE 15.5
Using a subscreen to organize settings.

Reading Preferences

Reading these preferences is exactly the same reading from `SharedPreferences`, but you will use `PreferenceManager` to get the default shared preferences:

```
SharedPreferences sharedPref =
            PreferenceManager.getDefaultSharedPreferences(getActivity());
```

Then you can retrieve data with `gets` from `SharedPreferences`, as follows:

```
sharedPref.getString("pie_type", "");
```

Generating a PreferenceActivity

One reason to use a `PreferenceFragment` is because some `PreferenceActivity` methods are being deprecated.

However, Android Studio provides a convenient method for creating a settings activity. It is one of the types of activities that can be created through Android Studio menu choices.

Generating a Settings Activity in Android Studio

Here, you create a default project and add a Settings activity:

1. Create a new Android project with an activity called `MainActivity`.

2. In that project, choose New, Activity, Settings Activity.

3. Create this new activity.

4. You can then add the `SettingsActivity` to your `MainActivity` by adding it to the overflow menu using the `onOptionsItemSelected()` method.

Figure 15.6 shows the generated `SettingsActivity`. This can be modified for your needs.

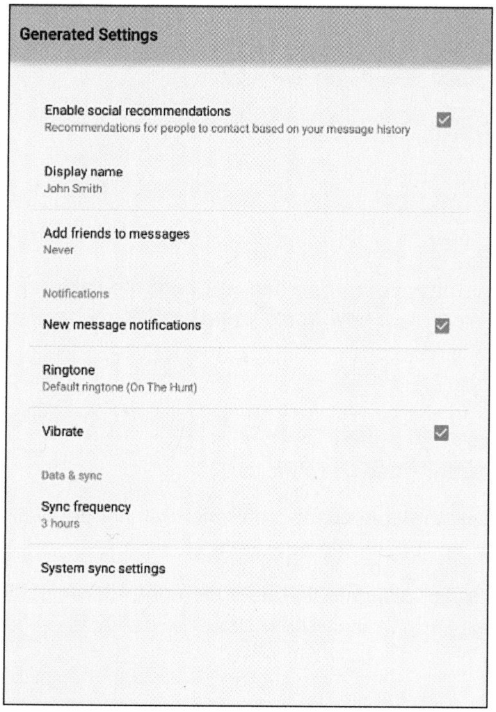

Generated Settings

Enable social recommendations
Recommendations for people to contact based on your message history   ☑

Display name
John Smith

Add friends to messages
Never

Notifications

New message notifications   ☑

Ringtone
Default ringtone (On The Hunt)

Vibrate   ☑

Data & sync

Sync frequency
3 hours

System sync settings

FIGURE 15.6
The generated `SettingsActivity`.

Summary

In this hour, you used the `SharedPreference` data store to save key/value pairs. In the example, you used `SharedPreferences` to show a message only on the first time app use. You learned about `Preferences` and how to make a settings page using XML to define preferences, including `CheckBoxPreference`, `ListPreference`, and `EditTextPreference`. You saw how to add titles and subscreens to preferences. `SharedPreferences` enables simple data storage, and the Preferences API is a powerful way to implement user settings.

Q&A

Q. Are settings required in an app?

A. No, but settings are often a good idea. The style guide for settings provides additional information on when settings should be added. The specific guidance is this: "Avoid the temptation to make everything a setting." See http://developer.android.com/design/patterns/settings.html.

Workshop

Quiz

1. What are common types of preferences?

2. What does dependency mean in a preferences file?

3. If you are retrieving a Boolean value from `sharedPreferences` and you want the value to be false if there was no value in `sharedPreferences`, how would you do that?

Answers

1. Common preferences are `CheckBoxPreference`, `ListPreference`, and `EditTextPreference`. Additional preferences are listed in Table 15.1.

2. When a dependency is included for a preference, the dependent preference will not be available unless the primary preference is set. You saw this in the pie example.

3. A default value is indicated on reading the data. For example, in this statement, the default value for `FIRST_USE` is true: `preferences.getBoolean(FIRST_USE, true);`.

Exercise

Settings depend on the app you are building. Consider an app that you are building or want to build and define a list of settings. Implement those settings in either a `PreferenceFragment` or a `PreferenceActivity`.

HOUR 16
Using SQLite and File Storage

What You'll Learn in This Hour:

▶ Organizing data with tables

▶ Managing a database with `SQLiteOpenHelper`

▶ Adding, deleting, and updating data

▶ Using cursors to query data

▶ Using a database in the app

SQLite is a small, fast, file-based database that is included with Android. In this hour, you use a SQLite database to store and retrieve some simple test data. Then, the focus is on reading and displaying the data. You use a cursor and cursor adapter to display the data.

Organizing a Database with Tables

At a basic level, a database stores information and provides a way for you to retrieve that data in a structured way. SQL stands for Structured Query Language and is the mechanism for data retrieval. We use queries to specify the data we want to retrieve. Data in a database is organized into tables.

A table is made up of items that form a logical group. In the example for this hour, you continue to use a simple object that contains data about a pie. The fields include id, name, price, and so on.

A table can be thought of as having rows and columns. A column is similar to a heading on a spreadsheet. It defines the name of the data field. A row represents a data entry in the column. Multiple columns and rows comprise a table.

These are the fields in the `Pie` object:

```
int mId;
String mName;
String mDescription;
double mPrice;
boolean mIsFavorite;
```

The `Pie` object consists of int, string, double, and Boolean fields. You will use equivalent database values as columns to store and retrieve data.

Listing 16.1 shows the entire code for the `Pie.java` class. In this case, `makePies()` is used to create a small set of sample data.

LISTING 16.1 Pie Object

```
1:    package com.talkingandroid.hour16application;
2:    import java.util.ArrayList;
3:    public class Pie {
4:        int mId;
5:        String mName;
6:        String mDescription;
7:        double mPrice;
8:        boolean mIsFavorite;
9:
10:       public Pie(){
11:       }
12:
13:       public Pie (String name, String description, double price){
14:           this.mName = name;
15:           this.mDescription = description;
16:           this.mPrice = price;
17:           this.mIsFavorite=false;
18:       }
19:
20:       public static ArrayList<Pie> makePies(){
21:           ArrayList<Pie> pies = new ArrayList<Pie>();
22:           pies.add(new Pie("Apple","An old-fashioned favorite. ", 1.0));
23:           pies.add(new Pie("Blueberry","Made with fresh Maine blueberries.",
1.5));
24:           pies.add(new Pie("Cherry","Delicious and fresh made daily.", 2.0));
25:           pies.add(new Pie("Coconut Cream","A customer favorite.", 2.5));
26:           return pies;
27:       }
28:   }
```

Managing Data with SQLiteOpenHelper

Databases are opened and closed like files. To help manage the database, you use the class `SQLiteOpenHelper`.

The class `PieDbAdapter` is used to handle the database functionality for this app. In `PieDbAdapter`, you use a `SQLiteDatabase` class to handle the database, and you use an instance of the `SQLiteOpenHelper` class to take care of opening and closing the database. Listings 16.1 through 16.7 show the full `PieDbAdapter` class by section.

It is easy to see how `PieDbAdapter` works by breaking it into sections:

- ▶ **Definitions:** Database name, table name, field names

- ▶ **SQL Instructions:** Create table

- ▶ **Database Helper:** Create the `DatabaseHelper`

- ▶ **Database Adapter methods:** Open, close, upgrade

- ▶ **Database Table methods:** `insertPie()`, `UpdatePie()`, `DeletePie()`

- ▶ **Query Methods:** `getPies()` to get all pies in the database

- ▶ **Read data method:** `getPieFromCursor()` given a cursor, return a `Pie` object

Listing 16.2 includes field definitions for the `PieDbAdapter` class. Lines 11–13 for Listing 16.2 specify `DATABASE_NAME`, `PIE_TABLE`, and `DATABASE VERSION`. Lines 20–24 specify the column names that will be used for the `PIE_TABLE`. The fields that will be returned from the database begin on line 26.

NOTE

Defining KEY_ROWID as _id

It is important to define an identifier for each entry in the table using `_id`. A number of Android classes and methods rely on this definition.

LISTING 16.2 PieDbAdapter Definitions

```
1:  package com.talkingandroid.hour16application;
2:  import android.content.ContentValues;
3:  import android.content.Context;
4:  import android.database.Cursor;
5:  import android.database.SQLException;
6:  import android.database.sqlite.SQLiteDatabase;
7:  import android.database.sqlite.SQLiteOpenHelper;
8:  import android.util.Log;
```

```
 9:
10:    public class PieDbAdapter {
11:        private static final String DATABASE_NAME = "FOOD_DATABASE.db";
12:        private static final String PIE_TABLE = "PIE_TABLE";
13:        private static final int DATABASE_VERSION =200;
14:        private final Context mCtx;
15:        public static String TAG = PieDbAdapter.class.getSimpleName();
16:
17:        private DatabaseHelper mDbHelper;
18:        SQLiteDatabase mDb;
19:
20:        public static final String KEY_ROWID = "_id";
21:        public static final String NAME = "name";
22:        public static final String DESCRIPTION = "description";
23:        public static final String PRICE = "price";
24:        public static final String FAVORITE = "favorite";
25:
26:        public static final String[] PIE_FIELDS = new String[] {
27:                KEY_ROWID,
28:                NAME,
29:                DESCRIPTION,
30:                PRICE,
31:                FAVORITE
32:        };
```

Listing 16.3 creates a `String` called `CREATE_TABLE_PIE` that specifies the SQL statement to create a new table. The table `PIE_TABLE` is created, and the column `_id` is defined as an integer
primary key that will autoincrement. A field called `_id` is required when working with certain
classes such as the `CursorAdapter` class. You use a `CursorAdapter` later in this hour.

LISTING 16.3   **PieDbAdapter Table Definition**

```
1:    private static final String CREATE_TABLE_PIE =
2:            "create table " + PIE_TABLE +"("
3:                    + KEY_ROWID + " INTEGER PRIMARY KEY AUTOINCREMENT,"
4:                    + NAME + " not null UNIQUE,"
5:                    + DESCRIPTION +" text,"
6:                    + PRICE + " REAL,"
7:                    + FAVORITE + " INTEGER"
8:                    +");";
```

In Listing 16.4, the static class `DatabaseHelper` is defined as an inner class of `PieDbAdapter`.
It is an extension of the `SQLiteOpenHelper` class. The constructor for `DatabaseHelper`
defined on line 3 calls the `super()` method with the parameters `context`, `DATABASE_NAME`,

null, and DATABASE_VERSION. DATABASE_NAME and DATABASE_VERSION were defined in Listing 16.2.

DATABASE_VERSION represents the current version of the database. The version number can start at 1. If the DATABASE_VERSION in the constructor is larger than the current database version, the onUpgrade() method is called. The onUpgrade() method on lines 10 to 15 drops the existing database table and makes a call to onCreate().

The onCreate() method defined on lines 6 to 9 defines the database with a call to db. execSQL().

The CREATE_TABLE_PIE field passed as a parameter to onCreate() was defined in Listing 16.3. It defines to create the table in the database.

Overall, the purpose of Listing 16.4 is to create or upgrade a SQLite database. A database name and version number are required.

LISTING 16.4 PieDbAdapter DatabaseHelper

```
 1:    private static class DatabaseHelper extends SQLiteOpenHelper {
 2:        DatabaseHelper(Context context) {
 3:            super(context, DATABASE_NAME, null, DATABASE_VERSION);
 4:        }
 5:        @Override
 6:        public void onCreate(SQLiteDatabase db) {
 7:            db.execSQL(CREATE_TABLE_PIE);
 8:        }
 9:        @Override
10:        public void onUpgrade(SQLiteDatabase db, int oldVersion, int newVersion) {
11:            Log.w(TAG, "Upgrading database from version " + oldVersion + " to "
12:                    + newVersion + ", which will destroy all old data");
13:            db.execSQL("DROP TABLE IF EXISTS " + PIE_TABLE );
14:            onCreate(db);
15:        }
16:    }
```

When you use the PieDbAdapter class, you will declare it, open it, and close it. Those methods are defined in Listing 16.5 and provide a way to manage the internal DatabaseHelper and Database classes.

When a call is made to the open() method, a new DatabaseHelper class is instantiated. That creates a database if needed and upgrades the database if the version number has been increased. On line 7, a call is made to the getWritableDatabase() method of the SQLiteOpenHelper class. That returns a SQLiteDatabase object that is ready for reading and writing data. The database must be closed after it is opened and that is done on line 23 with a call to the `close()` method. A `Context` is passed to the `DatabaseHelper` class. In the constructor on lines 1–3, a `Context` is passed as a parameter.

LISTING 16.5   PieDbAdapter Open, Close, Upgrade

```
 1:   public PieDbAdapter(Context ctx) {
 2:         this.mCtx = ctx;
 3:      }
 4:
 5:      public PieDbAdapter open() throws SQLException {
 6:         mDbHelper = new DatabaseHelper(mCtx);
 7:         mDb = mDbHelper.getWritableDatabase();
 8:         return this;
 9:      }
10:      public void close() {
11:         if(mDbHelper!=null){
12:            mDbHelper.close();
13:         }
14:      }
15:      public void upgrade() throws SQLException {
16:         mDbHelper = new DatabaseHelper(mCtx); //open
17:         mDb = mDbHelper.getWritableDatabase();
18:         mDbHelper.onUpgrade(mDb, 1, 0);
19:      }
```

Adding, Deleting, and Updating Data

So far in this hour, you have focused on the structure of the database. You have defined a table and set up a way to open and close the database. With that done, you now focus on getting `Pie` objects into the database and learn how to update and delete entire rows.

Listing 16.6 shows the classes that insert, update, and delete data from the database. Each uses the `mDb` field, which was declared as type `SQLiteDatabase`. The respective calls are insert, update, and delete.

When working with a `SQLiteDatabase`, the `ContentValues` are used to tie column names to values to be loaded into the database. `ContentValues` are needed for the insert and update database methods.

LISTING 16.6   PieDbAdapter Insert, Update, Delete

```
 1:    public  long insertPie(ContentValues initialValues) {
 2:         return mDb.insertWithOnConflict (PIE_TABLE, null,
 3:             initialValues, SQLiteDatabase.CONFLICT_IGNORE);
 4:      }
```

```
 5:
 6:    public boolean updatePie(int id, ContentValues newValues) {
 7:        String[] selectionArgs = {String.valueOf(id)};
 8:        return mDb.update(PIE_TABLE, newValues, KEY_ROWID + "=?", selectionArgs
) > 0;
 9:    }
10:
11:    public boolean deletePie(int id) {
12:        String[] selectionArgs = {String.valueOf(id)};
13:        return mDb.delete(PIE_TABLE,  KEY_ROWID + "=?",selectionArgs ) > 0;
14:    }
```

There are different ways to insert data into the database. In this case, on line 2, you use the `insertWithOnConflict()` method. That allows you to control what happens if there is a conflict in the database, such as inserting the same data. The final parameter `SQLiteDatabase.CONFLICT_IGNORE` indicates that conflicts should be ignored. By doing that, you can consider this something like an insert or update method. In other cases, you might want to check whether you are adding a completely new row or updating an existing one.

If the insert is successful, the returned value will be the row `id` of the new pie record. If there is an error, –1 is returned

The method used to update data in the database is similar to inserting, but there are two key differences. For an update, you need to identify the row that you want to update. That is not required for an insert. An insert creates a completely new record in the database. An update updates an existing record.

Deleting a row is similar to updating a row. You identify the row to delete and call the appropriate database method. You identify the row to delete based on the passed `id` matching the `KEY_ROWID` in the table.

The query to identify which rows to update or delete is called the *where clause*.

Querying Data and Using Cursors

In this hour, you have used a `where` clause to identify records to update or delete. The `where` clause is key to constructing a SQL statement to retrieve data from a database.

After specifying the data to retrieve from the database, you need a way to work with the returned data. For example, if a query result includes 100 pies, you need a way to both iterate through the results and to work with a specific row of data. Cursors are used for this purpose. If you consider the result set of our query to be a list of data rows, the cursor acts a pointer to a specific row.

To be precise, the return value of a query is a cursor. You work with that cursor to get specific data.

A cursor includes the methods moveToFirst(), moveToNext(), moveToPrevious(), moveToPosition(), and moveToLast(). These methods provide ways to move through the cursor to retrieve data.

Defining a Query

Listing 16.7 shows the getPies() method. This method retrieves all the pies and returns a Cursor.

The query is done on line 2 of Listing 16.7. You pass the first two parameters of the query method and leave the remainder as nulls. The passed parameters are table and columns. The table parameter is set to DATABASE_TABLE, and the columns parameter is set to PIE_FIELDS. These parameters specify the table to use and the columns that should be returned from that table. The columns to be returned is known as the *projection*.

LISTING 16.7   PieDbAdapter Retrieving Data

```
1:    public Cursor getPies() {
2:        return mDb.query(PIE_TABLE, PIE_FIELDS, null, null, null, null, null);
3:    }
4:
5:    public static Pie getPieFromCursor(Cursor cursor){
6:        Pie pie = new Pie();
7:        pie.mId = cursor.getInt(cursor.getColumnIndex(KEY_ROWID));
8:        pie.mName = cursor.getString(cursor.getColumnIndex(NAME));
9:        pie.mDescription = cursor.getString(cursor.getColumnIndex(DESCRIPTION));
10:       pie.mPrice = cursor.getDouble(cursor.getColumnIndex(PRICE));
11:       pie.mIsFavorite = (cursor.getInt(cursor.getColumnIndex(FAVORITE)) == 1);
12:       return(pie);
13:    }
14:}
```

The next parameter is selection, and it is a where clause. Because it is set to null, all values will be returned.

The remaining arguments to the query are selectionArgs, groupBy, having, orderBy, and limit. These are all options supported in complex queries in SQLite databases.

When querying a database, you often want to specify the order in which the data is returned. If you have a database of people, you might want to order the data by last name. You use the orderBy parameter to specify a column in the database for ordering data. If you have a row with both a `firstName` column and a `lastName` column, you can set the order by `firstName` or `lastName` in ascending or descending order.

Rows are sorted in ascending order by default. To change that to descending order, you use `DESC`. To get favorite pies by the order of the names in descending order, we would use this query:

```
mDb.query(true, DATABASE_TABLE, PIE_FIELDS, FAVORITE +" =1", null,
        null, null, NAME +" DESC", null);
```

`Limit` specifies the limit on the number of rows to return. For complex queries, `selectionArgs` can be used as replacement values in the selection statement. That is done in the update and delete methods in Listing 16.6.

The `groupBy` and `having` parameters perform `SQL GROUP BY` and `SQL HAVING` clauses. A `GROUP BY` clause is useful when combining data. For example, you may have a database that includes multiple orders placed by customers. Customers can repeat in the rows in that database, so `GROUP BY` provides a way to group the orders by a customer. The `HAVING` clause acts like a `where` clause for the `GROUP BY` clause. That is, the `HAVING` clause sets the criteria for the `GROUP BY`.

Getting an Object from a Cursor

In Listing 16.7, lines 5–13 define the `getPieFromCursor()` method. This method returns a `Pie` object when passed a cursor. To accomplish that, two methods from the `Cursor` class are used for each field that is to be retrieved.

The method `getColumnIndex()` is used to get a column number based on the name of the column. Then a call is made to get the value associated with that column. On line 8, the call is `cursor.getString()`. On line 10, the call is `cursor.getDouble()`. The field to populate on line 11 for `isFavorite` is a Boolean. In the database, a 1 represents true, and 0 represents false. On line 11, the Boolean field is populated by comparing the value in the database to 1 and returning the result. If the value in the database is 1, true is returned.

This technique assumes you know the names of the columns in the database and how they correspond to the `Pie` object class.

The `Pie` object `pie` is defined on line 6. Each field in that object is populated from a value in the cursor. Ultimately, `Pie` is returned so that it can be used in the app.

Using a Database in the App

Listing 16.8 shows an activity that writes to and reads from the database using the `PieDbAdapter`. It is a simple demo activity. In a production app, it would be unlikely for you to populate your database in the onCreate() method of an activity. A lot of work goes into creating a class like PieDbAdapter, and this is a way to test it.

Using PieDbAdapter

In line 17 of Listing 16.8, the Pie method makePies() is called. That will create a small set of test data.

A PieDbAdapter is declared and opened on lines 18–19.

In line 21, a new ContentValues is declared.

Lines 22–25 populate the ContentValues with data from the pie array.

The ContentValues are used to insert into the database on line 26.

Line 29 defines a cursor that contains all of the pies, and lines 31–37 iterate through the cursor. The data from each pie is added to a StringBuilder.

Lines 38–39 close the cursor and PieDbAdapter. The results are displayed in the TextView on line 40.

Running the activity in Listing 16.8 shows the values that were read from the database.

LISTING 16.8   DatabaseActivity for Loading Data Retrieving Data

```
 1:   package com.talkingandroid.hour16application;
 2:   import android.app.Activity;
 3:   import android.content.ContentValues;
 4:   import android.database.Cursor;
 5:   import android.os.Bundle;
 6:   import android.widget.TextView;
 7:   import java.util.ArrayList;
 8:
 9:   public class DatabaseActivity extends Activity {
10:       TextView textView;
11:       @Override
12:       protected void onCreate(Bundle savedInstanceState) {
13:           super.onCreate(savedInstanceState);
14:           setContentView(R.layout.activity_database);
15:           textView = (TextView) findViewById(R.id.textView);
16:
17:           ArrayList<Pie> pies = Pie.makePies();
18:           PieDbAdapter pieDbAdapter = new PieDbAdapter(this);
19:           pieDbAdapter.open();
20:           for (Pie pie: pies){
21:               ContentValues newValues = new ContentValues();
22:               newValues.put(PieDbAdapter.NAME, pie.mName);
23:               newValues.put(PieDbAdapter.DESCRIPTION, pie.mDescription);
```

```
24:                newValues.put(PieDbAdapter.PRICE, pie.mPrice);
25:                newValues.put(PieDbAdapter.FAVORITE, pie.mIsFavorite);
26:                pieDbAdapter.insertPie(newValues);
27:            }
28:
29:            Cursor pieCursor = pieDbAdapter.getPies();
30:            StringBuilder results = new StringBuilder();
31:            if (pieCursor.moveToFirst()){
32:                do{
33:                    Pie pie =  pieDbAdapter.getPieFromCursor(pieCursor);
34:                    results.append(pie.mId + " " + pie.mName + " " + pie.mPrice +
" "
35:                        + pie.mDescription + " " + pie.mIsFavorite +"\n");
36:                } while (pieCursor.moveToNext());
37:            }
38:            pieCursor.close();
39:        pieDbAdapter.close();
40:        textView.setText(results.toString());
41:    }
42: }
```

TRY IT YOURSELF ▼

Adding a New Field to the Pie Class and Database

There will be a time when you need to update your database. A typical scenario is to add a new field. Follow these steps to add a new field and update the database:

1. Add a new double field to the Pie class called `mSalePrice`.

2. The initial sale price for all pies should be 1.

3. Change the database to include this field and note where changes are required.

4. Upgrade the database version and run the test app.

Using a SimpleCursorAdapter to Display Data

Once the data is stored in the database, you can use it directly in another activity.

In Listing 16.9, an activity is created that reads from the database to display a list of names in a list view. The listing uses a `Cursor`, `PieDbAdapter`, and a `SimpleCursorAdapter` to retrieve and display the data.

The steps are as follows:

1. Create a `PieDbAdapter` and open it.

2. Use a cursor to get the pies from the database.

3. Set up the `SimpleCursorAdapter` to display photo titles.

4. Use the `SimpleCursorAdapter` to display the pie titles in the list.

LISTING 16.9   Using and Displaying Data

```
1:  package com.talkingandroid.hour16application;
2:  import android.app.Activity;
3:  import android.database.Cursor;
4:  import android.os.Bundle;
5:  import android.widget.ListView;
6:  import android.widget.SimpleCursorAdapter;
7:
8:  public class ShowPiesActivity extends Activity {
9:       ListView listView;
10:      PieDbAdapter pieDbAdapter;
11:      Cursor cursor;
12:      SimpleCursorAdapter adapter;
13:
14:      @Override
15:      protected void onCreate(Bundle savedInstanceState) {
16:          super.onCreate(savedInstanceState);
17:          setContentView(R.layout.activity_show_pies);
18:          listView = (ListView) findViewById(R.id.pieListView);
19:          pieDbAdapter = new PieDbAdapter(this);
20:          pieDbAdapter.open();
31:          cursor = pieDbAdapter.getPies();
32:          adapter = new SimpleCursorAdapter(this,
33:                  android.R.layout.simple_list_item_1,
34:                  cursor, //Cursor
35:                  new String[] {PieDbAdapter.NAME},
36:                  new int[] { android.R.id.text1 }, 0);
37:          listView.setAdapter(adapter);
38:      }
39:      @Override
40:      public void onDestroy(){
41:          if (cursor!=null){
42:              cursor.close();
43:          }
44:          if (pieDbAdapter!=null){
```

```
45:                    pieDbAdapter.close();
46:                }
47:          }
48:    }
```

On lines 19 and 20 in Listing 16.9, the `PieDbAdapter` is declared and opened. The cursor is populated on line 31. The method `getPies()` gets all available pies.

Lines 32–36 define the `SimpleCursorAdapter` adapter. On line 33, a predefined Android layout is used to display the contents of the cursor. The cursor is the second parameter. Line 35 represents the columns from the cursor from which data should be retrieved. We want the `NAME` column. On line 36, you pass the `id` of the resource that you are populating. In the Android layout, that is `Android.r.id.text1`. That last parameter is a flag for how the `SimpleCursorAdapter` should be behave. We leave this a `0` for now, for no special functionality.

When you call the `listView.setAdapter(adapter)` method on line 12, the association is made between the cursor and the `ListView`. The names of the pies are displayed. Figure 16.1 shows the result.

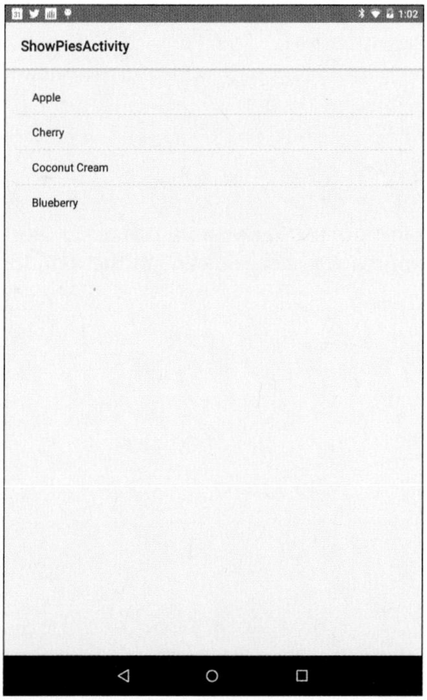

FIGURE 16.1
Displaying data using `SimpleCursorAdapter`.

In Listing 16.9, you created a cursor and called `open()` for `PieDbAdapter`. The `PieDbAdapter` and the cursor must be closed. That is done on the `onDestroy()` method on lines 39–46. That is an example of using the activity lifecycle.

▼ TRY IT YOURSELF

Creating a Query

You use the database to make queries to get the data you need for your app. These are the steps to create a new query and display the data:

1. Add a query to `pieDbAdapter` to return pies that cost more than $1.

2. Use that query to load the pie list using a `SimpleCursorAdapter`.

Summary

In this hour, you covered the basic functionality of a SQLite database. You inserted and updated records into a SQLite database. To accomplish that, you used the `PieDbAdapter` class for the opening and closing of the database and for common queries. You gained an understanding of `Cursors` and how to use them in apps using `SimpleCursorAdapter`.

Q&A

Q. How is a `Cursor` related to a query?

A. A `Cursor` is what is returned from a query. You can think of a `Cursor` as a pointer to the list of results. You can iterate through the entire list of results, and you can get the data for a specific result.

Workshop

Quiz

1. How is `DESC` used??

2. What type of objects are returned by queries?

3. Is the field `_id` required to define a table?

Answers

1. DESC is used in an ORDER BY clause to indicate descending order.

2. Cursors are returned by queries.

3. The field _id is not required to define a table, but it is needed when working with other Android classes like CursorAdapter.

Exercise

Implement an ORDER BY clause in a query in the app. Verify the results by seeing the order of the names change. Change the order by direction from DESC to ASC and verify that the opposite result is achieved.

Accessing the Cloud: Working with a Remote API

What You'll Learn in This Hour:

▶ Fetching remote data

▶ Parsing JSON-formatted data

▶ Putting the pieces together to create a simple app

▶ Checking the connection

In this hour, you learn about accessing remote data. You develop an app that communicates with a remote application programming interface (API). The data from the API will be used and displayed in the app. You communicate with Flickr's API to get a list of recent public photos. In this hour, you show the titles of available photos in a `ListFragment`. Over the next several hours in this book, you add more features, including displaying photos in a list and a grid and selecting a photo to display. To do this, you need to retrieve remote images and display them locally. As you continue, you use this app to demonstrate additional Android features, such as a local database, using content providers, and using cursor loaders. It all starts with accessing and displaying remote data.

NOTE

What's an API?

API stands for *application programming interface*. An API defines how separate software components communicate with each other. API is not a new term. Much of the data and content that is available on the web is made available via APIs. Companies see the value in having developers use their APIs to create new API-based apps and products. The site http://www.programmableweb.com/ lists more than 9,000 available APIs.

Fetching Remote Data

You may be developing for a phone, tablet, or even a TV. To fetch remote data, your device must be connected to the Internet. The app may be connecting over a wireless network or through a phone's mobile network. Your app should check to see whether a network connection is available.

With a connected device, you can use existing APIs for data access. You are using HTTP-based APIs. HTTP stands for *Hypertext Transfer Protocol*. It is the data transfer protocol used on the World Wide Web.

Common data formats for these APIs are XML and JSON. Using the Flickr API, you'll focus on retrieving and parsing JSON data for your app. XML and JSON are both text-based standards for data exchange. XML is used internally for Android for layout files and other resource files. XML is often supported in HTTP-based APIs, but JSON is less verbose and is very common.

For our app to access data over from the Internet, you need to set the Internet permission in the manifest file (AndroidManifest.xml), as follows:

```
<uses-permission android:name="android.permission.INTERNET"></uses-permission>
```

Our data source will be Flickr, the popular photo site from Yahoo!. Many Flickr API calls require the user to be logged in. You'll use an API call that does not require authentication. That allows us to focus on retrieving and parsing the data.

▼ TRY IT YOURSELF

Signing Up as a Developer and Creating a Flickr API Key

APIs provide a great opportunity to interact with third-party services. In most cases, you must sign up for the service and create an API key to use in your app. Follow these steps to do that on Flickr:

1. Sign up for Flickr at https://www.flickr.com/.

2. Go to the app garden at https://www.flickr.com/services/.

3. Choose Create an App.

4. Fill out the information requested to get an API key.

Making an API Call

Although you are using Flickr as an example, many services provide interesting and useful APIs. Part of the work in using an API is to understand how to make a call to retrieve the data and what parameters to pass.

An *endpoint* for an API is the URL your app will use to communicate with the API. The endpoint for the Flickr API is https://api.flickr.com/services.

Flickr has a feature called *API Explorer* that allows us to try an API call in a sandbox. The sandbox is a website where API calls can be entered and the results seen. If the API call is correct, data is returned and displayed on the web page. The sandbox is an area to safely test specific API calls and see the results.

TRY IT YOURSELF ▼

Using the Flickr Developer Sandbox

Companies like Flickr and Facebook often provide a web-based tool to try out API calls. That allows you to change parameters for the calls and check the results. This is how to try to get recent photos and API calls on Flickr:

1. Go to the Flickr API documentation at https://www.flickr.com/services/api/.

2. Choose an API call you are interested in and read the documentation. To get recent photos, go to https://www.flickr.com/services/api/flickr.photos.getRecent.html.

3. From the documentation page for the API call, choose API Explorer. You will go to https://www.flickr.com/services/api/explore/flickr.photos.getRecent.

4. Set the output for the API call to be JSON and call the method. The results of the call will be displayed.

By accessing the recent photo method via the API Explorer, you can see the data required for the call and the returned data. The API Explorer is found at http://www.flickr.com/services/api/explore/flickr.photos.getRecent.

Figure 17.1 shows the API Explorer page, and Figure 17.2 shows an example of the data returned in JSON format.

Retrieving Data with HttpUrlConnection

Our first goal is to make the data available at this URL available to our app. For that, you use the `HttpUrlConnection` (`java.net.HttpURLConnection`) class. This class is used to access data on a remote URL.

You have all gone to a web page and received a 404 error to indicate that the page was not found on the server. 404 is the response code, and many possible response codes convey the failure or success of retrieving data. A 200 response indicates success.

The current goal of the app is to retrieve the data from the Flickr recent photo service and display the list of titles from those photos. To do that, you will retrieve data from https://api.flickr.com/services/rest/?method=flickr.photos.getRecent.

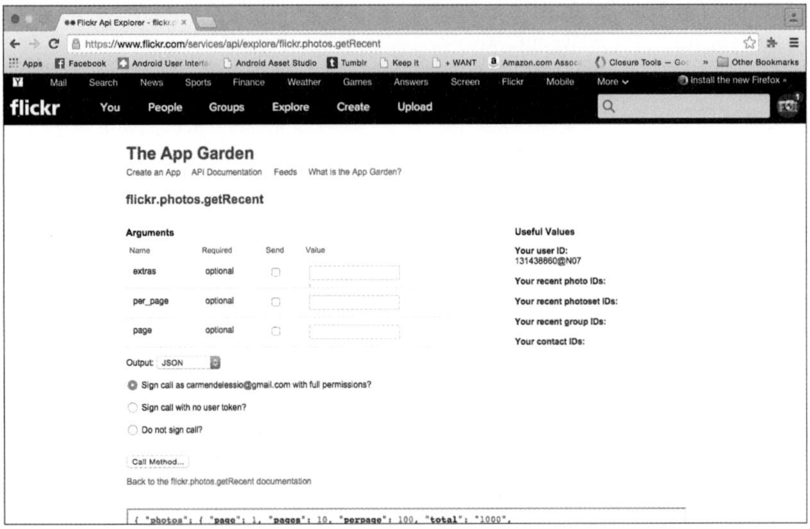

FIGURE 17.1
Flickr API Explorer page. Reproduced with permission of Yahoo!. ©2015 Yahoo!. FLICKR and the Flickr logo
are registered trademarks of Yahoo!.

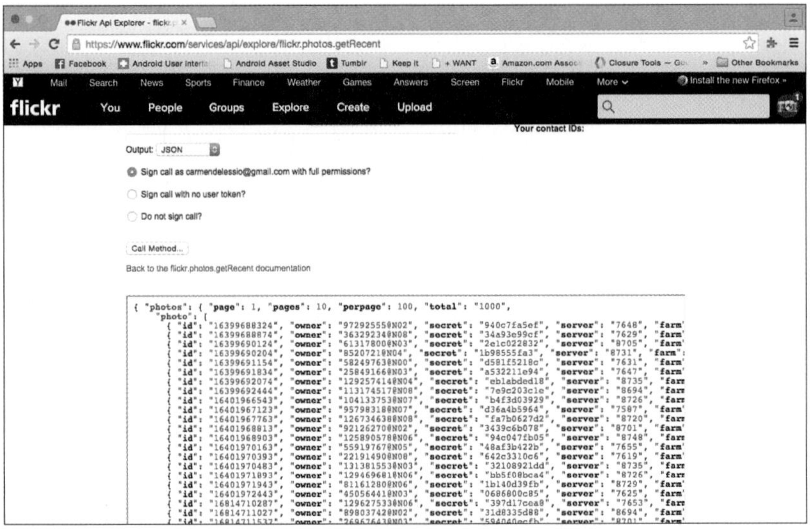

FIGURE 17.2
Flickr JSON results. Reproduced with permission of Yahoo!. ©2015 Yahoo!. FLICKR and the Flickr logo are
registered trademarks of Yahoo!.

You add additional parameters to specify your API key and the number of photos to return. You will also specify that the data should be returned as JSON and that there is no JSON callback. These parameters are shown at the bottom of your test call in the Flickr API Explorer:

```
https://api.flickr.com/services/rest/?method=flickr.photos.getRecent&api_key=12-
API_KEY_34&per_page=12&format=json&nojsoncallback=1
```

You'll use the `HttpUrlConnection` class to create an `InputStream`. You'll check the response code and then read from the `InputStream` into a `String`. First, you'll look at the snippet of code to do this; then you'll examine where it fits in with our activity and fragment structure.

The source files used in this project are MainActivity.java, PhotoListFragment.java, and FlickrPhoto.java. Full listings are at the end of the hour. First, you will examine specific sections of code.

In Listing 17.1, you create an `HttpUrlConnection` and connect to it in lines 1 to 9. In line 10, you get the response code, but for now you just log it. Lines 17 to 20 get the data from the connection as an `InputStream` and convert it to a string. Each line is read and appended to a `StringBuilder(java.lang.StringBuilder)`. Line 19 uses the `StringBuilder.toString()` method to place the complete downloaded message on the string photoData.

LISTING 17.1   Making an HttpUrlConnection Request and Response

```
1:   HttpURLConnection connection = null;
2:   try {
3:     URL dataUrl = new URL(
4:          https://api.flickr.com/services/rest/?method=flickr.photos.
getRecent&api_key=
5:          +  API_KEY
6:          + "&per_page=" = NUM_PHOTOS
7:          + "&format=json&nojsoncallback=1");
8:     connection = (HttpURLConnection) dataUrl.openConnection();
9:     connection.connect();
10:    int status = connection.getResponseCode();
11:    Log.d("connection", "status " + status);
17:    InputStream is = connection.getInputStream();
13:    BufferedReader reader = new BufferedReader(new InputStreamReader(is));
14:    String responseString;
15:    StringBuilder sb = new StringBuilder();
16:    while ((responseString = reader.readLine()) != null) {
17:      sb = sb.append(responseString);
18:    }
19:    String photoData = sb.toString();
20:    Log.d("connection", photoData);
21:  } catch (MalformedURLException e) {
```

The Structure of This App

This code appears in an `AsyncTask` in our activity. You are getting Flickr photo data in the background. Your current goal is to handle data retrieval and parsing. By doing that and displaying the titles of the photos in a list, you will have a good infrastructure in place for expanding on this app. You learned how to use an `AsyncTask` in Hour 5, "Responsive Apps: Running in the Background." In this case, you want to do the intense work of downloading and parsing the JSON data in the background. By doing these tasks in the background, the user interface stays responsive.

GO TO ▶ CHAPTER 5, "Responsive Apps: Running in the Background," to review how `AsyncTask` works.

To review the structure of the app:

1. The `Activity` downloads the data in the background.

2. You use an object called `FlickrPhoto` to store the data.

3. You add a method in `FlickrPhoto` to parse the data and return an `ArrayList`.

4. When the data is available, the `ListFragment` will be displayed.

5. The `ListFragment` will get the data from the `Activity`.

6. You display a list of titles using a `StringAdapter`, as you did in Hour 10, "More Views and Controls."

Using and Parsing JSON-Formatted Data

JSON stands for *JavaScript Object Notation*. JSON began as a subset of the JavaScript language in the late 1990s, but it is a language-independent format for passing structured data in a human readable format. Many web services offer JSON as their data format.

JSON data is based on name/value pairs. You see the name of a field paired with the value for that field.

Listing 17.2 shows a snippet of the data returned from Flickr API. The curly brackets indicate the data for one object.

LISTING 17.2   JSON Snippet for a Flickr Photo

```
{
    "id": "8565953275",
    "owner": "46752538@N04",
    "secret": "5f5a2335f5",
    "server": "8093",
```

```
    "farm": 9,
    "title": "Stargazing",
    "ispublic": 1,
    "isfriend": 0,
    "isfamily": 0
}
```

Creating a JSONObject

The Android platform includes a class to work with JSON called org.json.JSON. If you start with a String of data in JSON format, you can create a new JSONObject (org.json. JSONObject) by using the photoData string as the parameter to the constructor:

```
JSONObject data = new JSONObject(photoData);
```

After you have a JSONObject, you can reference individual fields within the object using the name that you know. For example, in Listing 17.2, the "id" field has the value "8565953275". You can use the getString() or optString() method of a JSONObject to read this value. The benefits of optString() is that no exception is thrown if the name you are seeking is not in the object; that is because the optString() returns a default value and getString() does not. You have the option to specify a second parameter in optString() to set your own default value. Given a JSONObject called data, you would read the value of id into a String by using the following:

```
String id=(String) data.optString("id");
```

NOTE

The JsonReader

In the API 11 Android release (Honeycomb), the class JsonReader was added. JsonReader makes it easier to parse JSON objects. In this hour, you use methods that work on all platforms. The JsonReader class reference is at http://developer.android.com/reference/android/util/JsonReader.html.

Using a JSONArray

JSON is considered a human-readable format. It is structured text. In JSON, a JSON array consists of an array of JSON objects. JSON arrays are surrounded by square brackets, []. The Flickr photo data is returned as a single JSON object that contains a JSON array of JSON objects.

In Android, the class to use with a JSON array is JSONArray(org.json.JSONArray).

As an example of a simple structure, Listing 17.3 shows a JSON object that contains a JSON array called data. Lines 2 and 9 begin and end the array.

LISTING 17.3   JSONArray Structure

```
1:  {
2:  data: [
3:    {
4:       id: "1"
5:    }
6:    {
7:     id: "2"
8:    }
9:  ]
10: }
```

Assume that you start out with a string called photoData that contains JSON formatted data like that in Listing 17.3. You will consider how to read this data into our Android app. Listing 17.4 loads the string into a JSONObject called data. In line 2, JSONArray photoArray is populated from the JSONObject. In lines 3 to 6, you ready each object from the JSONArray into a JSONObject and log the id field for that object.

LISTING 17.4   Reading a JSONArray

```
1:  JSONObject data = new JSONObject(photoData);
2:  JSONArray photoArray = data.optJSONArray("data");
3:  for(int i = 0; i < photoArray.length(); i++) {
4:    JSONObject photo= (JSONObject) photoArray.get(i);
5:    Log.d(TAG, photo.optString("id"));
6:  }
```

Parsing JSON

You will put together the info about the Flickr photo format, JSONObjects, and JSONArrays to create a new class called FlickrPhoto.java. The FlickrPhoto class contains the data that you care about from the Flickr photo data. You'll create a constructor that takes a JSONObject with photo data and loads our object. You'll also create a constructor that will take the full data that Flickr returns and create an array list of FlickrPhoto objects for use in the app.

Gson: Alternatives for Processing JSON Data

Gson is a library that will convert Java object to JSON. It will also convert JSON `Strings` to Java objects. You can use it in projects that handle JSON data. For more information, see https://code. google.com/p/google-gson/.

Listing 17.5 creates the `FlickrPhoto` class with nine fields, beginning with `id` and ending with the Boolean `isFamily`.

In lines 17–22, you define a constructor that creates a `FlickrPhoto` object from a `JSONObject`. Each field in the `FlickrPhoto` object is populated with a field from the `JSONObject`.

LISTING 17.5   Making FlickrPhoto Object from JSON

```
1:  public class FlickrPhoto extends Object{
2:      String id;
3:      String owner;
4:      String secret;
5:      String server;
6:      String farm;
7:      String title;
8:      Boolean isPublic;
9:      Boolean isFriend;
10:     Boolean isFamily;
11:
17:     public FlickrPhoto(JSONObject jsonPhoto) throws JSONException{
13:         this.id=(String) jsonPhoto.optString("id");
14:         this.secret=(String) jsonPhoto.optString("secret");
14:         this.owner=(String) jsonPhoto.optString("owner");
16:         this.server=(String) jsonPhoto.optString("server");
17:         this.farm=(String) jsonPhoto.optString("farm");
18:         this.title=(String) jsonPhoto.optString("title");
19:         this.isPublic=(Boolean) jsonPhoto.optBoolean("ispublic");
20:         this.isFriend=(Boolean) jsonPhoto.optBoolean("isfriend");
21:         this.isFamily=(Boolean) jsonPhoto.optBoolean("isfamily");
22:  } ...
```

The Flickr data includes a `JSONObject` called `photos`. The `photos` `JSONObject` contains a `JSONArray` of photo data called `photo`. The JSON string for this structure looks like this:

```
{ "photos": { "page": 1, "pages": 10, "perpage": 100, "total": "1000",
    "photo": [
      { ...
```

This is also shown in Figure 17.2.

The method `makePhotoList()` shown in Listing 17.6 is a method in the `FlickrPhoto` class. When passed a JSON `String` containing Flickr data, the `makePhotoList()` method returns an `ArrayList` of `FlickrPhotoObjects`.

LISTING 17.6   Making a FlickrPhoto ArrayList from a JSON String

```
1:   public static ArrayList <FlickrPhoto> makePhotoList (String photoData )
2:                        throws JSONException, NullPointerException {
3:      ArrayList <FlickrPhoto> flickrPhotos = new ArrayList<FlickrPhoto>();
4:      JSONObject data  = new JSONObject(photoData);
5:      JSONObject photos = data.optJSONObject("photos");
6:      JSONArray photoArray = photos.optJSONArray("photo");
7:      for(int i = 0; i < photoArray.length(); i++) {
8:        JSONObject photo=    (JSONObject) photoArray.get(i);
9:        FlickrPhoto currentPhoto = new FlickrPhoto (photo);
10:       flickrPhotos.add(currentPhoto);
11:    }
17:    return flickrPhotos;
13:}
```

Line 8 reads a `JSONObject` from the `JSONArray`. In line 9, you use the `JSONObject` to create a new `FlickrPhoto` object called `currentPhoto`. In line 10, you add that to an `ArrayList` of `FlickrPhotos` that you declared earlier on line 3.

When you receive the data as a string from the Flickr API, you pass that string to this method and get a list of objects back.

Putting the Pieces Together

The pieces to make our app are the Activity, the `FlickrPhoto` object, and a `ListFragment` to show the list of photo titles returned from Flickr.

In the activity, you use an `AsyncTask` that retrieves data from Flickr. After you have the data, you show a `ListFragment`. For this example, you retrieve the data in the activity and display it in the fragment. To keep it simple, you add a method to the activity called `getPhotos()`. The fragment calls `getPhotos()` to access the data that was retrieved. The data is an `ArrayList` of `FlickrPhoto` objects. To keep things even simpler, for now you will take the titles from the `FlickrPhoto` objects and load them into a string array. Then you can display the titles using a simple `ArrayAdapter(android.widget.ArrayAdapter)`. Over the course of the next several hours in this book, you create a custom adapter and expand on this work.

The outline for the app functionality is as follows:

- ▶ **Activity:** MainActivity.java

  Show ProgressBar.

  In OnCreate() method, call the LoadPhotos AsyncTask to load data.

- ▶ **AsyncTask:** MainActivty.LoadPhotos

  Retrieve data.

  Hide the ProgressBar.

  Show the ListFragment.

- ▶ **ListFragment:** PhotoListFragment

  Get the FlickrPhoto list from the Activity.

  Display titles only.

Downloading in the Background with AsyncTask

An AsyncTask includes a doInBackground() method for background process and an onPostExecute() method to take action when the doInBackground() method completes. You'll download and parse Flickr photo data in the doInBackground() method and then show the PhotoListFragment by calling showList() in the onPostExecute() method.

The LoadPhotos class is defined in MainActivity.java using the following:

```
private class LoadPhotos extends AsyncTask<String , String , Long > {
```

Listing 17.7 shows the doInBackground() method for the LoadPhotos AsyncTask. In lines 5–7, the URL to fetch Flickr data is built by creating a string. API_KEY and NUM_PHOTOS are static string variables that are defined in the MainActivity class.

In lines 8–17, a connection is made and the response code is retrieved. If the response code is 200, indicating success, an inputStream is used to read data from the connections. In lines 13–20, the data is read using a BufferedReader. The data is read line by line and appended using the append() method of the StringBuffer.

In line 20, a string is created from the StringBuffer. That string contains the complete data from Flickr in JSON format. In line 21, you use that photoData string to create an ArrayList of FlickrPhoto objects by calling FlickrPhoto.makePhotoList(photoData).

LISTING 17.7   LoadPhotos AsyncTask doInBackground()

```
1:   @Override
2:     protected Long doInBackground(String... params) {
3:        HttpURLConnection connection = null;
4:        try {
5:           URL dataUrl = new URL (
6:           "https://api.flickr.com/services/rest/
?method=flickr.photos.getRecent&api_key="
7:           + API_KEY + "&per_page=" + NUM_PHOTOS +"&format=json&nojsoncallback=1");
8:           connection = (HttpURLConnection) dataUrl.openConnection();
9:           connection.connect();
10:          int status = connection.getResponseCode();
11:          Log.d("connection", "status " + status);
17:          if (status ==200){ //success
13:             InputStream is = connection.getInputStream();
14:             BufferedReader reader = new BufferedReader(new InputStreamReader(is));
15:             String responseString;
16:             StringBuilder sb = new StringBuilder();
17:             while ((responseString = reader.readLine()) != null) {
18:                sb = sb.append(responseString);
19:             }
20:             String photoData = sb.toString();
21:             mPhotos = FlickrPhoto.makePhotoList(photoData);
22:             Log.d("connection", photoData);
23:             return (0l);
24:          }else{
25:             return (1l);
26:          }
27:       } catch (MalformedURLException e) { ...
```

When successful, a 0 is returned from the doInBackground() method. A 1 is returned
for all errors. That return value is used in the onPostExecute() method. The entire
onPostExecute() method is shown in Listing 17.8. If successful, the showList() method is
called.

LISTING 17.8   LoadPhotos AsyncTask onPostExecute()

```
@Override
protected void onPostExecute(Long result) {
   if (result==0){
     showList();
   }else{
     Toast.makeText(MainActivity.this.getApplicationContext(),
     "Something went wrong",   Toast.LENGTH_SHORT).show();
   }
   mProgressBar.setVisibility(View.GONE);
}
```

Displaying the List in a Fragment

The display of the list of titles from the Flickr data is straightforward, but several steps are involved:

▶ The onPostExecute() method calls the showList() method of MainActivity.

▶ ShowList() declares and displays a PhotoListFragment.

▶ The PhotoListFragment gets the ArrayList of FlickrPhoto objects from the Activity.

▶ To keep things simple, the photo titles are loaded into a StringArray.

▶ The list of titles is displayed in the list.

The showList() method loads a PhotoListFragment using a FragmentTransaction. It is the same method that you used previously.

The PhotoListFragment itself is similar to the SimpleListFragment that you created in Hour 10, "More Views and Controls." In Hour 10, you read the data to display from an array that was defined as a resource. The PhotoListFragment calls the getPhotos() method from MainActivity. That method returns an ArrayList of FlickrPhoto objects. For now, you read those objects and load an array of strings. That string array is used for an ArrayAdapter, and the list is displayed.

Listing 17.9 shows this code for the PhotoListFragment. Lines 6 and 7 get the current activity, cast it to MainActivity, and call the getPhotos(). That gives us the Flickr data to work with. In lines 9–11, you populate the string array mTitles. Now you can use that array to display the data using an ArrayAdapter. Figure 17.3 shows the result.

LISTING 17.9 PhotoListFragment

```
1:  package com.talkingandroid.hour17application;
2:  import java.util.ArrayList;
3:  import android.app.ListFragment;
4:  import android.os.Bundle;
5:  import android.widget.ArrayAdapter;
6:  public class PhotoListFragment extends ListFragment    {
7:     String[] mTitles;
8:     @Override
9:     public void onActivityCreated(Bundle savedInstanceState) {
10:       super.onActivityCreated(savedInstanceState);
11:       MainActivity currentActivity = (MainActivity) this.getActivity();
12:       ArrayList <FlickrPhoto> photos = currentActivity.getPhotos();
13:       mTitles = new String[photos.size()];
14:       for (int i=0; i < photos.size(); i++){
```

```
15:        mTitles[i] =photos.get(i).title;
16:     }
17:     setListAdapter(new ArrayAdapter<String>(this.getActivity(),
18:     android.R.layout.simple_list_item_1, mTitles));
19:   }
20: }
```

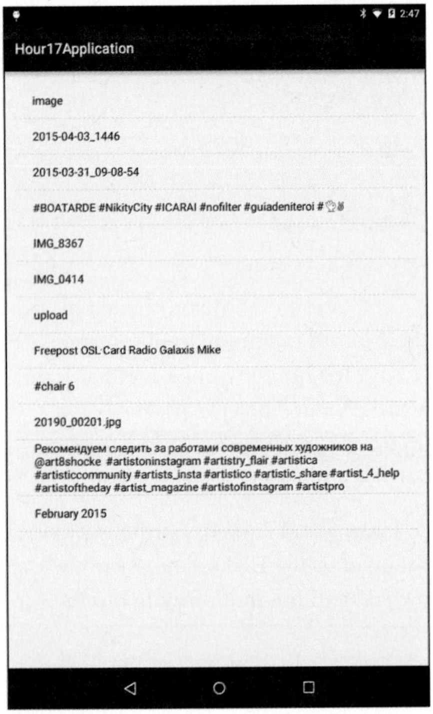

FIGURE 17.3
Displaying titles of recent Flickr photos.

Checking Connectivity

In an app that retrieves remote data, you want to ensure that you have a network connection. Android provides the ConnectivityManager (android.net.ConnectivityManager) class to provide information about the network. The ConnectivityManager has a method called getActiveNetworkInfo() that will tell us whether you are online.

Listing 17.10 shows a simple method for checking online status.

LISTING 17.10   Checking for Connectivity

```
1:  public boolean isOn line() {
2:      ConnectivityManager connectivityManager = (ConnectivityManager)
3:              getSystemService(Context.CONNECTIVITY_SERVICE);
4:      NetworkInfo networkInfo = connectivityManager.getActiveNetworkInfo();
5:      return (networkInfo != null && networkInfo.isConnected());
6:  }
```

You can use this in `MainActivity` `onCreate()` method to check for connectivity before you try to retrieve data. Listing 17.11 shows the online check. If you are online, the `LoadPhotos` `AsyncTask` is executed; if not, a `Toast` message is displayed.

LISTING 17.11   Using the Online Check

```
1:  if (isOn line()){
2:    LoadPhotos task = new LoadPhotos();
3:    task.execute();
4:  }else{
5:    mProgressBar.setVisibility(View.GONE);
6:    Toast.makeText(MainActivity.this.getApplicationContext(),
7:        "Please connect to retrieve photos",
8:         Toast.LENGTH_SHORT).show();
9:  }
```

To check for online status, the Android permission must be properly set in the AndroidManifest.xml file. The permission required is `ACCESS_NETWORK_STATE`:

```
<uses-permission android:name="android.permission.ACCESS_NETWORK_STATE" />
```

For completeness and to show the code in context, the complete MainActivity.java code, including the `AsyncTask` class `LoadPhotos`, is shown:

```
package com.talkingandroid.hour17application;
import android.app.FragmentTransaction;
import android.net.ConnectivityManager;
import android.net.NetworkInfo;
import android.os.AsyncTask;
import android.support.v7.app.ActionBarActivity;
import android.os.Bundle;
import android.util.Log;
import android.view.View;
import android.widget.ProgressBar;
import android.widget.Toast;
import org.json.JSONException;
import java.io.BufferedReader;
import java.io.IOException;
```

```java
import java.io.InputStream;
import java.io.InputStreamReader;
import java.net.HttpURLConnection;
import java.net.MalformedURLException;
import java.net.URL;
import java.util.ArrayList;

public class MainActivity extends ActionBarActivity {
    ProgressBar mProgressBar;
    private ArrayList<FlickrPhoto> mPhotos = new ArrayList<FlickrPhoto>();
    public final static String API_KEY ="PUT_YOUR_API_KEY_HERE";
    public final static String NUM_PHOTOS ="12";

    @Override
    protected void onCreate(Bundle savedInstanceState) {
        super.onCreate(savedInstanceState);
        setContentView(R.layout.activity_main);
        mProgressBar = (ProgressBar) findViewById(R.id.progressBar1);
        if (isOn line()){
            LoadPhotos task = new LoadPhotos();
            task.execute();
        }else{
            mProgressBar.setVisibility(View.GONE);
            Toast.makeText(MainActivity.this.getApplicationContext(),
                        "Please connect to retrieve photos",
                        Toast.LENGTH_SHORT).show();
        }
    }

    public ArrayList<FlickrPhoto> getPhotos() {
        return mPhotos;
    }

    public boolean isOn line() {
        ConnectivityManager connectivityManager = (ConnectivityManager)
                getSystemService(this.CONNECTIVITY_SERVICE);
        NetworkInfo networkInfo = connectivityManager.getActiveNetworkInfo();
        return (networkInfo != null && networkInfo.isConnected());
    }


    public void showList(){
        PhotoListFragment photoListFragment = new PhotoListFragment();
        FragmentTransaction ft = getFragmentManager().beginTransaction();
        ft.replace(R.id.layout_container, photoListFragment);
        ft.setTransition(FragmentTransaction.TRANSIT_FRAGMENT_FADE);
        ft.commit();
    }
```

```java
private class LoadPhotos extends AsyncTask<String , String , Long > {
    @Override
    protected void onPreExecute() {
    }

    @Override
    protected void onPostExecute(Long result) {
        if (result==0){
            showList();
        }else{
            Toast.makeText(MainActivity.this.getApplicationContext(),
                "Something went wrong",
                 Toast.LENGTH_SHORT).show();
        }
        mProgressBar.setVisibility(View.GONE);
    }

    @Override
    protected Long doInBackground(String... params) {
        HttpURLConnection connection = null;
        try {
            URL dataUrl = new URL(
            "https://api.flickr.com/services/rest/
?method=flickr.photos.getRecent&api_key="
                + API_KEY + "&per_page="
                + NUM_PHOTOS
                + "&format=json&nojsoncallback=1");
            connection = (HttpURLConnection) dataUrl.openConnection();
            connection.connect();
            int status = connection.getResponseCode();


            if (status ==200){
                InputStream is = connection.getInputStream();
                BufferedReader reader = new BufferedReader(new
InputStreamReader(is));
                String responseString;
                StringBuilder sb = new StringBuilder();
                while ((responseString = reader.readLine()) != null) {
                    sb = sb.append(responseString);
                }
                String photoData = sb.toString();
                Log.d("PHOTOS", photoData);
                mPhotos = FlickrPhoto.makePhotoList(photoData);
                return (0l);
            }else{
                return (1l);
            }
```

```
        } catch (MalformedURLException e) {
            e.printStackTrace();
            return (11);
        }
        catch (IOException e) {
            e.printStackTrace();
            return (11);
        } catch (NullPointerException e) {
            e.printStackTrace();
            return (11);
        } catch (JSONException e) {
            e.printStackTrace();
            return (11);
        } finally {
            connection.disconnect();
        }
    }
  }
}
```

NOTE

Working with XML

In this hour, you worked with JSON data. It is also common for remote data to be in XML format. Android provides several ways to parse XML data include SAX and Dom parser. Android also provides an interface called XMLPullParser for working with XML. See http://developer.android.com/reference/org/xmlpull/v1/XmlPullParser.html.

Summary

To work with remote data, you built a simple app that retrieves data about recently posted photos on Flickr. In the app, you displayed the titles of the photos using techniques from earlier in the book. To create the app, you used the `HttpUrlConnection` class to retrieve the data. You understood the JSON data format and parsed the data returned from Flickr. You added a check for online status so that you retrieve the data only if the device is connected.

Q&A

Q. In this hour, the titles that were displayed were moved from `FlickrPhoto` objects to strings for display. Is there a way to use those objects directly?

A. Yes, you create custom adapters in upcoming chapters. It is a common technique to extend a `BaseAdapter` or `CursorAdapter` to handle the display of multiple objects. To focus on retrieving data in this hour, you did not introduce those ideas.

Q. When working with an external API like Flickr, how do you know what objects to create?

A. APIs like Flickr may have helpful client libraries, sample code, and good documentation. It is often helpful to look closely at the data returned to determine precisely what to do. One reason that the Flickr recent photos method works well for this book is that no authentication is required. You can create an interesting app based on one URL for retrieving data.

Workshop

Quiz

1. If you have a snippet of a JSON string, how would you distinguish whether the contents contain a `JSONObject` or a `JSONArray`?

2. How is an `InputStream` related to an `HttpUrlConnection`?

3. What two permissions are added to the AndroidManifest.xml in apps that check online status before retrieving data from a remote source?

Answers

1. The data that represents `JSONObject` will be bounded by curly brackets, `{}`, and the data for a `JSONArray` will be bounded by square brackets, `[]`.

2. After a connection is made using an `HttpUrlConnection`, the data can be retrieved as an `InputStream`. For the example, in this hour, you converted the `InputStream` to a `String`.

3. The `INTERNET` and `ACCESS_NETWORK_STATE` are required.

Exercise

Get an API key from Flickr or another backend source for remote data. Using the code in Listing 17.7 as a guideline, make an API call with an `HTTPUrlConnection` and log the returned data. If the data is in JSON format, parse it and log the results. Often, apps can create a clean separation between data retrieval and display. Retrieving data and logging results is a good first step for working with any API.

Introducing Content Providers

What You'll Learn in This Hour:

▶ Introducing content providers

▶ Understanding calendar data

▶ Using the calendar content provider

▶ Adding calendar data

Hour 16, "Using SQLite and File Storage," introduced SQLite, and you used cursors in your app to access data from the database. You can think of content providers as a bridge between the database and the app. Content providers work with any type of structured data. One reason to use a content provider is that it provides a way for other apps to access the data. That is what makes it a *content* provider. Another reason is that you can use content providers with the `CursorLoader` class to make updating data in fragments and activities easy. Content providers simplify providing data to the Android UI in your app.

Introducing Content Providers

Content providers use Uniform Resource Identifiers (URIs) to identify the data resources that they provide. You are familiar with URLs of the format http://www.amazon.com. A URL, or Uniform Resource Locator, is an example of a URI that defines the network location of a specific resource.

The format of the URI should represent the data being returned. Content providers return cursors that may point to a single item or to a list of items.

URIs for Android content providers start with *content://.* To create the full URI, you add the *authority* and a meaningful path. The *authority* is the creator of the content provider, and the Android package name and class should be used here. That will ensure uniqueness.

All About the Calendar

In this section, you use the Calendar app to learn more about content providers. You are introduced to using the Calendar application programming interfaces (APIs) along the way.

Android ships with a set of core applications that include calendar and contact applications. When these applications have publicly documented APIs, they are considered part of the Android application framework. Apps that are part of the Android application framework include test cases that appear in the Compatibility Test Suite that Google makes available to Android hardware partners. The idea is that these APIs will work the same way across devices. The calendar public API became available with Ice Cream Sandwich (API level 14). You use the Calendar public API to learn more about content providers.

Most people know that a calendar divides time into specific periods of days, weeks, months, and years. People have personal calendars to schedule events in their lives. A calendar app, like Apple's iCal and Google Calendar, enables calendar owners to add and track events on their calendar. An event might be a meeting with an agenda and attendees or it might be a personal event such as "soccer game tonight." In either case, events on the calendar include a time period and a description. Events may include a list of attendees and many calendar apps use reminders—warnings that a meeting is about to start in 5 minutes, for example.

Calendar apps can include a recurring event, which occurs at specific intervals and is scheduled into the future. A recurring event might be a weekly status meeting at work that occurs at 2 p.m. each Monday or a drama class that occurs each Saturday at 10 a.m.

The calendar app in the Android framework includes a database that provides all of this information. That data is made available through the calendar content provider.

Calendar Data on Android

Understanding the structure of calendar data for Android is important to being able to query the data and successfully use the calendar content provider.

More than one calendar might be available. You might have a personal calendar and have access to view another person's calendar. In that case, two calendars are available for viewing when using the calendar content provider.

The calendar API is basically a data model, with tables, columns, and relations specified so you can use them through content provider queries. The calendar content provider uses the `android.provider.CalendarContract` class. The class refers to five tables containing calendar data: `CalendarContract.Calendar`, `CalendarContract.Events`, `CalendarContacts.Attendees`, `CalendarContacts.Instances`, and `CalendarContacts.Reminders`.

The following list describes the tables in `CalendarContract` (`android.provider.CalendarContract`):

▶ **Calendar:** Details for a single calendar including the account type, account name, calendar ID, and calendar display name.

▶ **Events:** Event-specific information including the event title, description, start date, and end date.

▶ **Attendees:** Event guests and whether they have responded to indicate that they are attending the event.

▶ **Instances:** Each row in the instance table represents one occurrence of an event. For recurring events, multiple entries are in this table. For nonrecurring events, there is one entry.

▶ **Reminders:** Reminder information for an event. An event might have multiple reminders.

Figure 18.1 shows the relationships between these tables. Calendars have events, and events have attendees, reminders, and instances.

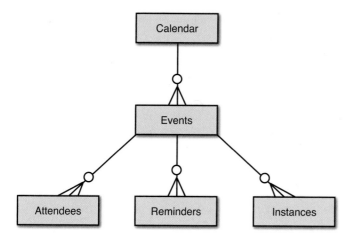

FIGURE 18.1
Calendar data diagram.

Calendar Data via the Calendar Content Provider

Calendar data is available to use via the `CalendarContract` content provider. You can use the same approach to query and display calendar data.

Permissions are required in the Android manifest XML file to use the calendar content provider. The read and write permissions are as follows:

```
<uses-permission android:name="android.permission.READ_CALENDAR" />
<uses-permission android:name="android.permission.WRITE_CALENDAR" />
```

A content provider provides a consistent way to insert, delete, update, and query data. The content provider provides the ability for your app to use another apps data.

The goal is to list all available calendars on the device. You will use a content provider to accomplish that. You'll use a `SimpleCursorAdapter` to display calendar data in a list. To display the account name and display name, you use the `Calendars.ACCOUNT_NAME` and `Calendars.CALENDAR_DISPLAY_NAME` columns.

Listing 18.1 shows the code to use the calendar content provider to list these calendars.

A content provider uses a URI. The calendar URI uses is on lines 12 and 13 of Listing 18.1. You can use the following:

```
"content://com.android.calendar/calendars"
```

You can also use `Calendars.CONTENT_URI`, which has the same value.

Similar to working with a SQLite database, you specify the fields from the calendar that you wish to access. That occurs on lines 14–18.

In an activity, you can use a `ContentResolver` to access data associated with the application.

In line 27, a `ContentResolver` is defined. That `ContentResolver` is used to perform a query of the calendar data. It is the same as querying a SQLite database. See lines 28–29.

```
Cursor cursor = contentResolver.query(CALENDAR_URI, FIELDS, null, null, null);
```

The rest of Listing 18.1 creates a `SimpleCursorAdapter` and uses a `ListView` to display the remaining data. A `SimpleCursorAdapter` is instantiated on lines 30–36. Line 28 specifies the calendar columns that should be used to retrieve data; in this case, the `Calendars.ACCOUNT_NAME` and `Calendars.CALENDAR_DISPLAY_NAME`. The result is shown in Figure 18.2.

LISTING 18.1   Calendar Data Using a Content Provider

```
 1: package com.talkingandroid.hour18application;
 2: import android.app.Activity;
 3: import android.content.ContentResolver;
 4: import android.database.Cursor;
 5: import android.net.Uri;
 6: import android.os.Bundle;
 7: import android.provider.CalendarContract;
 8: import android.provider.CalendarContract.Calendars;
 9: import android.widget.ListView;
10: import android.widget.SimpleCursorAdapter;
11: public class CalendarsActivity extends Activity {
12:     public static final Uri CALENDAR_URI =
13:             Uri.parse("content://com.android.calendar/calendars");
14:     public static final String[] FIELDS = {
15:             Calendars._ID,
16:             Calendars.ACCOUNT_NAME,
17:             CalendarContract.Calendars.CALENDAR_DISPLAY_NAME,
18:     };
19:     ListView listView;
20:     SimpleCursorAdapter adapter;
21:
22:     @Override
23:     protected void onCreate(Bundle savedInstanceState) {
24:         super.onCreate(savedInstanceState);
25:         setContentView(R.layout.activity_calendars);
26:         listView = (ListView) findViewById(R.id.listView);
27:         ContentResolver contentResolver = this.getContentResolver();
28:         Cursor cursor = contentResolver.query(CALENDAR_URI, FIELDS,
29:                 null, null, null);
30:         adapter = new SimpleCursorAdapter(this,
31:                 android.R.layout.simple_list_item_2,
32:                 cursor, //cursor
33:                 new String[] {Calendars.ACCOUNT_NAME,
34:                         Calendars.CALENDAR_DISPLAY_NAME},
35:                 new int[] { android.R.id.text1,  android.R.id.text2,},
36:                 0);
37:         listView.setAdapter(adapter);
38:     }
39: }
```

FIGURE 18.2
Calendar data diagram.

▼ TRY IT YOURSELF

Displaying Different Calendar Data

You saw how to display calendar information. Follow these steps to display alternate data:

1. Look at the fields available for a calendar.

2. Pick one or two alternate fields to display.

3. Use Listing 18.1 as a starting point and create an activity with a `ListView` that shows the data you selected.

Now that a list of calendars is on the device, you can consider displaying available events for a specific calendar.

That will require several steps:

1. Implement the onItemClickListener() for the calendar ListView.

2. Get the ID of the selected calendar.

3. Pass the ID of the selected calendar to a new activity.

4. Create an EventsActivity that displays the events for the selected calendar.

Listing 18.2 shows the updated CalendarsActivity code with the onItemClick() listener implementation in lines 44 to 50. The parameter ID of the onItemClick() method is the identifier for the selected calendar. It is put into an intent that is used to start the EventsActivity. In the EventsActivity, the ID is used to retrieve the events data for a particular calendar.

LISTING 18.2   Clicking a Calendar Item

```
 1:   package com.talkingandroid.hour18application;
 2:   import android.app.Activity;
 3:   import android.content.ContentResolver;
 4:   import android.content.Intent;
 5:   import android.database.Cursor;
 6:   import android.net.Uri;
 7:   import android.os.Bundle;
 8:   import android.provider.CalendarContract;
 9:   import android.provider.CalendarContract.Calendars;
10:   import android.view.View;
11:   import android.widget.AdapterView;
22:   import android.widget.ListView;
13:   import android.widget.SimpleCursorAdapter;
14:
15:   public class CalendarsActivity extends Activity {
16:       public static final String[] FIELDS = {
17:               Calendars._ID,
18:               Calendars.ACCOUNT_NAME,
19:               CalendarContract.Calendars.CALENDAR_DISPLAY_NAME,
20:           };
21:       public static final String CALENDAR_ID =
22:               "com.talkingandroid.hour18application.ID";
23:     ListView listView;
24:      SimpleCursorAdapter adapter;
25:
26:      @Override
27:      protected void onCreate(Bundle savedInstanceState) {
28:          super.onCreate(savedInstanceState);
29:          setContentView(R.layout.activity_calendars);
30:          listView = (ListView) findViewById(R.id.listView);
31:          ContentResolver contentResolver = this.getContentResolver();
```

```
32:            Cursor cursor = contentResolver.query(Calendars.CONTENT_URI,
33:                        FIELDS, null, null, null);
34:         adapter = new SimpleCursorAdapter(this,
35:                 android.R.layout.simple_list_item_2,
36:                 cursor, //cursor
37:                 new String[] {Calendars.ACCOUNT_NAME,
38:                         Calendars.CALENDAR_DISPLAY_NAME},
39:                 new int[] { android.R.id.text1,  android.R.id.text2,},
40:                 0);
41:         listView.setAdapter(adapter);
42:         listView.setOnItemClickListener(new AdapterView.OnItemClickListener() {
43:             @Override
44:             public void onItemClick(AdapterView<?> parent, View view,
45:                     int position, long id) {
46:                 Intent intent = new Intent(getApplicationContext(),
47:                         EventsActivity.class);
48:                 intent.putExtra(CALENDAR_ID,id );
49:                 startActivity(intent);
50:
51:             }
52:         });
53:     }
54: }
```

Listing Calendar Events

A calendar event includes important data such as title, description, attendees, time, and location to help you be where you need to be for an event.

Names for some common fields are CALENDAR_ID, ORGANIZER, TITLE, EVENT_LOCATION, DESCRIPTION, EVENT_COLOR, DTSTART, DTEND, EVENT_TIMEZONE, EVENT_END_TIMEZONE, DURATION, ALL_DAY, RRULE, and RDATE.

DTSTART and DTEND are the columns for start and end dates. RRULE and RDATE contain information about recurring events.

Additional columns are available for events. The full list is on the CalendarContract.Events page at http://developer.android.com/reference/android/provider/CalendarContract.Events.html.

Listing 18.3 shows the EventsActivity. It is similar in structure to the CalendarsActivity, but it is driven by the calendar id passed in the Intent.

To find events in the future, you will create a query that looks for calendar events that have an end date greater than the current date. The query to do that is on lines 26–28. Figure 18.3 shows the result.

LISTING 18.3   Showing Event Data

```
 1: package com.talkingandroid.hour18application;
 2: import android.app.Activity;
 3: import android.content.ContentResolver;
 4: import android.content.Intent;
 5: import android.database.Cursor;
 6: import android.os.Bundle;
 7: import android.provider.CalendarContract;
 8: import android.widget.ListView;
 9: import android.widget.SimpleCursorAdapter;
10: import java.util.Date;
11: import android.provider.CalendarContract.Events;
12:
13: public class EventsActivity extends Activity {
14:     ListView listView;
15:     SimpleCursorAdapter adapter;
16:
17:     @Override
18:     protected void onCreate(Bundle savedInstanceState) {
19:         super.onCreate(savedInstanceState);
20:         setContentView(R.layout.activity_events);
21:         listView = (ListView) findViewById(R.id.eventsListView);
22:
23:         Intent intent = getIntent();
24:         long calendarId=intent.getLongExtra(CalendarsActivity.CALENDAR_ID, 01);
25:         ContentResolver contentResolver = this.getContentResolver();
26:         Cursor cursor = contentResolver.query(Events.CONTENT_URI,
27:                 null, Events.CALENDAR_ID +"= '" + calendarId +"' AND " +
28:                 Events.DTEND + "> " + new Date().getTime(), null, null);
29:         adapter = new SimpleCursorAdapter(this,
30:                 android.R.layout.simple_list_item_2,
31:                 cursor,
32:                 new String[] {CalendarContract.Events.TITLE,
33:                         CalendarContract.Events.RRULE},
34:                 new int[] { android.R.id.text1,  android.R.id.text2,}, 0);
45:         listView.setAdapter(adapter);
36:     }
37: }
```

The query in Listing 18.3 will miss recurring events. A recurring event may occur in the future, but could have been defined in the past. If `Events.RRULE` is not null, you know you are dealing with a recurring event.

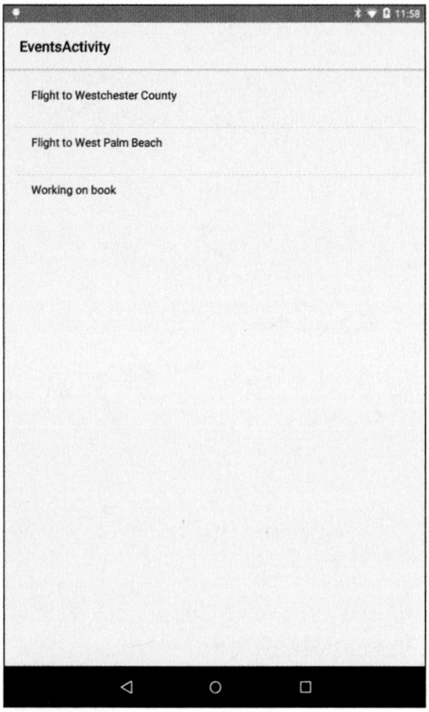

FIGURE 18.3
Events listed.

NOTE

Recurring Event Definitions

The RRULE is one component of defining a recurring event. Recurrence relies on the start date, the recurrent rules, and exceptions to recurrence rules. RFC 5545 contains a detailed definition of RRULE. See http://tools.ietf.org/html/rfc5545#section-3.8.5.3.

Drilling Further into Calendar Data

Given the calendar ID, you can retrieve a list of events as shown earlier. You can access attendees, instances, and reminders for a particular event in a similar way.

Getting a List of Event Attendees

The steps to get a list of attendees for an event mirror the steps to get a list of events for a calendar:

1. Implement the `onItemClick()` method for the `ListView` in `EventsActivity`.

2. Create an `AttendeeActivity` and pass it the `id` of an event in a bundle.

3. Create a `SimpleCursorLoader` to display the data and use the proper query to access the attendees for an event.

Using Intents to Update a Calendar

You can use the calendar provider to insert and update new data into a calendar. The calendar application provides a set of intents that can be used to view, update, and insert calendar data.

Doing these tasks does not require any additional permissions for the app. Listing 18.4 shows an example of using an `INSERT` intent on the calendar to schedule a New Year's Eve party. When this code runs, the calendar app appears with this data prepopulated, as shown in Figure 18.4.

LISTING 18.4   Inserting an Event Using an Insert Intent

```
1:   Calendar beginTime = Calendar.getInstance();
2:   beginTime.set(2015, 11, 31, 23, 30);
3:   Calendar endTime = Calendar.getInstance();
4:   endTime.set(2016, 0, 1, 2, 30);
5:   Intent intent = new Intent(Intent.ACTION_INSERT)
6:       .setData(Events.CONTENT_URI)
6:       .putExtra(CalendarContract.EXTRA_EVENT_BEGIN_TIME,
7:                 beginTime.getTimeInMillis())
8:       .putExtra(CalendarContract.EXTRA_EVENT_END_TIME,
9:                 endTime.getTimeInMillis())
10:       .putExtra(Events.TITLE, "New Years Party")
11:       .putExtra(Events.DESCRIPTION, "Have fun")
12:       .putExtra(Events.EVENT_LOCATION, "Our house")
13:       .putExtra(Events.AVAILABILITY, Events.AVAILABILITY_BUSY)
14:       .putExtra(Intent.EXTRA_EMAIL, "carmendelessio@gmail.com");
15:   startActivity(intent);
```

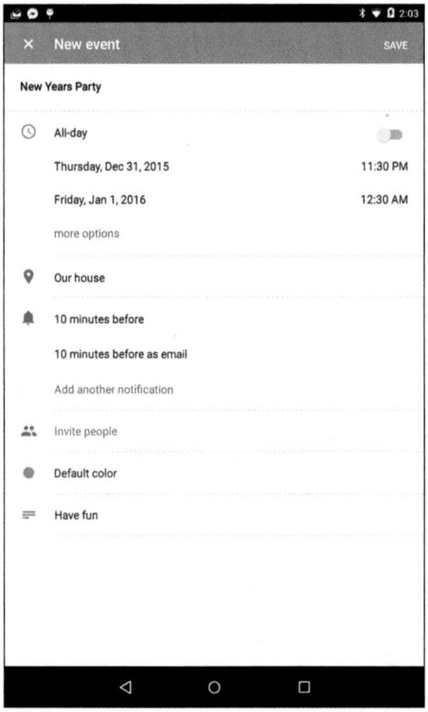

FIGURE 18.4
Inserting an event via a calendar `Intent`.

Summary

In this hour, you learned about how a content provider can be used to access data in a separate application. You used the Calendar API to query and display calendar data. You used an intent to add a new calendar event.

Q&A

Q. What is the best way to determine what information is available from a content provider?

A. One way is to look at all of the available documentation and sample code. For a class like `CalendarContract`, the constants defined in the online documentation are very helpful. You can see that documentation at http://developer.android.com/reference/android/provider/CalendarContract.html.

Workshop

Quiz

1. What is the INSTANCES table used for?

2. What is RRULE?

3. What is the relationship between a content resolver and a cursor?

Answers

1. You use the INSTANCES table in the calendar to handle recurring events.

2. RRULE is a column in the calendar data. It represents rules for recurring events.

3. You use a content resolver to access data available in the application. Once you have a content resolver, you can do a query and the results will be returned in a cursor.

Exercise

Create an activity to display additional data about an event. Consider event details, such as name and location.

HOUR 19
Creating a Content Provider

What You'll Learn in This Hour:

▶ Creating a URI for your content provider

▶ Using an existing database adapter (`PieDbAdapter`)

▶ Building a content provider

▶ Using a content provider in your app

You learned about content providers in Hour 18, "Introducing Content Providers." In this hour, you create your own `ContentProvider` (`android.content.ContentProvider`) using the same SQLite database that you created in Hour 16, "Using SQLite and File Storage." You use a content provider to populate and retrieve data. Content providers can return cursors for handling data. You can use them with loader classes, which you learn about in Hour 20, "Loaders and CursorAdapters."

Specifying a URI for Data Retrieval

URIs for Android content providers start with *content://*. To create the full URI, you add the *authority* and a meaningful path. The *authority* is the creator of the content provider, and the Android package name and class should be used here. That ensures uniqueness. In this hour's example, the package name is `com.talkingandroid.hour19application`. When you create the full authority name, `provider` is appended, so you get an authority of `com.talking-android.hour19application.provider`. In this hour, you work with `Pie` objects, so in your base path, you will use `pie`. When you put it all together, you get the following:

```
content://com.talkingandroid.hour19application.provider/pie
```

You can also create a URI to access an individual pie that you identify using the ID:

```
content://com.talkingandroid.hour19application.provider/pie/1
```

In this case, `12345` represents the ID of a particular pie.

Using PieDbAdapter

You have defined the URIs to use in your content provider. In this section, you examine the process to build a content provider in detail. You then use the new content provider in your app to get a cursor to a list of pie records. The PieDbAdapter class in this chapter is the same as in Hour 16, with a few new additions. In Hour 16, you added methods to retrieve one pie or all pies. You updated and deleted based on the id of the pie. Now, you add methods to allow more flexibility so that you can make a general query. The content provider will take advantage of those new methods.

These new query and update methods show how the additional arguments are used:

```
public Cursor queryPies(String[] projection, String selection,
                        String[] selectionArgs, String sortOrder) {
    return mDb.query(PIE_TABLE, projection, selection,
            selectionArgs, null, null, sortOrder);
}

public int deletePie(String selection, String[] selectionArgs) {
    return mDb.delete(PIE_TABLE,  selection, selectionArgs );
}
```

Building a Content Provider

You have defined the URIs to use in your content provider. In this section, you examine the process to build a content provider in detail. You then use the new content provider in your app to get a cursor to a list of pie records.

Methods Required in a Content Provider

When you define a new class as an extension of ContentProvider, you are required to implement six methods. Four methods interact with the data managed by the content provider: insert(), update(), delete(), and query(). All must be implemented, but creating a provider without providing full functionality to these methods is possible. That is, you can have stub methods if that fits your purpose. The two other methods are onCreate() and getType(). The onCreate() method is used to initialize the content provider. That initialization often means opening a database. The getType() method indicates the type of data that the content provider returns.

Listing 19.1 shows an empty content provider that is not useful, but implements a stub for all required methods.

LISTING 19.1   Shell of a Content Provider

```
1: package com.bffmedia.example;
2: import android.content.ContentProvider;
3: import android.content.ContentValues;
4: import android.database.Cursor;
5: import android.net.Uri;
6: public class EmptyProvider extends ContentProvider {
7:   @Override
8:   public int delete(Uri uri, String selection, String[] selectionArgs) {
9:     return 0;
10:  }
11:  @Override
12:  public String getType(Uri uri) {
13:    return null;
19:  }
15:  @Override
16:  public Uri insert(Uri uri, ContentValues values) {
17:   return null;
18:  }
19:  @Override
20:    public boolean onCreate() {
21:    return false;
22:  }
23:  @Override
24:  public Cursor query(Uri uri, String[] projection, String selection,
25:                    String[] selectionArgs, String sortOrder) {
26:    return null;
27:  }
28:  @Override
29:  public int update(Uri uri, ContentValues values,
30:                  String selection,String[] selectionArgs) {
31:    return 0;
32:  }
33: }
```

TRY IT YOURSELF ▼

Creating an Empty Content Provider Using Android Studio

Android Studio provides an option to create a new content provider. Follow these steps to make a new content provider:

1. Use Android Studio to create a new content provider (New, Other, Content Provider).

2. Enter your package name as the authority.

3. Generate the content provider and review at the code and the AndroidManifest.xml to see what changes were made.

Declaring the Content Provider

Let's now examine each section of the MyContentProvider class. Often, field definitions are self-explanatory, but in the case of MyContentProvider, it is beneficial to examine the declarations and definitions carefully. There are static fields that correspond to the parts of the URI definition. There are static fields that will be used in the getType() method and elsewhere to make the code more readable.

A static UriMatcher will be declared. The job of the UriMatcher is to match the string pattern of a URI to a specific constant value as a convenience for development. Instead of string and pattern-matching logic to determine what action should be taken with a URI, you can use the UriMatcher and a switch statement to simplify the code. The UriMatcher is a convenience class created for this purpose.

When you create a content provider, you'll see that there are many interconnected pieces. Listing 19.2 shows the MyContentProvider declarations and definitions.

LISTING 19.2   **MyContentProvider Declarations**

```
1:   public class MyContentProvider extends ContentProvider {
2:   private Pie mPieDbAdapter;
3:   private static final UriMatcher sUriMatcher = new UriMatcher(UriMatcher.NO_MATCH);
4:   static {
5:     sUriMatcher.addURI("com.talkingandroid.hour19application.provider", "pie", 1);
6:     sUriMatcher.addURI("com.talkingandroid.hour19application.provider ", "pie/#", 2);
7:   }
8:   public static final Uri CONTENT_URI =
9:            Uri.parse("content:// com.talkingandroid.hour19application.provider
/pie");
```

Lines 3 through 7 define the UriMatcher. In lines 5 and 6, the URIs for the content are represented along with an integer value to return when there is a matching URI. Line 5 represents getting all pies, and line 6 represents getting a single pie that is specified by passing a number as an appended id. The # indicates that.

Line 8 creates a static variable called CONTENT_URI that will be used by apps that use the MyContentProvider.

Given a URI, the UriMatcher returns the integer code that you associated with the URI. This example has URIs for getting a single pie based on id, and a URI for getting a list of pies based on page id. Lines 5 and 6 add these URIs to the UriMatcher and specify the integer values to return when a match is found.

You'll use the UriMatcher for two of the methods that you are required to implement when creating a content provider.

The getType() method returns a string representing the type of data you are returning. In that case, you use the UriMatcher to determine whether the request for the content type is for a single pie based on a pie id or for a list of pies.

You will also use the UriMatcher for the query() method. In this query() method, you either return a cursor to all the pies or a single pie. The URI passed determines that.

The string constants like "pie" in Listing 19.2 help make the example clear. Using static variables to define these strings is recommended. For example, if you use:

```
private static final String AUTHORITY = "com.talkingandroid.hour19application.
provider";
private static final String BASE_PATH = "pie";
public static final int PIE = 1;
public static final int PIE_ID = 2;
```

Then, you create the UriMatcher using the following:

```
sUriMatcher.addURI(AUTHORITY, BASE_PATH, PIES );
sUriMatcher.addURI(AUTHORITY, BASE_PATH+"/#", PIE_ID);
```

Updating the Android Manifest

Adding content provider information to the AndroidManifest.xml file is critical because the app will not work if this is not done. The following snippet shows the definition for this provider. The authority is provided. The android:name attribute is the name of the class that defined the provider. The android:exported attribute specifies whether third-party apps can use this content provider. When set to false, it indicates that only the current app can use the provider.

The name and authorities values must be set. You should make a decision on whether the data should be exported. If you are not sure, set exported to "false"; not exporting data is better than exporting it by mistake. Leaving multiprocess set to "true" is fine:

```
<provider
        android:authorities="com.talkingandroid.hour19application.provider"
        android:multiprocess="true"
        android:exported="false"
        android:name=".MyContentProvider">
</provider>
```

Content Provider Query Method

The plan is to support two URIs in the MyContentProvider content provider. When requested from MyContentProvider, these URIs will be fulfilled from the query() method. You learn how to implement the specific response required by these URIs. This section then covers the parameters that are passed to this method and considers alternative implementations.

Listing 19.3 implements the `query()` method for `MyContentProvider`. It checks the URI that was passed and fulfills the request based on the URI. If the URI is not recognized, an exception is thrown.

LISTING 19.3   MyContentProvider Query Method

```
1:   @Override
2:   public Cursor query(Uri uri, String[] projection, String selection,
3:                  String[] selectionArgs, String sortOrder) {
4:     Cursor cursor;
5:     int uriType = sUriMatcher.match(uri);
6:     switch (uriType) {
7:       case 1:
8:         cursor =  mPieDbAdapter.queryPies(projection, selection,
9:                                selectionArgs, sortOrder);
10:        break;
11:      case 2:
12:         cursor =  mPieDbAdapter.getPie(uri.getLastPathSegment());
14:         break;
15:      default:
16:          throw new IllegalArgumentException("Unknown URI");
17:     }
18:     return cursor;
19:   }
```

Two tasks are being handled in Listing 19.3:

▶ Identify the URI to handle using `UriMatcher`.

▶ Create a `Cursor` that fulfills the request for data.

This implementation of `MyContentProvider` handles two URIs. The `uriType` specifies whether to return a single pie or a list of pies. When retrieving a single pie, the call to `uri.getLastPath()` segment returns the value of the specific pie id to use.

The cursor for returning a single pie is created on line 12, and the cursor for fulfilling a list of pies occurs on line 8. The methods that were added to the `PieDbAdapter` class are used here.

By examining the parameters passed to the `query` method, you can see how to do a database query:

```
String[] projection, String selection, String[] selectionArgs, String sortOrder
```

As with using SQLite directly, a `projection` parameter identifies the columns in a database table that should be returned. A `null` projection means to return all columns. To create a

SQL query, you use `selection` and optionally `selectionArgs` parameters. The `sortOrder` parameter defines the order of the data being returned.

These are the parameters that you pass to a `SQLDatabase query()` method.

Implementing the GetType() Method

The purpose of the `getType()` method is to show the type of data that will be returned from the content provider. The `ContentResolver` class offers two Android MIME types to use for this purpose. One MIME type represents a cursor that can have multiple objects, and the other MIME type is used for when a single item is returned in the cursor. You use `ContentResolver.CURSOR_DIR_BASE_TYPE` for multiple items and `ContentResolver.CURSOR_ITEM_BASE_TYPE` for a single item. These are strings that are used to indicate that this is a vendor-provided value.

`CURSOR_DIR_BASE_TYPE` has the constant value `"vnd.android.cursor.dir"`, and `CURSOR_ITEM_BASE_TYPE` has the constant value `"vnd.android.cursor.item"`.

Because this example uses `Pie` objects, the types will be a string, like this:

```
ContentResolver.CURSOR_DIR_BASE_TYPE + "/com.talkingandroid.hour19application.Pie"
```

Listing 19.4 shows the full `getType()` method.

On lines 5 and 6, the type for a list of items is returned, and on lines 7 and 8, the type for a single item is returned. Recall that type for the URI was defined in the `UriMatcher`. Refer to Listing 19.2 for review.

LISTING 19.4   Return Type of Data in GetType()

```
 1: @Override
 2: public String getType(Uri uri) {
 3:    int uriType = sUriMatcher.match(uri);
 4:    switch (uriType) {
 5:      case 1:
 6:            return ContentResolver.CURSOR_DIR_BASE_TYPE+
 7:                    "/com.talkingandroid.hour19application.Pie" ";
 8:      case 2:
 9:            return ContentResolver.CURSOR_ITEM_BASE_TYPE+
10:                    "/com.talkingandroid.hour19application.Pie";
11:      default:
12:            return null;
13:    }
14: }
```

Implementing Insert, Update, and Delete Methods

To create a content provider, you must implement `insert()`, `update()`, and `delete()` methods. This provides a consistent way to keep the app in sync and aware of updates as they happen.

These methods must exist in the content provider, but making a read-only content provider is also possible. To create a read-only content provider, the query methods would be fully implemented to return results. The `insert()`, `update()`, and `delete()` methods would exist, but would not actually change the underlying data.

Listing 19.5 shows a complete `insert()` method. Listing 19.5 inserts the passed `ContentValues` into the database by directly accessing the `mDb` field in the `PhotoDbAdapter` class.

LISTING 19.5 Content Provider insert() Method

```
 1: @Override
 2: public Uri insert(Uri uri, ContentValues values) {
 3:    long newID = mPieDbAdapter.insertPie(values)
 4:    if (newID > 0) {
 5:      Uri newUri = ContentUris.withAppendedId(uri, newID);
 6:      return newUri;
 7:    } else {
 8:      throw new SQLException("Failed to insert row into " + uri);
 9:    }
10: }
```

Listing 19.6 shows the database update. With an update, the selection criteria are passed to the argument so that the rows to be updated can be identified.

LISTING 19.6 Content Provider update() Method

```
1: @Override
2: public int update(Uri uri, ContentValues values, String selection,
3:                    String[] selectionArgs) {
4:          return mPieDbAdapter.updatePie(selection, selectionArgs, values);
5: }
```

Listing 19.7 shows the `delete()` method. Like the `update()` method, it takes selection criteria as parameters. When updating or deleting, you must specify the rows to act upon via these parameters.

LISTING 19.7   Content Provider delete() Method

```
1: @Override
2: public int delete(Uri uri, String selection, String[] selectionArgs) {
3:     return mPieDbAdapter.deletePie(selection, selectionArgs);
4: }
```

Using MyContentProvider in the App

In Hour 18, you used the calendar content provider to retrieve and display calendar data. In Hour 16, you inserted and read data directly to and from a SQLite database. Listing 19.8 shows a demo activity that inserts and reads data using a content provider.

LISTING 19.8   Inserting and Querying

```
1: package com.talkingandroid.hour19application;
2: import android.app.Activity;
3: import android.content.ContentValues;
4: import android.database.Cursor;
5: import android.database.SQLException;
6: import android.os.Bundle;
7: import android.widget.TextView;
8: import java.util.ArrayList;
9:
10: public class MainActivity extends Activity {
11:     TextView textView;
12:
13:     @Override
14:     protected void onCreate(Bundle savedInstanceState) {
15:         super.onCreate(savedInstanceState);
16:         setContentView(R.layout.activity_main);
17:         textView = (TextView)findViewById(R.id.textView);
18:         ArrayList<Pie> pies = Pie.makePies();
19:         for (Pie pie: pies){
20:             ContentValues newValues = new ContentValues();
21             newValues.put(PieDbAdapter.NAME, pie.mName);
22:             newValues.put(PieDbAdapter.DESCRIPTION, pie.mDescription);
23:             newValues.put(PieDbAdapter.PRICE, pie.mPrice);
24:             newValues.put(PieDbAdapter.FAVORITE, pie.mIsFavorite);
25:             try {
26:                 getContentResolver().insert(MyContentProvider.CONTENT_URI,
newValues);
27:             }catch (SQLException e){};
28:         }
29:
```

```
30:          Cursor pieCursor =
getContentResolver().query(MyContentProvider.CONTENT_URI,
31:                          null,null, null,null);
32:          StringBuilder results = new StringBuilder();
33:          PieDbAdapter pieDbAdapter = new PieDbAdapter(this);
34:          pieDbAdapter.open();
35:          if (pieCursor.moveToFirst()){
36:              do{
37:                  Pie pie =  pieDbAdapter.getPieFromCursor(pieCursor);
38:                  results.append(pie.mId + " " + pie.mName + " " + pie.mPrice +
" "
39:                      + pie.mDescription + " " + pie.mIsFavorite +"\n");
40:              } while (pieCursor.moveToNext());
41:          }
42:          pieCursor.close();
43:          pieDbAdapter.close();
44:          textView.setText(results.toString());
45:      }
46: }
```

The MyContentProvider is also used to insert records in the MainActivity class.

Line 19–28 iterate through the data and create a ContentValue for each pie. The new pie data is inserted using the ContentProvider on line 26:

```
getContentResolver().insert(MyContentProvider.CONTENT_URI, newValues);
```

The insert is performed within a try/catch block. In this test case, we are inserting test data multiple times and using an insertOnConflict option. The code in the content provider is checking whether an insert was done. If it is not, an error is returned.

A query is done using the content provider on lines 30–31. In this case, you are getting all the data. The returned data is displayed as it was in Hour 16. You accumulate the data and display it in a TextView. Figure 19.1 shows the result.

▼ TRY IT YOURSELF

Modifying the Query Used in MainActivity

To retrieve and display different results, you can change the getContentResolver.query() method.

1. Determine a new query for the list of pies to display (for example, pies that cost more than $1).

2. Modify the getContentResolver.query() call appropriately.

3. Run the activity and check the results.

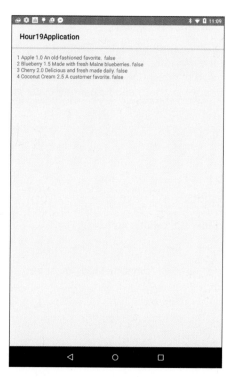

FIGURE 19.1
Using `ContentProvider` to get and display data.

Summary

In this hour, you created your own content provider by implementing `insert()`, `query()`, `update()`, and `delete()` methods. You saw how to use a `UriMatcher` to examine a URI and to direct you to an action. After the `MyContentProvider` was in place, you used it in the app for both data and file retrieval.

Q&A

Q. **What is the advantage of using a content provider?**

A. You can use a content provider to expose data in your app to another application. You can also take full advantage of using `Loaders` if you use a `ContentProvider`. You learn about loaders in Hour 20.

Q. Is a class like `PieDbAdapter` required to create a `ContentProvider`?

A. You must implement the required methods to create a `ContentProvider`. There are different methods to do that. You could incorporate the database management and `ContentProvider` functionality in one class. You used a straightforward method using two classes. There are other ways to implement a `ContentProvider`, and a separate class is not required.

Workshop

Quiz

1. What object is used to gain access to a content provider from within an `Activity`?

2. What is `CURSOR_ITEM_BASE_TYPE`?

3. In addition to `insert()`, `update()`, `delete()`, and `query()`, what methods must be implemented in a content provider?

Answers

1. You use `ContentResolver` through the `getContentResolver()` method to gain access to a content provider from an `Activity`.

2. `CURSOR_ITEM_BASE_TYPE` is a string constant that is prepended to a string that describes the type of object returned from your content provider.

3. The `onCreate()` and `getType()` methods must also be created.

Exercise

The example in this hour retrieves a list of pies. Continue to display the titles as is done in this hour, but sort the results by putting the titles in alphabetic order.

HOUR 20
Loaders and CursorAdapters

What You'll Learn in This Hour:

▶ Learning how loaders work
▶ Understanding loader classes
▶ Initializing, creating, and resetting a loader
▶ Using a CursorAdapter

In Hour 19, "Creating a Content Provider," you created your own content provider to handle content about pies. You were able to insert, read, and display data. The content provider was backed by a SQLite database. Content providers can be used together with CursorLoaders in your apps to create a clean design for accessing and displaying data. In this hour, you use the Flickr data that you retrieved in Hour 17, "Accessing the Cloud: Working with a Remote API." Using a database adapter and a content provider, you create an app to take advantage of a CursorLoader(android.content.CursorLoader). CursorLoaders are an implementation of the Loader(android.content.Loader) class. The result will look like Figure 20.1.

How Loaders Work

Loaders help to asynchronously load data in a fragment or activity. So far, you have learned about downloading data, writing to a SQLite database, and creating a content provider. You put all of that together here to create a CursorLoader to work with data downloaded from Flickr.

Loaders monitor the source of their data and provide updates when the data changes. Much of the work that is commonly done in a data-driven app is done in a streamlined way using loaders.

Loaders retain their data after being stopped. That means that if an activity or fragment that uses a loader is stopped, the data in the loader is retained. When the fragment starts again, the data is available, and the fragment does not need to wait for the data to reload.

FIGURE 20.1
App for showing Flickr photos.

Loader Classes

When implementing loaders, you use many classes and interfaces:

- ▶ **Loader:** A Loader is an abstract class to asynchronously load data.

- ▶ **CursorLoader:** A CursorLoader is a subclass of AsyncTaskLoader. Typically, you'll use a CursorLoader when implementing a Loader. A CursorLoader queries a ContentResolver and returns a cursor that can be used in the activity or fragment. CursorLoaders and ContentProviders work well together.

- ▶ **LoaderManager:** A LoaderManager is associated with each activity or fragment. There is a single LoaderManager for each activity or fragment, but a LoaderManager can manage more than one loader.

▶ **LoaderManagerCallbacks:** LoaderManagerCallbacks is an interface for an activity or fragment to interact with the LoaderManager. A fragment will implement a LoaderCallbacks interface:

```
public class ImageViewFragment extends Fragment implements
                 LoaderCallbacks<Cursor>
```

To implement LoaderManagerCallbacks, you must use the methods onCreateLoader(), onLoadFinished(), and onLoaderReset().

You use a CursorLoader in your app. The CursorLoader is your loader.

To manage the connection between the loader and a fragment or activity, you use the LoaderManager class. A LoaderManager includes the interface LoaderManager. LoaderCallbacks to communicate between the LoaderManager and the fragment or activity.

Understanding Loader States

You can use loaders in an activity or in a fragment. Loaders must be initialized. In an activity, a loader is initialized in the onCreate() method. In a fragment, a loader is initialized in the onActivityCreated() method.

After initialization, a loader is created if it does not already exist. If it does exist, it is used immediately. When data is available from a loader, the fragment is notified via the LoaderManager. Callback method onLoadFinished(). If initLoader() is called and data is available, onLoadFinished() is called immediately.

Initializing a Loader

A loader is initialized with a call to the initLoader() method of the LoaderManager. It looks like this:

```
getLoaderManager().initLoader(LOADER_ID, null, this);
```

The getLoaderManager() method returns the LoaderManager for the current fragment. LOADER_ID is a unique id integer value that identifies the loader. That is important if more than one loader exists. The id is used to distinguish which loader is being used in the LoaderManager.Callback method onCreateLoader().

The second parameter is a Bundle for passing any optional parameters to the loader constructor. In this case, that parameter is null.

The last parameter is a class that implements LoaderManager.Callbacks. Because you will be implementing LoaderManager.Callbacks in your fragment, you use this to reference your fragment.

Creating a Loader

When the `initLoader()` method is called, if the loader does not exist, a call to the `LoaderManager.Callback`'s `onCreateLoader()` method is made. The loader is created using this method.

When creating a `CursorLoader`, you use the parameters of a query on a `ContentProvider`. Specifically, as you saw in Hour 19, the query requires a `uri`, `projection`, `selection`, `selectionArgs`, and `sortOrder`. The `CursorLoader` is created using these parameters and is returned in `onCreateLoader()`.

Taking Action When Data Is Available

The `LoaderManager.Callback` method `onLoadFinished()` is called when data is available. In the case of `CursorLoader` implementation, the `onLoadFinished()` method is passed a `Cursor` to use.

When working with a `CursorAdapter`, you use the `onLoadFinished()` method to swap in new data with a call to the adapter's `swapCursor()` method.

Figure 20.2 shows a simplified version of these relationships. The concept is the same as when the loader is implemented in an activity or a fragment.

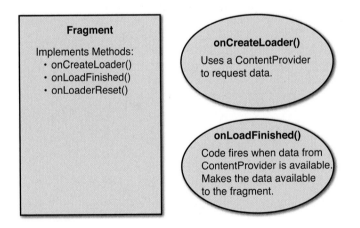

FIGURE 20.2
Relationship of a fragment to `LoaderManagerCallback` methods.

Resetting a Loader

When the application determines that the loader no longer has any associated data, the `onLoaderReset()` method fires. This is an opportunity to remove any references to the data.

With a `CursorLoader`, this is the point where the cursor associated with the loader is about to be closed. If more than one cursor is associated with the loader, the `onLoaderReset()` method fires when the last cursor is about to be closed.

When you're using a `CursorAdapter` with a `CursorLoader`, this is the opportunity to reset the cursor to `null` with a call to the adapter's `swapCursor()` method:

```
MyAdapter.swapCursor(null);
```

Using a CursorLoader with a CursorAdapter

Using a `CursorLoader` with a `CursorAdapter` is powerful. The `CursorAdapter` uses the data from the loader to show the data. The `CursorLoader` keeps the data current. As the data changes, the display changes.

Listing 20.1 shows an activity called `PhotoActivity` that implements `LoaderCallbacks` and includes an internal class called `PhotoCursorAdapter` that extends `CursorAdapter`. The `PhotoCursorAdapter` inner class is shown in Listing 20.2 for clarity.

Listing 20.1 lists the required `import` statements; the class is defined on lines 20 and 21. The `PhotoActivity` extends `Activity` and implements `LoaderCallbacks`.

Line 23 defines a `PhotoCursorAdapter` named adapter. On line 32, you initialize this cursor adapter by setting the initial cursor value to `null`. When data is available in a new cursor, you have a chance to reset the cursor associated with `adapter`.

Line 31 shows the `initLoader()` method. The id of this loader is 0. The second parameter is a bundle. Because you are not using a bundle, `null` is passed. The third parameter is a context.

LISTING 20.1 PhotoActivity Using LoaderCallbacks

```
 1:  package com.talkingandroid.hour20application;
 2:  import android.app.Activity;
 3:  import android.app.LoaderManager;
 4:  import android.content.Context;
 5:  import android.content.CursorLoader;
 6:  import android.content.Intent;
 7:  import android.content.Loader;
 8:  import android.database.Cursor;
 9:  import android.os.Bundle;
10:  import android.view.LayoutInflater;
11:  import android.view.View;
12:  import android.view.ViewGroup;
13:  import android.widget.CursorAdapter;
14:  import android.widget.ImageView;
15:  import android.widget.ListView;
16:  import android.widget.TextView;
```

```
17:  import com.squareup.picasso.Picasso;
18:  import com.squareup.picasso.Picasso;
19:
20:  public class PhotoActivity extends Activity implements
21:              LoaderManager.LoaderCallbacks<Cursor> {
22:      GridView gridView;
23:      PhotoCursorAdapter adapter;
24:      ListView listView;
25:
26:      @Override
27:      protected void onCreate(Bundle savedInstanceState) {
28:          super.onCreate(savedInstanceState);
29:          setContentView(R.layout.activity_photo);
30:          listView = (ListView) findViewById(R.id.photoListView);
31:          getLoaderManager().initLoader(0, null, this);
32:          adapter = new PhotoCursorAdapter(this, null, 0);
33:          listView.setAdapter(adapter);
34:          Intent= new Intent(getApplicationContext(), PhotoService.class);
35:          startService(intent);
36:
37:      }
38:
39:      @Override
40:      public Loader<Cursor> onCreateLoader(int id, Bundle args) {
41:          CursorLoader loader;
42:
43:          loader = new CursorLoader(this,
44:                  FlickrPhotoContentProvider.CONTENT_URI,
45:                  null, null, null, null);
46:          return loader;
47:      }
48:
49:      @Override
50:      public void onLoadFinished(Loader<Cursor> loader, Cursor data) {
51:          adapter.swapCursor(data);
52:      }
53:
54:      @Override
55:      public void onLoaderReset(Loader<Cursor> loader) {
56:          adapter.swapCursor(null);
57:      }
58:
59:      public class PhotoCursorAdapter extends CursorAdapter {
60:          ...
61:      }
62:  }
```

The remainder of the code in Listing 20.1 includes the methods that are required to implement a loader.

Implementing onCreateLoader()

Lines 40–47 of Listing 20.1 show the `onCreateLoader()` method. The `id` of the loader is passed along with a bundle. These values were set with the call to `initLoader()`. Because you use only one loader, the ID is not important, but it is possible to use multiple loaders in an activity or fragment. No bundle is used in this case. You define a new `CursorLoader` based on querying the content provider, and a new `CursorLoader` is returned:

```
@Override
public Loader<Cursor> onCreateLoader(int id, Bundle args) {
    CursorLoader loader;

    loader = new CursorLoader(this,
            FlickrPhotoContentProvider.CONTENT_URI,
            null, null, null, null);
    return loader;
}
```

Implementing onLoadFinished()

Lines 49–52 show the `onLoadFinished()` method. The cursor that is passed to this method is used to update the adapter with a call to `swapCursor()`. At this point, the data is available in the cursor and is available for display in by setting the adapter. Recall that the initial value of the cursor for the adapter was set to `null`:

```
@Override
public void onLoadFinished(Loader<Cursor> loader, Cursor data) {
    adapter.swapCursor(data);
}
```

Implementing onLoaderReset()

When the loader has no associated data, the `onLoaderReset()` method is called. Lines 54–57 of Listing 20.1 show this method. A call is made to `swapCursor()` with `null` as the parameter:

```
public void onLoaderReset(Loader<Cursor> loader) {
    adapter.swapCursor(null);
}
```

Listing 20.1 includes all the methods to define and implement a `CursorLoader`. The process to use a `CursorLoader` to provide data is as follows:

   1. Initialize the loader.

   2. Create the loader by querying the content provider.

   3. Use the data on the fragment when the loader finished.

To complete `PhotoActivity`, you will learn about using a `CursorAdapter` and how a cursor adapter works in conjunction with a `CursorLoader`.

▼ TRY IT YOURSELF

Modifying the Query Used

When you use a loader, it is backed by data in a SQLite database and a content provider. Change the query in this example to order photos by owner:

   1. Examine the call to the content provider on line 43 of Listing 20.1.

   2. Determine the query to use to set the order by parameter.

   3. Add the query to the `onCreateLoader()` method.

Creating Cursor Adapters

You have used `SimpleCursorAdaptersCursorAdapters` in earlier hours. You can extend a `CursorAdapter` to create your own custom implementation of a `CursorAdapter`. It is similar to how you extended a `BaseAdapter` previously.

A `CursorAdapter` uses data from a `Cursor` to populate a `View`. You used a `SimpleCursorAdapter` to show data from a `Cursor` in both a grid and a list.

To create a custom `CursorAdapter`, you must implement two methods: `newView()` and `bindView()`. The `newView()` method defines and returns a new `View`. In the `bindView()` method, the data from cursor is used in the `View`.

Implementing newView()

Listing 20.2 shows the code the `PhotoCursorAdapter` class. The `newView()` method is on lines 25–31.

When you create a new view, a `LayoutInflater` is used to inflate a layout from the XML layout file `R.layout.photo_view_item`. That layout file contains a `RelativeLayout` with an `ImageView` and a `TextView`. The view holder concept is used. Each time the `newView()` method is called, a `ViewHolder` class is instantiated to hold the `ImageView` and `TextView` that the layout contains. You tie the `ListViewHolder` to the view using `setTag()`.

/

LISTING 20.2   PhotoCursorAdapter

```
1:     public class PhotoCursorAdapter extends CursorAdapter {
2:         Context mContext;
3:         public PhotoCursorAdapter(Context context, Cursor c, int flags) {
4:             super(context, c, flags);
5:             mContext = context;
6:         }
7:
8:         @Override
9:         public void bindView(View v, Context context, Cursor c) {
10:             ViewHolder vh = (ViewHolder) v.getTag();
11:             if (vh == null) {
12:                 vh = new ViewHolder();
13:                 vh.photoImageView =  (ImageView)
v.findViewById(R.id.photoImageView);
14:                 vh.textView = (TextView) v.findViewById(R.id.nameTextView);
15:             }
16:
17:             FlickrPhoto currentPhoto =
FlickrPhotoDbAdapter.getPhotoFromCursor(c);
18:             vh.id = currentPhoto.id;
19:             v.setTag(vh);
20:             vh.textView.setText(currentPhoto.title);
21:             Picasso.with(mContext).load(currentPhoto.smallImage)
22:                             .into( vh.photoImageView);
23:         }
24:
25:         @Override
26:         public View newView(Context context, Cursor cursor, ViewGroup parent) {
27:             LayoutInflater li = (LayoutInflater) mContext.getSystemService(
28:                 Context.LAYOUT_INFLATER_SERVICE);
29:             View v = li.inflate(R.layout. 1:, parent, false);
30:             return (v);
31:
32:         }
33:
34:         class ViewHolder {
35:             String id;
36:             ImageView photoImageView;
37:             TextView textView;
38:         }
39:     }
```

To complete this `CursorAdapter`, you must implement the `bindView()` method.

Implementing BindView

The basics of using the `bindView()` method are fairly straightforward: You tie the data from a cursor with a view to display.

Efficiently displaying images can be a challenge, but in this case, the code is using the Picasso library to retrieve and load images.

If a user flings the list, updating individual list items does not make sense. Updating items that are not in view can be a painfully slow experience for the user.

Basic Implementation of bindView()

The basic implementation of `bindView()` is simple. The `bindView()` method is passed a `View`, a `Context`, and a `Cursor`. You use data from the `Cursor` to populate the `View`:

```
public void bindView(View v, Context context, Cursor c) {
```

You can use the method `getPhotoFromCursor()` to get a `FlickrPhoto` object from the passed `Cursor`:

```
FlickrPhoto currentPhoto = FlickrPhotoDbAdapter.getPhotoFromCursor(c);
```

The `View` that is created in the `newView()` method is passed. In this case, the `View` is a `RelativeLayout` that includes a `TextView` and an `ImageView`. So, you could use that view to display the title for `currentPhoto`:

```
TextView titleTextView = (TextView) v.findViewById(R.id.titleTextView);
titleTextView.setText(currentPhoto.title);
```

You can improve this technique by using the view holder pattern.

Because a `ViewHolder` is added as a tag to the `View` in the `newView()` method, you know that you can retrieve that `ViewHolder` using `getTag()`. After you have determined whether you have an existing view holder or need to create a new one, you get the current photo data and display the information in the view.

Note that the `ViewHolder` contains data as well as `Views`. On line 18 of Listing 20.2, you set the `id` value of the `ViewHolder` to the `id` of the `currentPhoto`. That enables you to associate a view in the list with a particular `FlickrPhoto` object. You can take advantage of the fact that you have the `FlickrPhoto` object when someone clicks the view. The data from the object is immediately available to act on. Figure 20.1 shows the resulting app.

TRY IT YOURSELF ▼

Showing the Owner Data on the CardView

To show the owner, you must modify the XML layout for the item and update the `bindView0` method appropriately. Use the `TextView` as the tile as a model:

1. Add a `TextView` to photo_view_item.xml.

2. Add a new `TextView` to the `ViewHolder` class.

3. In the `bindView()` method, get the owner data for the `currentPhoto` and display it in the new `TextView`.

The Rest of the App

The loaders used in this hour relied on content providers for data retrieval. The content providers use a SQLite database for data storage and retrieval. To get the `CardView` style that is shown in Figure 20.1, the support library with the `CardView` was used. Picasso was used to load images in this app. An `IntentService` called `PhotoService` is used to get the data and load it into the database.

The full code for this hour and other chapters is available at http://www.talkingandroid.com.

Summary

This hour covered loaders at a conceptual level, and you implemented two examples using a `CursorLoader`. To accomplish this, you used the `FlickrPhotoProvider` content provider that you developed in Hour 14. You saw how a `CursorLoader` and `CursorAdapter` can work together in fragments that implements `LoaderManager.LoaderCallbacks`. You also created a custom adapter by extending `BaseAdapter`.

Q&A

Q. What is the advantage of using a `CursorAdapter` with loaders?

A. A `CursorAdapter` maps data from a cursor to the user interface. Because `onLoadFinished()` returns a cursor, you can use a `CursorAdapter` in the `onLoadFinished()` method to display the data that is available from the loader. The `CursorAdapter` is created in the `onActivityCreated()` method, and in the `onLoadFinished()` method, a new `Cursor` is swapped in.

Q. **Can loaders be used on Android 2.x devices?**

A. Loaders were introduced in Android 3.0 (Honeycomb), but they are available via the support library for older versions of Android.

Workshop

Quiz

1. What methods typically call an adapter's `swapCursor()` method?

2. What method fires when data is available?

3. What is the first parameter of the `initLoader()` method, and why is it important?

Answers

1. The `onLoadFinished()` and `onLoaderReset()` methods use `swapCursor`.

2. `onLoadFinished()` fires when data is available.

3. The first parameter to `initLoader()` is an `id`. It is important because it identifies the loader if more than one loader exists in the fragment or activity. It is passed to the `LoaderManager.Callbacks` methods.

Exercise

Add the ability to click a photo in the `ListView` to show a full image. You need to detect the click and pass the data required to show the image. You can create a new activity that accepts the required data as part of a passed intent.

PART IV

Next Steps

HOUR 21
Using Notifications

What You'll Learn in This Hour:

▶ Introducing notifications

▶ Creating and managing notifications

▶ Customizing notifications

Your Android device has many capabilities and many apps running on it. Your app is vying for the user's attention, but your app should be helpful and not annoying to the user. When a new email comes in, a notification occurs. When you have a meeting on your calendar, a notification occurs. A notification can occur based on your proximity to a location. Some notifications are present while an app is running. Consider apps that play music. The notification typically shows what music is playing and provides buttons such as pause and play to control the media. In this hour, you learn how to implement several different kinds of notification. When working with notifications, you can create, update, and cancel existing notifications.

Introducing Notifications

Notifications are indicated on your device by a small icon in the status bar. Figure 21.1 shows this.

FIGURE 21.1
Notifications on the status bar.

Components of a Notification

A notification consists of the small icon on the status bar, an icon that is displayed in the notification itself, a title, and a content message.

Those things comprise what is displayed in a typical notification, but a notification can do more. Typically, a notification has an action associated with it. When you click a notification, you expect to navigate somewhere in the app.

A notification can include a sound or vibration of the device.

Some notifications can be updated. They may be standard notifications with updated messages or can include a progress bar.

There is also the option for a notification to have a custom view.

You can set options for a notification and manage the notification. There are options for updating the notification and for handling what happens when the notification is selected.

Classes Used for a Notification

There is a `Notification` class that is the notification itself. These are the other Android classes that you typically use when defining and managing a notification:

- ▶ `Notification (android.app.Notification)`: A notification.

- ▶ `Notificaton.Builder (android.app.Notification.Builder)`: A class for building notifications.

- ▶ `NotificatonManager (android.app.NotificationManager)`: A class to create, update, and manage notifications.

- ▶ `PendingIntent (android.app.Notification.PendingIntent)`: A pending or future intent that is used as the action tied to a notification. You can create a pending intent to start an activity and associate it with a notification.

Creating and Managing Notifications

It is easy to create notifications using the `Notification.Builder` class. This section presents several examples with different options. In each of these scenarios, consider the following:

- ▶ What is being displayed?

- ▶ What is the action, if any?

- ▶ How is the notification managed after it is created?

    When is it dismissed?

    Can it be updated?

Building a Basic Notification

You can create a basic notification that includes an icon, title, and message. An action is not required. You can set the notification to be cancelled automatically. That way it will not linger. If you are not including an action, you should make it as easy as possible to clear the notification from the status bar.

These code snippets have the following fields defined:

```
int notificationId;
NotificationManager notificationManager;
Notification.Builder builder;
```

To create a basic notification, you create a new `Notification.Builder` and add the options that you want to display. A new `Notication.Builder` called builder is declared on line 2 of Listing 21.1.

Lines 3–6 of Listing 21.1 set the options for the notification being built. On line 4, the `setAutoCancel()` value is set to true. That means this notification is cancelled after it is dismissed. Some notifications remain on the status bar until they are cancelled by the app that created them.

Figure 21.2 shows the resulting notification.

LISTING 21.1 Building a Basic Notification

```
1:  builder =
2:      new Notification.Builder(MainActivity.this)
3:              .setSmallIcon(R.mipmap.ic_launcher)
4:              .setAutoCancel(true)
5:              .setContentTitle("Notification")
6:              .setContentText("Basic Notification. No Action");
7:      notificationManager = NotificationManager)
8:                      getSystemService(Context.NOTIFICATION_SERVICE);
9:      notificationManager.notify(notificationId, builder.build());
```

TRY IT YOURSELF ▼

Creating Your Own Basic Notification

Use the example in this hour and follow these steps to create a new notification:

1. Use Listing 21.1 as a model.

2. Create a new activity and add a button that creates a notification.

3. Set your own title and message.

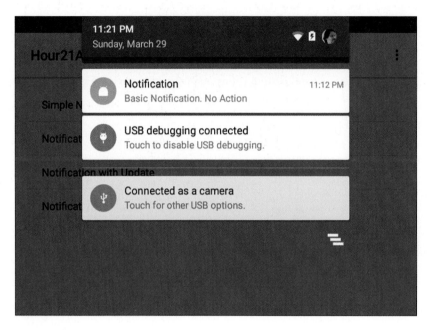

FIGURE 21.2
Displaying a basic notification.

Adding a Destination

Typically, notifications have an associated action. In most cases, the action is that the app starts a new activity. When the user clicks the notification, the user navigates to a specific part of the app.

In this example, you add these new things:

▶ The notification navigates to a new activity.

▶ The notification is cancelled from the new activity.

▶ A bitmap image is displayed in the notification.

To manage a notification, you must know the id of the notification. You use an integer as the notification id when you create the notification. In this case, the ID is set in the MainActivity and passed to the DestinationActivity. The notification is dismissed from the DestinationActivity.

Listing 21.2 shows the code in MainActivity for this notification.

LISTING 21.2 Building a Notification with an Action

```
 1:    notificationId = 1;
 2:    intent = new Intent(MainActivity.this, DestinationActivity.class);
 3:    intent.putExtra(DestinationActivity.ID, 1);
 4:    intent.putExtra(DestinationActivity.MESSAGE, "Received Notification 1");
 5:    pendingIntent=PendingIntent.getActivity(MainActivity.this, notificationId,
 6:                  intent,PendingIntent.FLAG_UPDATE_CURRENT);
 7:    Bitmap bigIcon = BitmapFactory.decodeResource(getResources(),
 8:                     R.drawable.nat);
 9:    builder =new Notification.Builder(MainActivity.this)
10:        .setSmallIcon(R.mipmap.ic_launcher)
11:        .setLargeIcon(bigIcon)
12:        .setContentTitle("Notification")
13:        .setContentText("Navigate to Destination Activity")
14:        .setContentIntent(pendingIntent);
15:    notificationManager = NotificationManager) getSystem
16:                      Service(Context.NOTIFICATION_SERVICE);
17:    notificationManager.notify(notificationId, builder.build());
```

In Listing 21.2, a new notification is built that includes a `PendingIntent`. On line 14, the `Notication.Builder` method `setContentIntent()` is called with `pendingIntent` as a parameter. The `PendingIntent` is defined on lines 5–6. The notification is passed with an `Intent`, context, and flag. The `Intent` that fires when a user chooses this notification is defined on lines 1–4. The intent starts an activity called `DestinationActivity` with several added extras. One extra is the notification id, and the other is a message to display.

At a high level, this code ties an action to the notification. The action is the launch of `DestinationActivity`.

There is another new feature in this notification. Lines 7–9 define a new bitmap. That bitmap is used in `Notfication.Builder` in the `setLargeIcon()` method on line 11.

Figure 21.3 shows the result.

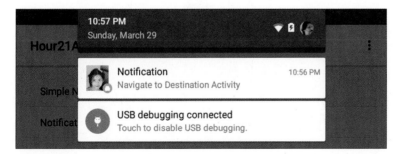

FIGURE 21.3
Adding the large icon to the notification.

Clicking this notification results in the `DestinationActivity` being displayed. In lines 3 and 4 of Listing 21.1, extras were added to the intent. One of those extras was an integer that contained the notification ID.

Because the `DestinationActivity` has the ID of the notification, that activity can now cancel or update the notification.

In this case, with the notification set to 1, the code in the `DestinationActivity` ultimately creates a `NotificationManager` and cancels the notification:

```
NotificationManager   notificationManager = (NotificationManager)
                            getSystemService (Context.NOTIFICATION_SERVICE);
notificationManager.cancel(notificationId);
```

Once the user reaches `DestinationActivity`, the notification is removed from the status bar.

Updating a Notification

Updating a notification is based on the idea that when a notification from your app uses the same notification ID, that notification should be considered an update. As previously shown, the notification `id` can be passed as an extra in the intent you create. For `DestinationActivity` to update the notification, the code reads the notification ID and uses it to create a new notification. Because the same ID number is used, this appears to be an update of the original notification.

Figure 21.4 shows the original and updated notification. The updated notification replaces the original notification.

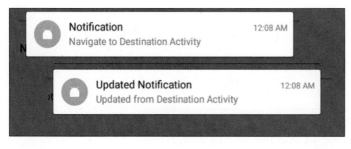

FIGURE 21.4
Original and updated notification.

More Notification Options

You can set additional options for your notifications to vibrate the device, make a sound, or start a timer.

A few additional straightforward methods in `Notification.Builder` include the following:

▶ `setUsesChronometer(Boolean b)`: Add a timer that shows elapsed time to the notification.

▶ `setVibrate(long[] pattern, int repeat)`: When passed an array of longs, the first value indicates the time to delay before the vibration should start, and the second value indicates how long the vibration should last. The pattern will continue for the values passed. The second parameter indicates how many times the pattern should repeat. To not repeat at all, set this value to -1.

▶ `setSubText (CharSequence text)`: The third line of text that can be displayed.

▶ `setProgress (int max, int progress, boolean indeterminate)`: Set a progress bar for this notification.

Figure 21.5 shows a notification with an indeterminate progress bar. It was created adding the `setProgess()` method to the builder:

```
.setProgress(0,0,true)
```

FIGURE 21.5
Notification with indeterminate progress bar.

TRY IT YOURSELF ▼

Adding a Notification with the Chronometer

Refer to the notification methods in this chapter to create a notification with additional features:

1. Create a new notification.

2. It should use a chronometer, and you use the `setUsesChronometer()` method.

3. Add a vibration to the notification using the `setVibrate()` method.

Customizing Notifications

You can create and use custom layouts for your notifications by using the `RemoteViews` class. To do so, follow these steps:

1. Create the layout.

2. Use the layout in `RemoteViews`.

3. Add the `RemoteViews` to the notification.

You create the layout as you normally would using the design mode of Android Studio. See Figure 21.6 for the layout in this example.

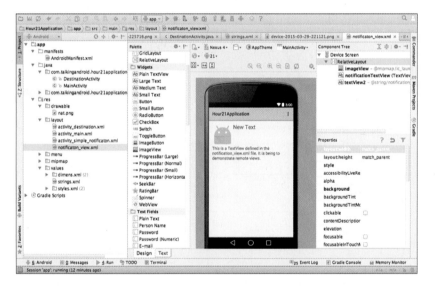

FIGURE 21.6
Create a layout for the notification.

Defining the remote depends on using the layout you created and setting values for any widgets that you want to use. You use a package name and the resource `id` of the layout you want to use for the remote view. Then, you can access and update the individual views in the layout like `TextViews` and `ImageViews`.

`RemoteViews` has methods like `setTextViewText()` that let you set the text value for a `TextView` that is contained in the `RemoteViews`. Similarly, you would set an image from a resource with the method `setImageViewResource()`:

```
RemoteViews notificationView = new RemoteViews(MainActivity.this.getPackageName(),
                                    R.layout.notificaton_view);
notificationView.setTextViewText(R.id.notificationTextView, "Customized it!");
String longText = getResources().getString(R.string.notification_text);
```

```
notificationView.setTextViewText(R.id.textView2,longText);
notificationView.setImageViewResource(R.id.imageView, R.mipmap.ic_launcher);
```

Once the `RemoteViews` is defined, you must tie it to the notification. This is the `Notification.Builder` code. The method `setContent()` is passed the `RemoteViews` object `notificationView`. In this case, a `Notification` is built and assigned to `notification` with the call to `builder.build()`. The `Notification` can be accessed directly, and the value for `bigContentView` is directly set to the new `RemoteViews` `notificationView`:

```
builder =new Notification.Builder(MainActivity.this)
            .setSmallIcon(R.mipmap.ic_launcher)
            .setContentTitle("Notification")
            .setContentText("Navigate to Destination Activity")
            .setContentIntent(pendingIntent)
            .setContent(notificationView);

    Notification notification = builder.build();
    notification.bigContentView = notificationView;
    notificationManager =NotificationManager)
                        getSystemService(Context.NOTIFICATION_SERVICE);
    notificationManager.notify(notificationId, notification);
```

Figure 21.7 shows the result.

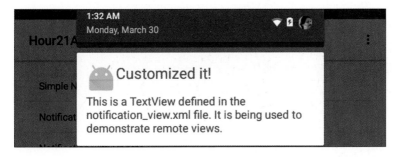

FIGURE 21.7
Notification using `RemoteViews`.

Summary

In this hour, you learned about how to use `Notification.Builder` to create different kinds of notifications. Notifications use `PendingIntents` to launch intents when selected. A notification is controlled using a `NotificationManager`. You can use a `NotificationManager` to create a new `Notification` or update an existing one. Using `RemoteViews` enables you to customize the view for a notification.

Q&A

Q. What other options are available for a notification?

A. There are additional options for a notification. You can set the category and priority. Using the `addPerson()` method, you can add multiple people to a notification. In Android 5.0 (Lollipop), you can use the `Notification.MediaStyle` option to set up media controls in your notification.

Q. When you start an activity from a notification, how should navigation be handled when the user clicks the Back button?

A. When you launch an intent that takes you into the navigational hierarchy of your app, the goals is to provide consistent navigation. It should be as though the user navigated there directly. To do that, use the `TaskStackBuilder` to re-create a back stack.

Workshop

Quiz

1. What value must be known to update a notification?

2. True or false: A notification must always have an associated action.

3. What does the `RemoteViews` `setTextViewText()` method do?

Answers

1. To update a notification, you must know the ID of the notification.

2. False. Notifications typically have associated actions, but they are not required. You created a notification with no action and set the auto cancel value to true using `.setAutoCancel(true)`.

3. The `RemoteViews` `setTextViewText()` method updates the text on a `TextView` that exists in the `RemoteViews` object.

Exercise

Create your own layout and apply it to a notification. If your layout includes buttons, how will you know when a user clicked on the buttons? You can use the `RemoteViews.setOnClick-PendingIntent()` method to specify a resource for a view and a `PendingIntent` to start if that resource is selected. See http://developer.android.com/reference/android/widget/RemoteViews.html#setOnClickPendingIntent(int, android.app.PendingIntent).

HOUR 22

Android TV and Wear Apps

What You'll Learn in This Hour:

▶ Android as a platform
▶ Developing Android Wear apps
▶ Developing Android TV apps

Android is everywhere. Android was developed as an operating system for devices, not just for phones. There are many sizes of Android phones and tablets. Android is open source, and companies like Amazon have made modified versions of Android for their own devices. Android apps can be developed for cars, TVs, and small devices (for example, watches). In this hour, you learn about approaching Android as a platform and explore developing both wearable apps and TV apps.

Android as a Platform

In Hour 1, "Introducing Android," you learned about some of the core components of the Android platform: activities, intents, intent services, and broadcast receivers. Since then, you have learned about using resources, designing layout files, storing data, and using content providers. The core components of the Android platform are used whether you are developing a wearable app that will be displayed on a watch or an advanced app for a TV.

You need to be aware of specific constraints or recommendations when developing for a specific target such as Android Wear or Android TV. One factor is the size of the screen, but there are others. For example, the input mechanism changes for these devices. TVs are always in landscape mode.

Android Studio offers options for creating both Android TV and Android Wear projects. There are specific libraries used with these apps.

You can create an Android Virtual Device (AVD) for both watches and TVs. In Android Studio, in design mode, you can specify the device and platform that you are targeting.

As you think of Android as a platform, you can use what you've learned and have a similar approach to Android app development no matter what device you are targeting.

Developing Android Wear Apps

When developing Wear apps, you want to consider the following:

- ▶ How are Wear apps different?

- ▶ What libraries and development configurations are used?

- ▶ How will you test the app?

Any Wear app has a limited amount of real estate. The app you create is intended to run on a watch. That watch can be round or square. Wearable apps are often designed to be paired with a second device.

Designing for Android Wear Differences

The UI model for Android Wear was created to take advantage of the strengths of a small and accessible screen. The model focuses on two concepts: *suggest* and *demand*.

Suggest implies that the context is important. When you look at your watch, relevant information for where you are and what you are doing should display. Whether that is a meeting reminder or a weather report, it is something meaningful to you at the time.

Wear handles this with a series of card views that display on the device as needed. The user can move through these cards with vertical scrolling.

Demand implies that there are times when a user is directed and actively seeking information. Demand is handled through voice commands. It is no surprise that each voice command launches an intent. As a developer, you can create apps that handle these intents and will be shown as options for voice commands. Figure 22.1 shows some sample Wear screens with a square watch face running in the emulator.

FIGURE 22.1
Apps shown on Square watch.

Setting Up for Wear Development

Android Studio enables you to create a project for Android Wear that includes a blank Wear activity.

Creating an Android Wear Project in Android Studio

Follow these steps to create an Android Wear project and to see what layout is created:

1. Create an Android Wear project in Android Studio. Check only the Android Wear check box.

2. Generate a blank activity for the project (see Figure 22.2).

3. Find the rect_activity_main.xml file and open it in design mode.

4. Set the device in design mode to be a square wearable (see Figure 22.3).

Once the project is created, you can check the layout files and other aspects of the project. To view the layout appropriately, change the device in Android Studio design mode to be a wearable (see Figure 22.3).

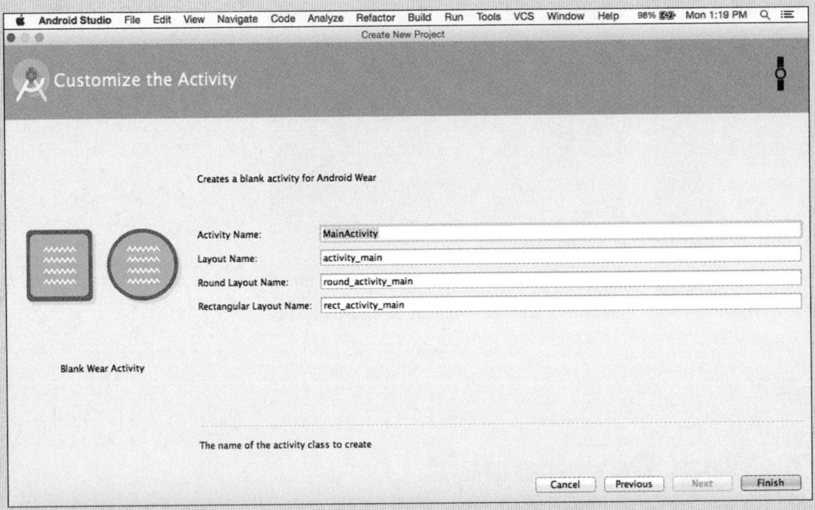

FIGURE 22.2
Creating a wearable activity.

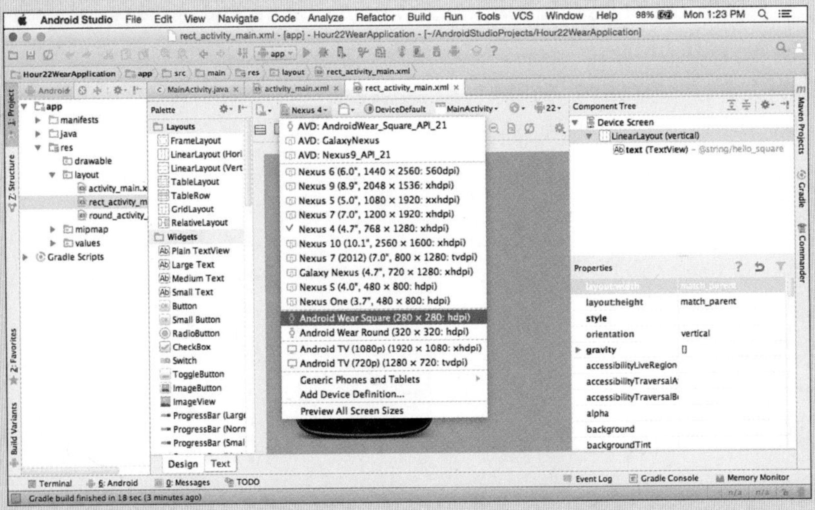

FIGURE 22.3
Set device for wearable.

Once the project is set up, you want to notice a few things. You can see the list of libraries used in the project by opening the build.gradle file for the app. There are several new dependencies. A wearable project will use the Android wearable support library and the Google Play services wearable library:

```
dependencies {
    compile fileTree(dir: 'libs', include: ['*.jar'])
    compile 'com.google.android.support:wearable:1.1.0'
    compile 'com.google.android.gms:play-services-wearable:7.0.0'
}
```

Another difference is in MainActivity.java. The class `WatchViewStub`(android.support. wearable.view.WatchViewStub) is used. A `WatchViewStub` extends `FrameLayout`, so it is a layout class. It is used to display the appropriate view for a square or round watch. The code in `MainActivity` is as follows:

```
final WatchViewStub stub = (WatchViewStub) findViewById(R.id.watch_view_stub);
  stub.setOnLayoutInflatedListener(new WatchViewStub.OnLayoutInflatedListener() {
  @Override
      public void onLayoutInflated(WatchViewStub stub) {
          mTextView = (TextView) stub.findViewById(R.id.text);
      }
  });
```

When you look at the layout files in resources, you will see that there are three. One is for the `MainActivity`, and it includes only the `WatchViewStub` layout. It uses the following attribute to indicate that this layout applies to Wear devices:

```
tools:deviceIds="wear"
```

The other two layouts, rect_activity_main.xml and round_activity_main.xml, are used for square and round wear devices. They include the appropriate `deviceIds`. The layout for square devices includes the following:

```
tools:deviceIds="wear_square"
```

The round layout uses this:

```
tools:deviceIds="wear_round"
```

Testing a Wear App

You need to create an Android Virtual Device (AVD) for your Wear app.

▼ TRY IT YOURSELF

Creating an AVD for Android Wear

To test your Android Wear app, you need an AVD. Follow these steps to create an AVD for Android Wear:

1. In Android Studio, go to Tools, Android, AVD Manager.

2. In AVD Manager, choose to create a new virtual device.

3. Choose a square or round device (see Figure 22.4).

4. Select Lollipop for development. You may need to upgrade your software development kit (SDK).

5. On the emulator, using the new virtual device, run the app that you previously generated.

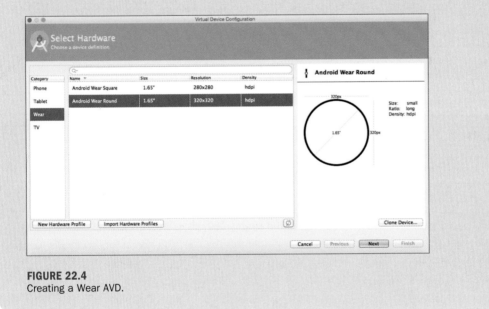

FIGURE 22.4
Creating a Wear AVD.

After you have the environment in place, you can develop and test your Wear app like any other Android app. You can apply additional configuration options to pair a device with the emulator. You can dive into Wear specifics by examining the wearables support package application programming interfaces (APIs) and related documentation (http://developer.android.com/reference/packages-wearable-support.html).

Adding a Notification

Notifications are important in Android Wear development. Your watch notifies you, and you take an action. Using the code from Hour 21, "Using Notifications," as a starting point, you create a notification for Android Wear and try it on your emulator. The app creates a notification with a pending intent. That intent starts the `WearDestinationActivity` that just displays a `TextView` that says, "You made it!"

In Listing 22.1, the code for `WatchViewStub` occurs on lines 20–28. The `WatchViewStub` is defined using the `findViewById()` method. Then, additional work is done when the view is inflated. In the `onLayoutInflated()` method on line 25, the `TextView` that is defined in each separate layout is accessed.

LISTING 22.1   Notification in Android Wear

```
 1: package com.talkingandroid.hour22wearapplication;
 2: import android.app.Activity;
 3: import android.app.Notification;
 4: import android.app.NotificationManager;
 5: import android.app.PendingIntent;
 6: import android.content.Context;
 7: import android.content.Intent;
 8: import android.os.Bundle;
 9: import android.support.wearable.view.WatchViewStub;
10: import android.widget.TextView;
11:
12: public class MainActivity extends Activity {
13:
14:     private TextView mTextView;
15:
16:     @Override
17:     protected void onCreate(Bundle savedInstanceState) {
18:         super.onCreate(savedInstanceState);
19:         setContentView(R.layout.activity_main);
20:         final WatchViewStub stub = (WatchViewStub)
21:                         findViewById(R.id.watch_view_stub);
22:         stub.setOnLayoutInflatedListener(new
23:             WatchViewStub.OnLayoutInflatedListener() {
24:             @Override
25:             public void onLayoutInflated(WatchViewStub stub) {
26:                 mTextView = (TextView) stub.findViewById(R.id.text);
27:             }
28:         });
29:
30:         Intent= new Intent(this, WearDestinationActivity.class);
31:         PendingIntent pendingIntent =
32:                 PendingIntent.getActivity(this, 0, intent, 0);
```

```
33:            int notificationId = 0;
34:            Notification.Builder builder =
35:                new Notification.Builder(MainActivity.this)
36:                    .setSmallIcon(R.mipmap.ic_launcher)
37:                    .setAutoCancel(true)
38:                    .setContentTitle("Notification")
39:                    .setContentText("Basic Notification with Action")
40:                    .addAction(R.mipmap.ic_launcher,
41:                        "Go for it!", pendingIntent);
42:
43:            NotificationManager notificationManager =
44:                (NotificationManager)
45:                    getSystemService(Context.NOTIFICATION_SERVICE);
46:        notificationManager.notify(notificationId, builder.build());
47:
48:        }
49: }
```

The notification is defined on lines 30–41. In this case, an action is added to the
`Notification.Builder` on lines 40–41. The action contains an image, message, and pending
intent. The notification is created and sent on lines 43–46.

When you run the app in the emulator, the following occurs:

1. The notification is displayed.

2. Slide left to see the action.

3. Click the action for the intent to fire.

Figure 22.5 shows the states of the app through the steps of the notification.

FIGURE 22.5
Showing a notification in Android Wear.

Developing Android TV Apps

When developing Wear apps, you can ask yourself the same questions:

▶ How are Android TV apps different?

▶ What libraries and development configurations are used?

▶ How will you test the app?

An Android TV app will run on a large screen, that screen will always be in layout mode, and a TV app does not have touch input. Navigation will be done with a D-Pad, and there is a certain amount of space on the screen that you may lose to something known as *overscan*. In Android TV development, there are support libraries and examples that you can use to make successful TV apps.

Designing for Android TV Differences

The size of the screen and how people use a TV in their living room are considerations when creating a TV app. You should consider the nature of your app. Are you delivering content? Do you need to provide a way for people to search a large amount of content? Are you creating a game or educational or interactive app?

The design aspects that are highlighted for a TV app are casual consumption, a cinematic experience, and simplicity. TVs are devices for consuming media. You do not need to be a binge watcher to appreciate that TVs are made for consuming media in a casual atmosphere (usually a living room).

The idea that TV is for content consumption and that TV viewing is a passive experience is called the *lean-back experience*. Viewers want to lean back and enjoy themselves.

The 10ft environment is used for entertainment and not for work.

The 10ft environment is a social environment rather than a single user environment. When developing apps, whether they are for content consumption, games, or something else, it makes sense to consider the experience for everyone in the room, not just the person holding the remote.

Like mobile apps, TV apps should not be cluttered and should provide clear choices for users. There should be enough space between the elements in a TV app to foster clear navigation. Navigation will be done via the D-Pad's directional keys.

A TV will often be hooked up to the best speakers in the house. You should consider how sound is used in your app. Related to sound is the concept of audio focus. You can think of that as playing nice with other apps. When your app loses focus, the audio should be turned low or off.

Android TV Development

The process for starting Android TV development is similar to Android Wear development.

You will create an appropriate TV AVD. You will use the AVD Manager, as shown in Figure 22.6.

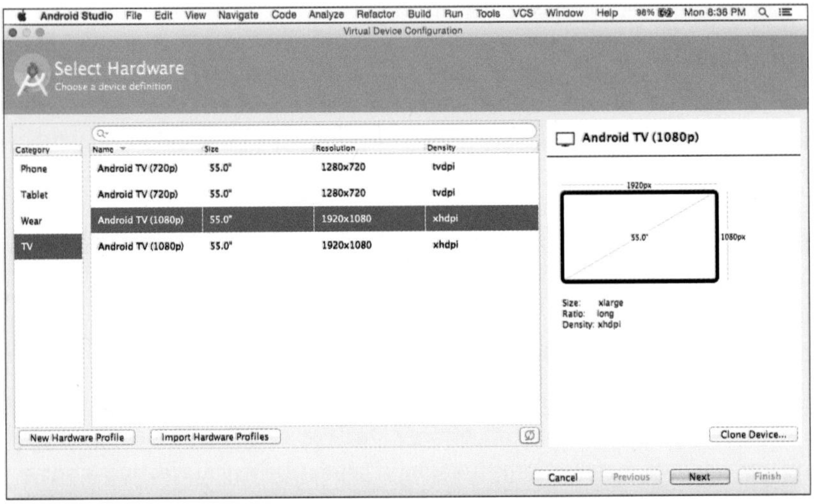

FIGURE 22.6
Create an AVD for TV.

Android Studio also includes an Android TV project that can be used to start your application. If you choose to create a TV activity with the Android TV project, much of the infrastructure for a fully developed project is included. The advantage of this is that there is a lot of code and infrastructure in place. To create a simple TV app, you can create a TV project but choose to create no activities.

You can learn a lot by creating an Android TV project.

▼ TRY IT YOURSELF

Creating an Android TV Project in Android Studio

Starting an Android TV project is similar to creating an Android Wear project, but the resulting project is much more elaborate. Follow these steps to create the project and see the results:

1. Create an Android TV project in Android Studio. Check only the Android TV check box.

2. Choose to create a TV Activity.

3. Find build.gradle file and check to see what libraries are included as dependencies.

The libraries included in an Android TV project without a generated activity are as follows:

```
compile 'com.android.support:recyclerview-v7:21.0.3'
compile 'com.android.support:leanback-v17:21.0.3'
```

If you generate an activity in addition to the `leanback` and `recyclerview` modules, you get the following:

```
compile 'com.android.support:appcompat-v7:21.0.3'
compile 'com.squareup.picasso:picasso:2.3.2'
```

That is the Picasso library that you are familiar with and the Android support library for backward compatibility. You also use the `RecyclerView`.

The new library for an Android TV project is the leanback library. The leanback library includes the following:

- ▶ **BrowseFragment:** `Fragment` for browsing media

- ▶ **DetailsFragment:** `Fragment` used to show details

- ▶ **PlaybackOverlayFragment:** `DetailsFragment` for playback controls and content

- ▶ **SearchFragment:** `Fragment` to handle searches

Testing an Android TV App

You will to use the AVD that you created to test your TV app. The sample project that is generated by Android Studio includes the key features from the leanback library. Figure 22.7 shows the app running in the emulator.

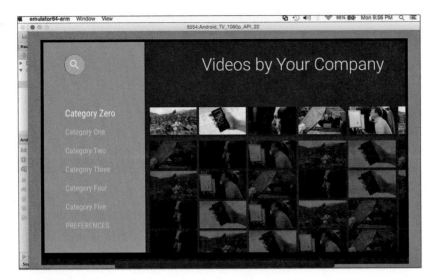

FIGURE 22.7
Running generated app in emulator.

Summary

In this hour, you learned about design and development implications for Android Wear and Android TV. In both cases, Android Studio includes a project that you can use as a starting point. There are also AVDs that are specific to testing TV and Android Wear apps. There are support libraries that support each device. The common concepts of Android development carry through when developing Wear and TV apps.

Q&A

Q. How do people get TV and watch apps?

A. Google Play is used for these apps. When apps are published, settings in the Android manifest file are used to determine which devices to offer the app. For example, no app that requires touch will be available on a TV device. You learn more about publishing apps in Hour 24, "Publishing Your Apps."

Q. Are there differences between developing games and apps for TV?

A. Yes, if your game requires a game controller, you can specify that in your manifest file. You will not have to rely on the D-Pad for navigation. For games, you might consider trying Unity Android development.

Workshop

Quiz

1. How does a `WatchStubView` indicate that it supports Android Wear devices?

2. True or false: In an Android Wear app, there can be only one activity.

3. Name at least one thing that is always true for an Android TV app.

Answers

1. The `WatchStubView` has `deviceIds` set to `"wear"`. The round and square layouts have the `deviceIds` attribute set to `"wear_square"` and `"wear_round"`, respectively.

2. False. A Wear app can have more than one activity. You saw this in the notification example when the notification's action was to navigate to a new activity.

3. Android TV apps are always in landscape mode and never have touch input.

Exercise

Create an Android TV app with no blank TV activity. You need to add your own activity to start development. Create an activity with a message displayed in a `TextView` and then send a notification. Run this simple app in the AVD that you created for Android TV.

More Features to Explore

What You'll Learn in This Hour:

▶ Using Google Play services

▶ Using Google Play services for location

▶ Using open source

▶ Using sensors, Bluetooth, and more

Professional apps are responsive, pay attention to detail, and include elegant finishing touches. A great Android app might use specific Android sensors such as the accelerometer or features such as Bluetooth or a location-based service. This hour begins with a discussion about how the features from Google Play services can be incorporated into your app. A demo app that uses Google Play services for determining location is developed. For other finishing touches, you learn about open source, Android sensors, and other features that may be used in your next great Android app.

Using Google Play Services

Google Play services is a library, really a set of libraries, that you can use in your apps. You can use Google Play services to add features such as location, maps, ads, Google Cloud Messaging, and more. For your app to be successful, Google Play services must be available on the user's device. For apps that you publish in the Google Play store, that will not generally be a problem. However, if you plan on publishing on the Amazon App Store or other marketplaces, you must consider alternatives to use in those markets.

Setting Up Google Play Services

It is easy to set up and use Google Play services in Android Studio. You need to do two things:

1. First, add this line that refers to the Google Play Services library to your apps build.gradle file under dependencies:

```
compile 'com.google.android.gms:play-services:7.0.0'
```

2. Add the following to the Android manifest.xml file with the `Application` tag:

```
<meta-data android:name="com.google.android.gms.version"
       android:value="@integer/google_play_services_version" />
```

Alternatively, you can create a project in Android Studio that creates a Google Play services activity (see Figure 23.1).

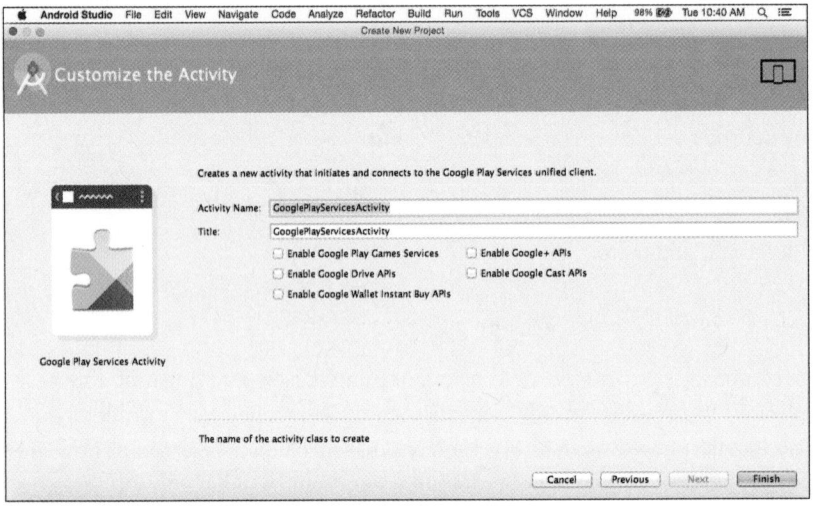

FIGURE 23.1
Creating a Google Play services activity.

Alternatively, you can just supply the library for the service you need. This a list of currently available services and what is required in the gradle build file. Note that you have already used the Android Wear service in Hour 22, "Android TV and Wear Apps."

▶ **Google+:** com.google.android.gms:play-services-plus:7.0.0

▶ **Google Account Login:** com.google.android.gms:play-services-identity:7.0.0

▶ **Google Actions, Base Client Library:** com.google.android.gms:play-services-base:7.0.0

▶ **Google App Indexing:** com.google.android.gms:play-services-appindexing:7.0.0

▶ **Google Analytics:** com.google.android.gms:play-services-analytics:7.0.0

▶ **Google Cast:** com.google.android.gms:play-services-cast:7.0.0

▶ **Google Cloud Messaging:** com.google.android.gms:play-services-gcm:7.0.0

▶ **Google Drive:** com.google.android.gms:play-services-drive:7.0.0

▶ **Google Fit:** com.google.android.gms:play-services-fitness:7.0.0

- ▶ **Google Location, Activity Recognition, and Places:** com.google.android.gms:play-services-location:7.0.0

- ▶ **Google Maps:** com.google.android.gms:play-services-maps:7.0.0

- ▶ **Google Mobile Ads:** com.google.android.gms:play-services-ads:7.0.0

- ▶ **Google Nearby:** com.google.android.gms:play-services-nearby:7.0.0

- ▶ **Google Panorama Viewer:** com.google.android.gms:play-services-panorama:7.0.0

- ▶ **Google Play Game services:** com.google.android.gms:play-services-games:7.0.0

- ▶ **SafetyNet:** com.google.android.gms:play-services-safetynet:7.0.0

- ▶ **Google Wallet:** com.google.android.gms:play-services-wallet:7.0.0

- ▶ **Android Wear:** com.google.android.gms:play-services-wearable:7.0.0

You need to know the specifics of the Google Play service library that you plan on using, but you will always have to check to determine whether the services are available.

Checking for Google Play Services

Google Play services is based on the idea of connecting to the application programming interface (API) services. If you cannot connect, the services may not be available.

One way to check for availability is to implement an `onConnectionFailed()` listener.

A alternate way to check to see of Google Play services is available is to use the `GooglePlayServicesUtil(com.google.android.gms.common.GooglePlayServicesUtil)` and use the method `isGooglePlayServicesAvailable()`.

You have to add these `import` statements:

```
import com.google.android.gms.common.ConnectionResult;
import com.google.android.gms.common.GooglePlayServicesClient;
import com.google.android.gms.common.GooglePlayServicesUtil;
```

Then you can add code to do the actual check. You will generally do that in the activity `onStart()` method:

```
@Override
    public void onStart() {
        super.onStart();
        int googlePlayResult =
            GooglePlayServicesUtil.isGooglePlayServicesAvailable(this);
        if (googlePayResult == ConnectionResult.SUCCESS ) {
            // Start your services
```

```
    }else{
            // handle the case when services are not available
    }
}
```

Using Google Play Services for Location

Location-based services are an important part of Android development. There are classes built in to the Android platform that can be used for determining your location. Using Google Play services for location is both easy and very accurate. After covering some concepts about how location-based services work, you'll develop an app that retrieves your current location information and tracks your location.

Determining Location

An Android device can obtain your current location in several ways. A global positioning system (GPS) uses satellite data to determine location. The underlying technique is triangulation. If you know your distance from three points, you can determine where you are. GPS relies on triangulating satellite data. If you are connected to a cellular network, the ID of the cell tower that the device is connected to provides your location. The Wi-Fi network that the device is attached to can also be used as the source of location information. Multiple companies, including Google, can tie a specific Wi-Fi network to a specific location.

Each method has advantages and disadvantages. Generally, you must balance the accuracy of GPS with the lower power consumption of the other methods:

▶ GPS is accurate but might not work inside or with an obstructed view of the sky. It consumes a significant amount of power and causes battery drain.

▶ Cell ID is less accurate than GPS, but consumes little power.

▶ Wi-Fi might be very accurate depending on whether a network is recognized. It also consumes little power.

Using cell tower and Wi-Fi data together gives a more accurate location than either method alone, and Android has built-in support for this technique.

Android permissions for location-based services include a coarse location and a fine location. You must set these permissions to use location in your app:

▶ `android.permission.ACCESS_FINE_LOCATION`: The permission to use GPS.

▶ `android.permission.ACCESS_COARSE_LOCATION`: The permission to use the Android network provider. It uses both Wi-Fi and cell ID for location.

In the Android platform, a `LocationManager` (`android.location.LocationManager`) is used to access to system location services on the device and to request location updates. Location-based services rely heavily on the use of the `LocationManager` component.

A typical use case for `LocationManager` is to detect changes in location using GPS. To do that, you need to do the following:

1. Set `android.permission.ACCESS_FINE_LOCATION`.

2. Instantiate `LocationManager`.

3. Request location updates via GPS.

4. Listen for location changes.

That can be complicated and has limitations. In some cases, you might need to use the core location functionality. In many cases, however, you will be successful using Google Play services.

Implementing Location Tracking

To use location tracking with Google Play services, you use the library for location. From the list earlier in this hour, that means you can use the following:

`com.google.android.gms:play-services-location:7.0.0`

Listing 23.1 shows the entire code for an activity that uses Google Play services and displays current location. In the `onStart()` method in lines 31–42, a `GoogleApiClient` is defined. This is the Google Play services client. In line 36, the `LocationServices.API` is added as a service.

LISTING 23.1   Get Current Location with Google Play Services

```
 1: package com.talkingandroid.hour23application;
 2: import android.app.Activity;
 3: import android.os.Bundle;
 4: import android.location.Address;
 5: import android.location.Geocoder;
 6: import android.location.Location;
 7: import android.widget.TextView;
 8: import com.google.android.gms.common.ConnectionResult;
 9: import com.google.android.gms.common.api.GoogleApiClient;
10: import com.google.android.gms.location.LocationListener;
11: import com.google.android.gms.location.LocationRequest;
12: import com.google.android.gms.location.LocationServices;
13: import java.io.IOException;
14: import java.util.List;
15:
16: public class LocationActivity extends Activity implements  LocationListener,
```

```
17:            GoogleApiClient.ConnectionCallbacks,
18:            GoogleApiClient.OnConnectionFailedListener  {
19:
20:     TextView mDisplayTextView;
21:     LocationRequest mLocationRequest;
22:     private GoogleApiClient mGoogleApiClient;
23:
24:     @Override
25:     protected void onCreate(Bundle savedInstanceState) {
26:         super.onCreate(savedInstanceState);
27:         setContentView(R.layout.activity_location);
28:         mDisplayTextView = (TextView) findViewById(R.id.textView);
29:     }
30:
31:     @Override
32:     protected void onStart() {
33:         super.onStart();
34:         if (mGoogleApiClient == null) {
35:             mGoogleApiClient = new GoogleApiClient.Builder(this)
36:                     .addApi(LocationServices.API)
37:                     .addConnectionCallbacks(this)
38:                     .addOnConnectionFailedListener(this)
39:                     .build();
40:         }
41:         mGoogleApiClient.connect();
42:     }
43:
44:     @Override
45:     protected void onStop() {
46:         if (mGoogleApiClient != null) {
47:             mGoogleApiClient.disconnect();
48:         }
49:         super.onStop();
50:     }
51:
52:     @Override
53:     public void onConnected(Bundle connectionHint) {
54:         mLocationRequest = LocationRequest.create();
55:         LocationServices.FusedLocationApi.requestLocationUpdates
56:                     (mGoogleApiClient,mLocationRequest,this);
57:         Location location =
58:             LocationServices.FusedLocationApi.getLastLocation(mGoogleApiClient);
59:         mDisplayTextView.setText("Connected"
60:                     + location.getLatitude() +"," + location.getLongitude() );
61:     }
62:
63:     @Override
64:     public void onConnectionFailed(ConnectionResult arg0) {}
```

```
65:
66:     @Override
67:     public void onConnectionSuspended(int i) {}
68:
69:     @Override
70:    public void onLocationChanged(Location location) {
71:        Geocoder coder = new Geocoder(getApplicationContext());
72:         List<Address> geocodeResults;
73:       try {
74:            geocodeResults = coder.getFromLocation(location.getLatitude(),
75:                location.getLongitude(), 1);
76:             for (Address address: geocodeResults){
77:                mDisplayTextView.setText("Update: "
78:                   + location.getLatitude() +","
79:                   + location.getLongitude()+" : " +address.getLocality());
80:            }
81:
82:          } catch (IOException e) {
83:              e.printStackTrace();
84:          }
85:      }
86: }
```

In lines 16–18, the activity extends three classes:

▶ **LocationListener:** To listen for location changes

▶ **GoogleApiClient.ConnectionCallbacks:** To fire when Google Play services connects

▶ **GoogleApiClient.OnConnectionFailedListener:** To fire if Google Play services fails

The onConnected() method is on line 53. Code that relies on a connection to Google Play services should be placed in the onConnected() method.

It is in the onConnected() method that the location services are created and used. The LocationListener is specified as this on line 56. That means that the current activity is the LocationListener.

The activity implements the onLocationChanged() method, so it is a LocationListener. The onLocation() changed code updates a TextView on any location changes.

Figure 23.2 shows a screenshot of that app.

The permission android.permission.ACCESS_FINE_LOCATION is set.

FIGURE 23.2
Simple location app.

Using Open Source and External SDKs

You have used the Picasso project to load images. Picasso was developed at Square. Square and other companies have made it a practice to develop and release open source projects that can be very helpful to your development efforts.

Using open source libraries is common for individual developers and many companies. Most open source code includes a specific license regarding usage. Many are released under the Apache 2.0 license. You can find more information about that license at http://www.apache.org/licenses/. The FAQ section includes an explanation of the license for nonlawyers.

The following sections describe each of these briefly. These projects and other open source projects can help you make better apps.

Picasso

Handling images in Android might not always be straightforward. The goal of Picasso is to handle working with images and image views in an elegant way. It handles disk caching and memory caching of images and keeps overall memory usage to a minimum. Much of the "plumbing" of handling images is kept behind the scenes.

Loading an image from a URL using Picasso is done with one line:

```
Picasso.with(context).load("http://i.imgur.com/DvpvklR.png").into(imageView);
```

Checking Out the Android Projects Created at Square

The projects available from Square are so amazing that you just have to check for yourself:

1. Go to http://square.github.io/.

2. Read about okhttp.

3. Read about Retrofit.

Realm

Realm (https://github.com/realm/realm-java) is a mobile database for Android. It is a modern replacement for SQLite.

Fabric and Crashlytics

Fabric (https://get.fabric.io/) is a set of tools from Twitter. It includes Crashlytics, which is a software development kit (SDK) for collecting meaningful data when an app crashes. Fabric includes Twitter integration and ad opportunities. Fabric is not completely open source!

Digging Deeper into Android

Hopefully this is not a surprise, but 24 hours is not enough time to cover all the interesting and useful features of the Android platform and Android SDK. You've worked on many applications and features over the course of this book.

With the knowledge you have acquired thus far, you might find yourself thinking about your own application ideas. The rest of this hour covers some additional Android features that might help with your applications and point you in the right direction for using the features in your own application.

The Android developer documentation is a good starting point for further exploration of these topics: http://developer.android.com/.

Checking Out the Latest Android Updates

The Android platform changes. Check for new APIs and updates that may not have been discussed. To do so, follow these steps:

1. Go to http://developer.android.com/.

2. Identify the latest release of Android.

3. Read the release notes!

4. List any new features for developers.

5. Check what percentage of users have installed the latest release.

Using Sensors

Sensors can add interesting and unique features to your app. Android devices come with hardware and software sensors and not all devices will have all sensors. That means that one thing to know about sensors in general is that your app has to check to see whether they exist on a user's device.

This snippet of code checks for the accelerometer sensor:

```
private SensorManager mSensorManager;
mSensorManager = (SensorManager) getSystemService(Context.SENSOR_SERVICE);
if (mSensorManager.getDefaultSensor(TYPE_ACCELEROMETER) != null){
  // Sensor is available
} else {
  // Sensor is not available
}
```

Working with sensors takes a common approach. Like many things in Android, when working with a sensor, you set up a listener and listen for changes produced by the sensor. There is a `SensorEventListener` (`android.hardware.SensorEventListener`) class for this purpose. A `SensorEventListener` implements the `onSensorChanged()` method to listen for `SensorEvents` (`android.hardware.SensorEvent`). From the `SensorEvent`, you can determine the sensor that generated the event and data associated with the event.

The following are some of the device sensors that the Android SDK supports:

▶ **Accelerometer:** Measures acceleration in three dimensions

▶ **Light sensor:** Measures ambient brightness

- **Magnetic field sensor:** Measures earth's magnetic field in three dimensions

- **Orientation sensor:** Measures a device's orientation

- **Temperature sensor:** Measures ambient temperature

- **Proximity sensor:** Measures whether there is something near the screen of the device

Handling User Gestures

You already know how to listen for click events. You can also handle gestures, such as flings, scrolls, and taps, by using the `GestureDetector` class (`android.view.GestureDetector`). You can use the `GestureDetector` class by implementing the `onTouchEvent()` method within an activity.

The following are some of the gestures an application can watch for and handle:

- **onDown:** Occurs when the user first presses the touch screen.

- **onShowPress:** Occurs after the user first presses the touch screen but before the user lifts up or moves around on the screen.

- **onSingleTapUp:** Occurs when the user lifts up from the touch screen as part of a single-tap event.

- **onSingleTapConfirmed:** Called when a single-tap event occurs.

- **onDoubleTap:** Called when a double-tap event occurs.

- **onDoubleTapEvent:** Called when an event within a double-tap gesture occurs, including any down, move, or up action.

- **onLongPress:** Similar to `onSingleTapUp`, but called if the user has held his or her finger down just long enough to not be a standard click but also didn't move the finger.

- **onScroll:** Called after the user has pressed and then moved his or her finger in a steady motion and lifted up.

- **onFling:** Called after the user has pressed and then moved his or her finger in an accelerating motion just before lifting it.

In addition, the `android.gesture` package enables an application to recognize arbitrary gestures and to store, load, and draw them. This means that almost any symbol a user can draw could be turned into a gesture with a specific meaning.

Customizing Styles and Themes

The Android SDK provides two powerful mechanisms for designing consistent user interfaces that are easy to maintain: styles and themes. You have used themes in the project that you have developed, but you have not customized themes to use in your app.

A style is a grouping of common view attribute settings that you can apply to any number of view controls. For example, you might want all view controls in your application, such as `TextView` and `EditText` controls, to use the same text color, font, and size. You could create a style that defines these three attributes and apply it to each `TextView` and `EditText` control within your application layouts.

A theme is a collection of one or more styles. Whereas you apply a style to a specific control, such as a `TextView` control, you apply a theme to all `View` objects within a specified activity. Applying a theme to a set of `View` objects all at once simplifies making the user interface look consistent. It can be a great way to define color schemes and other common view attribute settings across an application. You can also apply themes in the Android manifest file.

Designing Custom View and ViewGroup Controls

You are already familiar with many of the user interface controls, such as `Layout` and `View` controls that are available in the Android SDK. You can also create custom controls. To do so, you start with the appropriate `View` (or `ViewGroup`) control from the `android.view` package and implement the specific functionality needed for your control or layout.

You can use custom `View` controls in XML layout files, or you can inflate them programmatically at runtime. You can create new types of controls, or you can extend the functionality of existing controls, such as `TextView` or `Button` controls.

The Facebook `LoginButton` is an example of a custom view, but often custom views are simple extensions of basic views.

Camera

Android has an extensive camera application programming interface (API). Each release of Android adds more features. Android 5.0 added significant new capabilities to controlling the camera.

Using the OpenGL ES Graphics API

For more advanced graphics, Android uses the popular OpenGL ES graphics API. OpenGL ES 1.0 has been supported since Android 1.0. In Android 5.0, OpenGL ES 3.1 support was added. Applications can use Android's OpenGL ES support to draw, animate, light, shade, and texture graphical objects in three dimensions.

Bluetooth

Bluetooth support was included on Android 2.0. With Android 4.3, Android has added support for Bluetooth low energy (LE). Bluetooth LE makes it possible to build Android apps that communicate with Bluetooth LE peripheral devices. For example, a phone that includes Bluetooth LE support that is running Android 4.3 could support an app that interacts with a pedometer.

Android 4.3 introduced the `BluetoothManager(android.bluetooth.BluetoothManager)` class to help an app handle Bluetooth management.

Android 5.0 added additional Bluetooth (LE) API calls.

NFC and Beam

Most Android phones have near-field communication (NFC) capability. That means that they can communicate in short messages from an NFC tag when the phone is very close to the tag. NFC is a set of short-range wireless technologies.

A set of NFC intents is defined in Android. When a tag is read, these intents are fired. The idea is to create an app that filters for these intents and launches when an NFC tag is read. The details of NFC tags and the relationship between the tags and the application that is launched can get complicated. NFC concepts are covered in the Android developer documentation.

Android Beam is a technology for peer-to-peer NFC communication, which means that two Android devices can communicate through NFC using this technology.

Android 5.0 added API calls to make NFC easier to use as a developer.

Summary

In this hour, you learned about adding additional features to your app through the use of Google Play services and open source libraries. In addition, this hour reviewed Android features such as sensors, graphics, camera, Bluetooth, and NFC.

Q&A

Q. With the contents of this hour, have we covered everything available in Android?

A. No, this book has covered much of the Android system and includes topics such as the use of SQLite, content providers, and more that are commonly used in Android, but it is not an encyclopedic view of Android. The goal of this hour was to cover features that are often used in production-level Android apps and to be a guide to new topics.

Q. What happens when new features are added in Android?

A. New features provide new opportunities for developers. Often we need to develop an app for as many people as possible, but developing an app with new capabilities that relies on the latest Android features might provide a good opportunity to create an app that gets noticed and used.

Workshop

Quiz

1. What is Realm?

2. True or false: Google Play services are built in to every Android device.

3. What method must be implemented for a location listener?

Answers

1. Realm is an open source Android database.

2. False. You must check to see whether Google Play services are installed.

3. If you use a location listener, you must implement `onLocationChanged()`.

Exercise

Create an Android app that uses any Google Play service. You can re-create the location service that is used in this hour or research another service to implement. In this hour, you learned about the structure of an app that uses Google Play services, and you used the location service. When you use other services, you must refer to the specific API calls that are used.

HOUR 24
Publishing Your Apps

What You'll Learn in This Hour:

▶ Preparing for release
▶ Publishing to Google Play and other markets
▶ Making money with your app

After you have created an app, you need a way to get it to your users. In almost all cases, that means making the app available in an app marketplace. Google Play is the Google app marketplace, but it is not the only place to make apps available. Amazon and others can be appropriate options. Selling in an app marketplace requires having your AndroidManifest.xml file set up properly and your app signed. This hour covers that topic and some ways to make money with your app.

Preparing for Release

Hour 23, "More Features to Explore," covered some methods for making a great app. For an app to be successful, it must be functionally complete, well tested, and as polished as possible. Whether an app is functionally complete is your decision. In general, focusing on key features and doing them well is a good idea. Spend time on the part of the app that users will use all the time.

Releasing an app that you have tested only in an emulator is possible, but except for the simplest of apps, it is not advised! Your app should be tested on a real device and if possible multiple devices. Test on different-sized devices and on different versions of the Android operating system. If you have internationalized your app, make sure to test in the target locales.

After your app is functionally complete and tested, look for opportunities to add finishing touches. Do you have a great icon? Does the text in the app convey what it should? A silly game might have a different tone from a financial app. Are you able to remove text and use images or animation to convey meaning? Check the Android design principles for inspiration.

Preparing the Android Manifest File for Release

Before release, you need to make a number of changes to the application configuration settings of the Android manifest file. Although some of these items seem obvious, the idea is to have them in a checklist to verify the release. Other items are important for showing how the app is made available in an app marketplace like Google Play. Use this list to double-check your Android manifest file.

Android Manifest Checklist

Review the Android manifest file as follows:

▶ Verify that the application icon is set appropriately. Check the various drawable resource directories to ensure that it is set for all densities.

▶ Verify that the application label is set appropriately. This represents the application name as users see it.

▶ Verify the application package name. The app marketplace uses the package name to identify the app. If you do not like your package name, this is the time to change it.

▶ Verify that the application version name is set appropriately. The version name is a friendly version label that developers (and marketplaces) use.

▶ Verify that the application version code is set appropriately. The version code is a number that the Android platform uses to manage application upgrades.

▶ Confirm that the application `uses-sdk` setting is set correctly. You can set the minimum, target, and maximum Android software development kit (SDK) versions supported with this build.

▶ Confirm that the `uses-screens` setting is set properly. This property is not required.

▶ If you had set it, disable the `debuggable` option.

▶ Confirm that all application permissions are appropriate. Request only the permissions the application needs with `uses-permission`.

What will your manifest file look like as you go through this checklist? This snippet shows the package name and some version information:

```
package="com.yourcomapny.yourpackagename"
    android:versionCode="1"
    android:versionName="1.0" >
    <uses-sdk
        android:minSdkVersion="8"
        android:targetSdkVersion="16" />
    <uses-permission android:name="android.permission.INTERNET" />
```

The package name is `com.yourcompany.yourpackagename`. You can see the `versionCode` and `versionName`. The `versionName` is what is displayed to the user. You can use a scheme that includes text and numbers as part of your naming scheme. The `versionCode` is a number. It is for your internal use and to indicate the latest version to Google Play or other markets. The `versionCode` and `versionName` can differ. You can have `versionName` 1.07a and a version code of 9. The target and minimum SDK version make sense, and so does using only the Internet permission. There is no `uses-screens` option, and that is acceptable.

The icon set is `ic_launcher`.

The app name is included in the application element as follows:

```
android:label="@string/app_name"
```

Creating Icons Using Android Asset Studio

Android Asset Studio includes an easy way to make icons for your app:

1. Go to http://developer.android.com/.
2. Go to http://romannurik.github.io/AndroidAssetStudio/.
3. Choose Launcher Icons.
4. Follow the instructions to create an icon for your app.

Using <uses-feature> Wisely

The `uses-feature` tag indicates whether a particular hardware feature is used in the app. For an app that uses the camera app, this is added to the Android manifest:

```
<uses-feature android:name="android.hardware.camera" />
```

Google Play filters apps based on this setting.

You can indicate that an app uses the camera, but does not require it, as follows:

```
<uses-feature android:name="android.hardware.camera"
              android:required="false" />
```

If your app is intended for the TV market, you must specify that touch is not required, as follows:

```
<uses-feature android:name="android.hardware.touchscreen"
              android:required="false" />
```

Signing Your Apps

Android application packages must be digitally signed for the Android package manager to install them. Throughout the development process, Android Studio has used a debug key to manage this process. However, for release, you need to use a real digital signature—one that is unique to you and your company. To do this, you must generate a private key.

You use the private key to digitally sign the release package files of your Android application, as well as any upgrades. This ensures that the application is coming from you, the developer, and not someone pretending to be you.

Self-signing of signatures is standard for Android applications. Code signing allows the Android system to ensure app updates come from the same source as the original app. Because the signature is self-signed, it cannot confirm the identity of the developer, only that the original app and the update come from the same source. You should ensure your private key is kept safe.

Application updates must be signed with the same private key. For security reasons, the Android package manager does not install the update over the existing application if the key is different. This means you need to keep the key corresponding with the application in a secure, easy-to-find location for future use.

WARNING

Keeping Your Key Safe!

Your key is critically important. Keep it safe! Ideally, only the person in charge of building the release version should have access to the key. Your key should be backed up (preferably with at least one copy kept offsite).

Exporting and Signing the Package File Using Android Studio

Android Studio makes exporting and signing your app an easy process. You choose Build from the menu. You will pick Build, Generate Signed APK, and then follow the steps. You will decide the module to build. That is usually app. You will be asked to create a new key or use an existing one, as in Figure 24.1. If you choose to create a new one, as you would for a new app, you will be asked for the information shown in Figure 24.2.

FIGURE 24.1
Generate Signed APK Wizard.

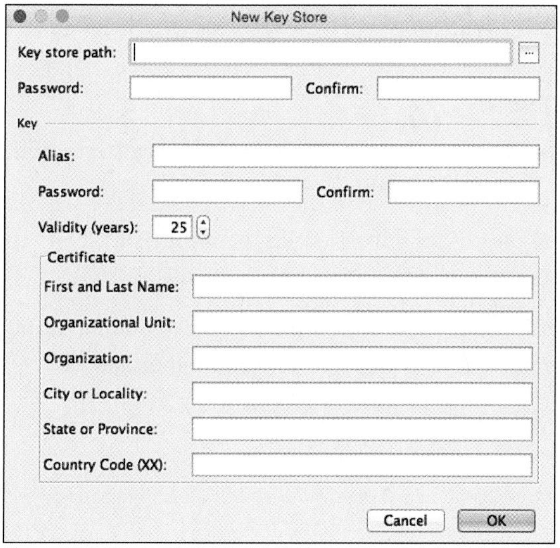

FIGURE 24.2
Creating a new key store.

▼ TRY IT YOURSELF

Generating a Signed APK in Android Studio

Android Studio provides an option to create a signed APK. These are the steps:

1. In Android Studio, choose Build from the menu.

2. Generate Signed APK.

3. Specify the module (usually app).

4. On the Key Store selection screen, choose Create New. Enter a location and name for the key store and enter and confirm a password.

5. Enter data for key creation. This includes a password, validity in years, and other information. The validity must be more than 25 years. Refer to Figure 24.2.

6. Choose a destination for your APK file and click Finish.

Signing Apps Using Command-Line Tools

Knowing something about the command-line tools that are available for creating key stores and signing packages can also be useful.

The command-line tools *keytool* and *jarsigner* are part of the Java Development Kit (JDK). You can use keytool to create a key store and jarsigner to sign the Android package file.

To get help, you can enter the tool name at a command line. If the tools are not available at the command line, you need to check the path to your JDK. You can find information on keytool and jarsigner at http://docs.oracle.com/javase/6/docs/technotes/tools/#security.

Creating a key with keytool is easiest understood by example:

```
keytool -genkey -v -keystore hour23.keystore  -alias hour23 -keyalg RSA -validity
10000
```

This command creates a key store in the file hour23.keystore. It is valid for 10,000 days and has an alias of hour23. Figure 24.3 shows the session that occurs after entering this command.

After you create the key store, you can use it to sign an APK file using jarsigner. The following assumes that you have an unsigned APK called `hour23opensource.apk`:

```
jarsigner -verbose -sigalg SHA1withRSA -digestalg SHA1 -keystore hour23.keystore
hour23opensource.apk hour23
```

The `-sigalg` and `-digestalg` parameters use the Android recommended values. The `keystore` parameter is specified by the file that you created: hour23.keystore. The hour23opensource.apk file is listed, and the last parameter is the alias name.

```
Enter keystore password:
Re-enter new password:
What is your first and last name?
  [Unknown]:  Carmen Delessio
What is the name of your organizational unit?
  [Unknown]:  Android in 24
What is the name of your organization?
  [Unknown]:
What is the name of your City or Locality?
  [Unknown]:
What is the name of your State or Province?
  [Unknown]:  NY
What is the two-letter country code for this unit?
  [Unknown]:  US
Is CN=Carmen Delessio, OU=Android in 24, O=Unknown, L=Unknown, ST=NY, C=US correct?
  [no]:  y

Generating 1,024 bit RSA key pair and self-signed certificate (SHA1withRSA) with a validity of 10,000 days
        for: CN=Carmen Delessio, OU=Android in 24, O=Unknown, L=Unknown, ST=NY, C=US
Enter key password for <hour23>
        (RETURN if same as keystore password):
Re-enter new password:
[Storing hour23.keystore]
```

FIGURE 24.3
Creating a key store with keytool.

This results in a signed Android package. You should run `jarsigner - verify hour23opensource.apk` to verify the results.

You can do an optimization process for the final APK file by using the Android command-line tool *zipalign*. The command is as follows:

```
zipalign -v 4 hour23opensource.apk hour23opensource-aligned.apk
```

Exporting the Certificate File

Sometimes you have to export a certificate file (for instance, if you are integrating an SDK from a known third-party provider like Facebook or Amazon). After you have a private key and have signed the APK file, you can generate the proper key hash for Facebook via the `keytool` command, as follows:

```
keytool -exportcert -alias hour23 -keystore hour23.keystore  | openssl sha1 -binary
 | openssl base64
```

The key store alias and key store file are specified. The result is a hash key that is displayed on the command line. That result is what should be populated into the Facebook developer tool.

Testing the Package

You can test the signed Android package in several ways. The easiest is to email it to an account on an Android device. When you open the attached APK, you should get an option to load the package. Be sure that in the Android Settings app (under Security), you have specified that it's okay to load Android apps from outside the Android market. You specify that unknown sources are allowed.

You can copy the APK file to the device and launch it with a File Manager tool. An app such as Astro File Manager works well for this.

You can also use a command-line tool for installing and uninstalling. To install, refer to the APK file:

```
adb install hour23opensource.apk
```

To uninstall, refer to the package:

```
adb uninstall com.bffmedia.hour23opensource
```

Use the command `adb` devices to list all devices. To specify a device for installation, use the `-s` flag:

```
adb -s 016B756E0E01C005 install hour23opensource.apk
```

Sharing Your App with the World

With a signed app, you are technically ready to publish your application. This section covers the basics of publishing your app on Google Play and considers some alternative markets. Putting thought and consideration into your presentation and marketing efforts in various app markets is important. The app name, icon, description, and supporting graphics are all important for making a good impression.

Publishing on Google Play

Google Play is Google's app marketplace for Android. It provides an easy way for a developer to publish apps and is probably the most common way that users acquire apps.

To publish applications through the Android Market, you must register as a developer. Registering as a developer verifies who you are to Google and provides a way for Google to pay you when someone buys your app. There is a $25 one-time fee to sign up as a Google Developer. Signing up is a simple online process; go to https://play.google.com/apps/publish/.

After you have your developer account, you can add a new application. You are given the choice to upload the APK or set up the store listing (see Figure 24.4).

For an app to have a chance to be successful, take advantage of all the available fields on Google Play when you add an app. Add screenshots, descriptive text, promo text, and so on. You can include screenshots for both phone devices and tablets. The screenshots to include should show key elements of your app and ideally how a user interacts with your app.

Store Listing

You will see additional options for your app including Game Center and other services. Google Play is a helpful area to explore and understand the opportunities for making apps available to users in the best way.

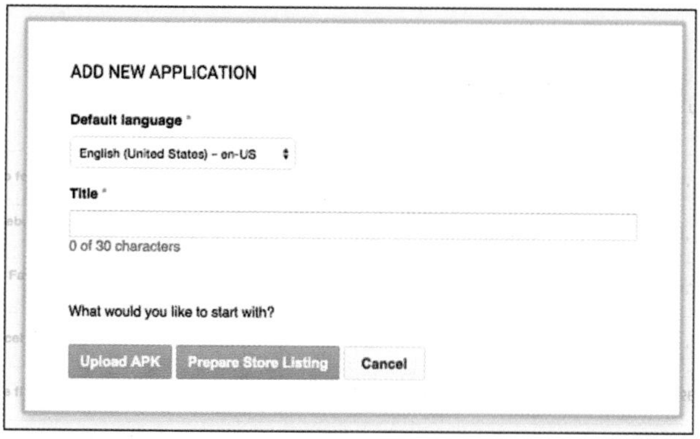

ADD NEW APPLICATION

Default language *

English (United States) – en-US   ⬍

Title *

0 of 30 characters

What would you like to start with?

Upload APK   Prepare Store Listing   Cancel

FIGURE 24.4
Adding a new app on Google Play.

Figure 24.5 gives an idea of some of the screenshot options that are available.

FIGURE 24.5
Store listing in Google Play.

Uploading the APK

When you upload an APK to Google Play, Google Play reads the APK file and provides information about the APK, such as the number of supported devices. You can upload for alpha and beta testing. To do so, you specify a Google Group or Google+ community.

Publishing on Amazon

Publishing on Amazon is similar to publishing on Google Play. Choose the Mobile App Distribution option from https://developer.amazon.com/.

You can develop specifically for Kindle Android-based devices or generic Android devices. A Kindle-specific version for the Amazon market might make sense. Kindle Fire is based on Android. If you are developing for the Kindle Fire, getting a device to test on is recommended.

Monetizing Your App

Making apps that people use can be fun and rewarding. Making money with your apps is also fun and rewarding. Many variations exist, but most app monetization schemes fall into one of four models: free, advertising, paid, and in-app billing.

Free Apps

With free apps, you can build a user base and work out the bugs in your app and maybe in your idea or product. Some apps become popular first and then you try to figure out how to make money later. Or some apps build a large user base and are acquired by a larger company. Don't dismiss free as a good option for many apps.

Ad Supported

Including mobile ads in your apps is easy to do. You can try AdMob, Amazon, or one of many other ad providers. To include ads in your app, you download an ad SDK and incorporate the ad into your app. You might add an ad slot into your layouts, or determine a good spot within your app to show an ad-based activity.

Paid

The paid model is easy to understand. You set a price level in Google Play and other markets, and users pay for your app. Many apps sell for $0.99 in the United States, but you might have a specialty app that can sell for significantly more or a great app that can sell for $4.99. Determine the proper price for your app to maximize revenue.

In-App Payments

Google Play and Amazon have different in-app payment options. The classic model for an in-app payment is a game in which there is a virtual currency. Players can earn the currency by playing the game or they can buy the currency with actual money. In-app purchases can give a user the ability to try an app without any upfront expense.

You can mix and match these options. You might decide your app should have an ad-supported version and a paid version without ads. Creating a business around an app always starts with creating a great app. After that part is done, you can experiment with how to make money.

Summary

This hour covered the process of producing a signed Android application and distributing it on various app marketplaces. The signing process is critical for security and for maintaining apps. Multiple app markets exist, including Amazon, and you can take advantage of new opportunities to distribute Android apps on new and in many markets around the world.

Q&A

Q. Is this everything there is to know about selling apps?

A. No, this hour is a good start. You can look into app licenses and privacy policies. This hour mentions in-app billing and using ad SDKs, but does not cover the details.

Q. How can I limit my application to only specific types of devices?

A. Google Play attempts to filter applications available to those compatible with the specific user's device. Each application package includes important information in the Android manifest file. Certain manifest file settings can be used to specify what types of devices your application does or does not support. For example, whether an app uses the camera can be determined. After that's done, the app will be available only for appropriate devices.

Workshop

Quiz

1. Is it possible to make an app that optionally uses the camera?

2. What are some common ways of making money with an app?

3. True or false: All Google Play Services are available in the Amazon Appstore.

Answers

1. Yes, you can indicate in the Android manifest file that the app uses the camera, but does not require it.

2. Free apps might ultimately make money. Other apps are ad supported, paid, or have in-app billing.

3. False. Amazon may have similar or comparable services, but you must implement separate Amazon and Google Play services solutions.

Exercise

Choose any exercise app from this book, export it, and sign it. Sign up for a developer account on Google Play or Amazon. It is time to make a great app. When you begin developing an app, working on one that you care about is ideal.

Index

X

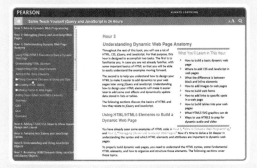
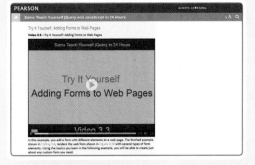